Digital Transformation in Sports

The sports industry is one of the most robust and competitive sectors in the world. Over the last decade, the integration of technology into sports has dramatically transformed the dynamics of how the sports industry operates. Sports analytics (i.e., the integration of data science and sports) is at the forefront of this digital transformation. Sports analytics encompasses the applications of innovative technologies and advanced analytical techniques to assess and enhance performance of players and teams, improve decision-making across diverse aspects, and bolster competitive advantages and strategies.

Digital Transformation in Sports explores the key driving forces and emerging trends that are fueling the digital transformation of the sports industry. It presents a collection of chapters that delve into state-of-the-art research and real-world applications of sports analytics, providing a diverse perspective on its transformative impact across different sports sectors. It showcases how advanced technologies such as the Internet of Things (IoT), machine learning (ML), and artificial intelligence (AI) are revolutionizing player performance, strategic decision-making, fan engagement, and operational efficiency. For example, by utilizing sensors, wearable technologies, tracking devices, and 5G networks, IoT technologies can collect an unprecedented amount of data in real time and enable the near-instantaneous transmission of this data to the centralized platforms for analysis. Sophisticated analytics powered by AI and ML enable the extraction of actionable insights from this raw data, transforming it into valuable intelligence that drives better decision-making.

By offering a bridge between theoretical frameworks and practical applications, this book demonstrates how such concepts as technology acceptance theories inform the successful implementation and adoption of analytics solutions. By drawing upon interdisciplinary insights, the chapters provide valuable tools and frameworks for researchers, analysts, practitioners, and stakeholders, delivering actionable guidance to harness the full potential of analytics in the rapidly evolving sports landscape.

Jillian McNiff Villemaire joined the Flagler College faculty in 2014. She teaches a variety of courses in the Department of Applied Management. Her primary interests include marketing, communications, and social media in the sports industry. Before devoting herself to undergraduate teaching, Dr. McNiff Villemaire worked in marketing for Boston University's Fitness and Recreation Center and for the New England Patriots, the New England Revolution, and Gillette Stadium. She brings a passion for applied sport management learning strategies to her role as teacher and adviser.

Haiyan Huang earned a PhD in information sciences and technology at the Pennsylvania State University. Her primary research and teaching interests include data science and analytics, web usability and user experiences, IT adoption, diversity of the IT workforce, and global information systems development. Before joining Flagler College, Dr. Huang taught at Michigan Technological University, Purdue University Calumet, and the Pennsylvania State University. She has published more than 40 journal articles, book chapters, and conference papers.

Data Analytics Applications

Series Editor, Jay Liebowitz

Teaching Data Analytics: Pedagogy and Program Design
by Susan Vowels and Katherine Leaming Goldberg

Data Analytics Applications in Gaming and Entertainment
by Günter Wallner

Developing Informed Intuition for Decision-Making
by Jay Liebowitz

Management in the Era of Big Data: Issues and Challenges
by Joanna Paliszkiewicz

Data Analytics and AI
by Jay Liebowitz

Closing the Analytics Talent Gap: An Executive's Guide to Working with Universities
by Jennifer Priestley and Robert McGrath

Online Learning Analytics
by Jay Liebowitz

Pivoting Government through Digital Transformation
by Jay Liebowitz

Data Analytics in Marketing, Entrepreneurship, and Innovation
by Mounir Kehal and Shahira El Alfy

Business Models: Innovation, Digital Transformation, and Analytics
by Iwona Otola and Marlena Grabowska

Developing the Intuitive Executive: Using Analytics and Intuition for Success
by Jay Liebowitz

Data Analytics in Finance
by Huijian Dong

Digital Transformation in Sports
by Jillian McNiff Villemaire and Haiyan Huang

For more information about this series, please visit: www.routledge.com/Data-Analytics-Applications/book-series/CRCDATANAAPP

Digital Transformation in Sports

Edited by
Jillian McNiff Villemaire and Haiyan Huang

CRC Press
Taylor & Francis Group

AN AUERBACH BOOK

Designed cover image: Shutterstock

First edition published 2026
by CRC Press
2385 NW Executive Center Drive, Suite 320, Boca Raton FL 33431

and by CRC Press
4 Park Square, Milton Park, Abingdon, Oxon, OX14 4RN

CRC Press is an imprint of Informa UK Limited

British Library Cataloguing-in-Publication Data
A catalogue record for this book is available from the British Library

ISBN: 978-1-032-64818-7 (hbk)
ISBN: 978-1-032-64240-6 (pbk)
ISBN: 978-1-032-66519-1 (ebk)

DOI: 10.1201/9781032665191

Typeset in Minion
by Newgen Publishing UK

Contents

Contributors..ix

Chapter 1 Introduction..1

Haiyan Huang

Chapter 2 Golf Analytics: It's More than Just a Stick and a Ball..........6

*Christopher Cain, Junghoon Lee, Eric Handley, Daniel Merrell,
Justin Ehrlich, and Rodney Paul*

Chapter 3 Analytics Democratization: How the NFL Fosters
a Pipeline of Future Analysts through Digital Data
Accessibility...31

Bradley J. Congelio

Chapter 4 Surveying Various Information Systems Theories
Used in the Context of AI and IoT in Sports.....................50

Mukesh Chaware and Sreejith Alathur

Chapter 5 Artificial Intelligence (AI): A New Window to Smart
Stadiums..87

*Sardar Mohammadi, Seyyed Iman Ghaffarisadr, and
Manuel Alonso Dos Santos*

Chapter 6 Game Theory in the Digital Age 110

Yvan J. Kelly

Chapter 7 Computational Approaches to Sport Outcome
Prediction..123

Sadegh Sulaimany and Sardar Mohammadi

Chapter 8 Analytics in Sports: A Review and Exploration of Financial and On-Field Performance of Football Clubs..138

Ziad Zein, Ashish Kumar Jha, and K. Mohammed Jasim

Chapter 9 Summary..169

Jillian McNiff Villemaire

Index...171

Contributors

Sreejith Alathur
Faculty in Information Systems
Indian Institute of Management
Kozhikode, Kerala, India

Christopher Cain
PGA University Program
Harrah College of Hospitality
University of Nevada
Las Vegas, Nevada, United States

Mukesh Chaware
Research Scholar in Information
    Systems
Indian Institute of Management
Kozhikode, Kerala, India

Bradley J. Congelio
Kutztown University of Pennsylvania
Kutztown, Pennsylvania,
    United States

Justin Ehrlich
Department of Sport Management
Syracuse University's Falk College
Syracuse, New York, United States

Seyyed Iman Ghaffarisadr
Sport Management
University of Mohaghegh Ardabili
Ardabil, Iran

Eric Handley
Golf Teaching and Research Center
College of Health and Human
    Development
The Pennsylvania State University
State College, Pennsylvania,
    United States

K. Mohammed Jasim
Trinity College Dublin
Dublin, Ireland

Ashish Kumar Jha
Trinity College Dublin
Dublin, Ireland

Yvan J. Kelly
Accounting, Economics, and
    Finance
School of Business
Flagler College
St. Augustine, Florida, United States

Junghoon Lee
PGA Golf Management University
    Program
Harrah College of Hospitality
University of Nevada
Las Vegas, Nevada, United States

Daniel Merrell
College of Health and Human
Development
The Pennsylvania State University
State College, Pennsylvania,
United States

Sardar Mohammadi
Department of Physical Education
Faculty of Humanities and Social
Science
University of Kurdistan
Sanandaj, Iran

Rodney Paul
Department of Sport Management
and Analytics
Falk College of Sport and Human
Dynamics
Syracuse University
Syracuse, New York, United States

Manuel Alonso Dos Santos
Department of Marketing and
Market Research
University of Granada
Granada, Spain

Sadegh Sulaimany
Social and Biological Network
Analysis Laboratory
Department of Computer
Engineering
University of Kurdistan
Sanandaj, Iran

Ziad Zein
Trinity College Dublin
Dublin, Ireland

1

Introduction

Haiyan Huang

The sports industry is one of the most robust and competitive sectors in the world. Over the last decade, the integration of technology into sports has dramatically transformed the dynamics of how the sports industry operates. Sports analytics (the integration of data science and sports) is at the forefront of this digital transformation. Sports analytics encompasses the applications of innovative technologies and advanced analytical techniques to assess and enhance the performance of players and teams, improve decision-making across diverse aspects, and bolster competitive advantages and strategies. On the one hand, using sensors, wearable technologies, tracking devices, and 5G networks, Internet of Things (IoT) technologies can collect an unprecedented, vast amount of data in real time and enable the near-instantaneous transmission of this data to centralized platforms for analysis. On the other hand, sophisticated analytics powered by artificial intelligence (AI) and machine learning (ML) enables the extraction of actionable insights from raw data, transforming it into valuable intelligence that drives better decision-making.

This book seeks to explore the key driving forces and emerging trends that are fueling the digital transformation of the sports industry. It presents a collection of chapters that delve into the state-of-the-art research and real-world applications of sports analytics, providing a diverse perspective on its transformative impact across different sports sectors.

The use of analytics in golf has evolved significantly, providing players, coaches, and analysts valuable insights to improve performance and refine the strategic aspects of the game. Chapter 2 illustrates how technological advancements are shaping the golf industry by empowering players to fine-tune their technique, leading to new levels of performance and success. The chapter begins by examining how analytics has changed the teaching,

DOI: 10.1201/9781032665191-1

coaching, and assessing of performance outcomes in golf, with the help of advanced monitoring systems such as FlightScope, Trackman, simulation rooms, and biomechanic data technologies. It then explores the growing acceptance of technology among professional golfers and their coaches, who are leveraging these tools to optimize body movement, increase force and speed, and prevent injuries. A particular focus of this chapter is on the "Strokes Gained" analysis, which employs data collected from ShotLink+ and combines with various machine learning algorithms to offer granular insights into a golfer's performance. By offering a detailed breakdown of performance, Strokes Gained helps players and coaches identify strengths and weaknesses, predict outcomes, personalize training regimens, and enhance overall performance. Furthermore, the chapter highlights the essential role of interdisciplinary collaborations in driving the future success of golf analytics.

Chapter 3 highlights an important application of sports analytics in the National Football League (NFL), the Big Data Bowl. The chapter begins by outlining the unique challenges faced by the NFL during the 2010s, when the league relied largely on conventional wisdom and teams were often hesitant to fully embrace advanced analytics. A critical turning point came in the 2017 season when the Philadelphia Eagles credited their Super Bowl LII victory to the use of data-driven analytics. This shift marked a pivotal moment in the NFL's acceptance of data and analytics. The NFL launched Big Data Bowl in 2019, which has become an annual competition where data scientists, students, and analysts are challenged to use NFL's publicly accessible Next Gen Stats data and apply machine learning techniques to answer questions about player performance, game outcomes, and strategy optimization. The open nature of Big Data Bowl democratizes sports analytics by giving anyone with the necessary skills and creativity the opportunity to contribute insights for challenging problems. The NFL regularly incorporates the findings from the Big Data Bowl into their operations, allowing teams to benefit from cutting-edge research and fresh perspectives. The chapter concludes by emphasizing how the NFL Big Data Bowl serves as a vital tool in the democratization of sports analytics. By making complex data more accessible and encouraging open competition, the NFL has not only fostered a new generation of analysts but also fundamentally transformed the way the game is understood and played.

As IoT devices and AI technologies continue to gain traction in the sports industry, understanding the factors that influence their adoption is crucial. Chapter 4 applies a set of information systems theories to examine the behavioral, psychological, and organizational factors driving the integration of these technologies in sports. The chapter mainly focuses on a set of technology acceptance theories, including Technology Acceptance Model (TAM), Diffusion of Innovations (DOI), Theory of Planned Behavior (TPB), and Value-Based Adoption Model (VAM). The Technology of Acceptance Model provides insights into how the ease of use and perceived usefulness of these technologies affect their acceptance within sports domains. The Diffusion of Innovations theory presents a valuable framework for understanding the adoption of technologies in sports, particularly AI and IoT solutions, which are transforming various aspects of the industry, including injury prevention and player safety. The Theory of Planned Behavior helps to explore the attitudes, intentions, and perceived control that athletes, coaches, and managers have toward adopting IoT and AI tools. The Value-Based Adoption Model highlights the importance of perceived value (functional, economic, social or/and emotional value) in technology adoption. By synthesizing these information systems theories, the chapter provides a comprehensive overview for understanding the adoption of IoT and AI technologies, offering an in-depth look at how these innovations are reshaping the sports industry.

The application of artificial intelligence in smart stadiums is fostering a wide range of opportunities to improve stadium operational effectiveness and enhance fan engagement. Chapter 5 explores the transformative role of artificial intelligence in shaping the development of smart venues. It begins by examining the convergence of artificial intelligence technologies and the smart stadiums concept. The chapter then provides a detailed discussion on how AI contributes to stadium operations, particularly in the areas of safety and security, and environmental sustainability. AI technologies, such as IoT devices, surveillance systems, video analytics, facial recognition, and predictive analytics, can analyze patterns of behavior, detect anomalies, identify potential threats, and provide early warnings to enable faster and more effective responses, enhancing stadium safety and security. In addition to safety, AI can also be applied to analyze and optimize energy consumption to lower the cost. Another major application of AI in smart stadiums is to revolutionize fan engagement and experiences. Virtual reality and augmented reality technologies are making stadiums more interactive and immersive, offering fans tailored, personalized experiences of live events. The chapter also examines the dual impact of the COVID-19 pandemic on AI adoption in stadiums. While the pandemic posed challenges, it also accelerated the implementation of AI solutions for enhancing health and safety. Finally, the chapter highlights the key players in the smart stadiums market, from both the industry and regional perspectives.

Chapter 6 provides an overview of game theory and unpacks its applications in sports analytics. The chapter begins with an introduction to the origins and foundations of game theory, exploring how it is applied in non-cooperative games. A central concept in game theory is the Nash equilibrium, which provides a mathematical framework for analyzing competitive strategies where each player in a game chooses their optimal strategy while considering the strategies of the other players. For example, in tennis, a player's offensive strategy might be influenced by the opponent's defensive positioning, and vice versa, with both players striving to achieve Nash equilibria in their play choices. Both players adjust their tactics to find an equilibrium where neither player benefits from changing their strategy unilaterally. Next, the chapter discusses mixed strategy solutions, a game theory approach where players randomize their decisions to prevent opponents from predicting their moves. In sports analytics, game theory has demonstrated to be a powerful tool for analyzing competitive behavior and optimizing decision-making. This chapter exemplifies the applications of game theory in various common decision-making scenarios in baseball, football, and tennis. Toward the end, the chapter acknowledges the limitations of applying game theory in sports analytics due to simplified assumptions and unpredictable gaming conditions. It concludes by emphasizing that the true potential of game theory in sports analytics lies in its integration with big data analytics.

In the wide spectrum of sports analytics, the frontier of predictive analytics is increasingly driven by the advancements of machine learning techniques that analyze historical and current data, player metrics, and gaming statistics to help teams forecast outcomes and gain strategic advantages. Chapter 7 examines the holistic process of such computational approaches and the related techniques for outcome predictions in sports. The process begins with collecting data from multiple sources, followed by preprocessing the data to ensure data quality and integrity. Next, relevant features or dimensions are selected to focus on the most significant variables for analysis. Finally, analytical machine learning algorithms (ranging from supervised machine learning to deep learning) are applied to uncover patterns, make predictions, and generate actionable insights. This systematic process, spanning from data collection to advanced analysis, enables a deeper understanding of complex systems and supports informed decision-making across various sports fields, from the major markets like basketball and baseball to niche ones such as horse racing and chess. The chapter concludes by discussing the challenges in implementing predictive analytics effectively, highlighting potential barriers and areas for improvement in future.

Chapter 8 explores the intricate relationships between on-field performance and the financial data of sports clubs. The research is divided into two parts, descriptive analysis and explanatory (predictive) analysis. In the descriptive analysis, the chapter presents a correlation heatmap that visually represents the relationships between various on-field performance metrics (such as Games Played, Wins, Losses, etc.) and off-field financial data (including Total Revenue, Matchday Revenue, and Social Media Followers, etc.) for 19 European football clubs in 2021. This heatmap offers valuable insights into the potential connections between a club's on-field success and its financial health. The chapter also employs *K*-means clustering analysis to segment the 19 clubs into two distinct clusters, one cluster consisting of 9 elite clubs with superior on-field and financial performance, while the second cluster includes 10 clubs with modest performance. The explanatory analysis focuses on forecasting future financial outcomes based on historical revenue data. The chapter applies four forecasting methods: the naive method, exponential smoothing, Holt-Winter's method, and auto-ARIMA. These techniques are used to analyze the revenue data from 2020 to 2021 and estimate the revenues from 2022 to 2024 for three selected clubs. It demonstrates the value of different forecasting approaches, each suited to different types of data and trends. While many studies have looked at either financial outcomes or on-field metrics separately, this chapter integrates both to provide a more comprehensive view of how sports clubs operate and how success in one area can lead to improved results in the other.

This collection of research chapters provides a comprehensive exploration of the transformative impact of digital technologies across various domains within the sports industry. It showcases how advanced technologies such as the Internet of Things, machine learning, and artificial intelligence are revolutionizing player performance, strategic decision-making, fan engagement, and operational efficiency. By addressing diverse aspects, ranging from real-time data collection in golf to democratized analytics in the NFL's Big Data Bowl and the integration of game theory for strategic optimization, these chapters offer a holistic view of how data and analytics are driving innovation in sports. Moreover, the collection bridges the gap between theoretical frameworks and practical applications, demonstrating how concepts like technology acceptance theories inform the successful implementation and adoption of analytics solutions. Drawing upon those interdisciplinary insights, the chapters provide valuable tools and frameworks for researchers, analysts, practitioners, and stakeholders, delivering actionable guidance to harness the full potential of analytics in the rapidly evolving sports landscape.

2

Golf Analytics: It's More than Just a Stick and a Ball

Christopher Cain, Junghoon Lee, Eric Handley,
Daniel Merrell, Justin Ehrlich, and Rodney Paul

In recent years, technology and advanced data collection and data analytics methods have been used more frequently in golf teaching and coaching applications. Before venturing into a discussion about how and when technology and these methods are useful in golf instruction, it is worthwhile to share how their application has set the stage for growth within the golf industry.

Technology is not only contributing to growth and diversity; simultaneously, it is also contributing to market specialization in teaching and coaching. It is within this specialization we see uniquely educated professionals using sophisticated data collection and analytics equipment and applications to understand the nuances of golf swing kinematics and kinetics.

2.1 THE ROLE OF TECHNOLOGY IN THE GROWTH OF GOLF

The game of golf has seen unprecedented growth over the past two decades, with a direct economic impact of $101.7B representing a 60% increase since 2000. The game's growth has also stimulated a deeper layer of economic activity – with indirect and induced effects, inclusive of golf tourism and real estate, driving total impact to $226.5B in the U.S. This impact supports 1.65M jobs with $80.1B in wages and benefits (NGF, 2023f).

As may be suspected from the overall economic impact, golf's reach is also at an all-time high, with 123M Americans reporting that they have played, watched, or read about the game. This reach represents a 30% increase since

DOI: 10.1201/9781032665191-2

2016. This surge has also influenced the total number of golf participants, with 45M Americans experiencing the game either on or off course. This swell in participation represents a 53% increase in the past 10 years (NGF, 2023a). These figures bode well for both an increase in the diversity of participants playing the sport and the potential for long-run gains, given it is a sport which participants can play well into retirement.

Economic and participation gains have been complemented by golf experiences off course. These experiences are represented by play through simulators like Full Swing and Trackman and socio-technological driving range experiences like TopGolf, Drive Shack, and Atomic Golf. These off-course technology-driven experiences account for 27.9M participants and have transferred 2.5M participants to on course (25.6M participants) in the U.S. (NGF, 2023c). In fact, it has been estimated that roughly 6.2 million Americans used a golf simulator in 2023, up 73% from pre-pandemic levels (NGF, 2023d). Additionally, studies have shown that simulators strengthen interest in on-course participation for golfers who have used simulators (NGF, 2023d), as these technologies are used to increase play time, socialization, and skills.

As the culture of the U.S. becomes increasingly reliant on technology for all aspects of life, recent research has demonstrated that "fewer than 10% of on-course players said they believe someone should begin their 'golf journey' at the golf course, with 80% saying a driving range or entertainment golf facility is the best option" (NGF, 2023c). Moreover, technology like social media is positively influencing perceptions of golf (NGF, 2023b). Still, roughly 80% of the population that actively engages with golf content on social networks do not currently participate in any kind of golf-related activity (NGF, 2023b).

Technology beyond that found in simulated play, such as golf-related applications for mobile devices, have also captured a younger demographic. Those under the age of 50 compared to those over 50 years of age are more likely to use a mobile application for: reserving tee times (56% vs. 33%); following major golf championships (57% vs. 31%); measuring yardage on the golf course (49% vs. 33%); recording playing statistics to manage their own game (52% vs. 22%); receiving golf-related news (34% vs. 20%); using golf video games (28% vs. 10%); and receiving golf instruction (13% vs. 7%) (NGF, 2018).

Age is also a factor to consider when examining the differences of participation in technologically enriched off-course environments versus traditional on-course environments. The average age of participants playing exclusively off-course is 31 compared to exclusively on-course at 46. However, age is not the only socioeconomic demographic to consider. Off-course exclusive participants versus on-course exclusive participants are more likely to be female (41% vs. 28%) and non-white (40% vs. 22%). This comparison also demonstrates participants in the off-course setting are less likely to report household incomes of more than $100k (40% vs. 42%) and a feeling of being financially comfortable (51% vs. 54%) (NGF, 2023e).

The transfer of off-course to on-course play is gaining traction as roughly 10% of current golfers are playing as a direct result of their off-course experiences (NGF, 2023c). Since 2016, golf has seen an 8% increase in on-course activity with 25.6M participants. On-course participation is supported by nearly 16,000 golf courses, which is more than the number of Starbucks or McDonald's locations nationwide. While golf courses represent 38,000 facilities globally, the U.S. still captures the lion's share of the market, with 5 times the number of golf courses than any other country.

2.2 THE ROLE OF TECHNOLOGY IN THE SPECIALIZATION OF TEACHING AND COACHING

As golf's consumer base continues to swell, diversify, and include a greater population of enthusiasts that embrace technology, there are also numerous golf instruction technologies to help the novice golfer and the seasoned professional alike enhance their playing ability and prevent injury.

With regard to performance enhancement, launch monitor systems like Flight Scope and Trackman record golf ball ballistics through radar and camera technologies to produce data to identify swing path, face angle, and club and ball speed as well as to measure the impact of the ball on the clubface. Prior to these objective data points and tools, this information was a subjective measure that relied on a trained instructor's eye or ear.

In addition to launch monitor systems, golf simulation rooms with motion capture technology analyze kinematics and kinetics. For example, Qualisys offers three-dimensional cameras, markers, and a software package that captures full body movements. This system can capture fine motor movement with a high level of accuracy that is ample to identify the nuances of a golf swing within a time series of data. This three-dimensional capture can also be paired with the capture of the force the golfer inhibits with the ground to generate swing velocity. Three-dimensional capture has several advantages over the traditional two-dimensional capture: it can identify positions like over- or under-rotation of the shoulder, hips, and wrists; the location of all body parts at the time of impact; other useful data points that aid in swing correction and enhancement; and it can prevent injury (Cain & Cain, 2022).

Advanced golf biomechanics technology is found in golf swing laboratories like the ones housed in the Dwaine Knight Center for Golf Management at the University of Nevada, Las Vegas (UNLV) or the biomechanics laboratory found in The Suzy and Jim Broadhurst Golf Teaching and Research Center at The Pennsylvania State University (PennState).

Data collection and analytics in golf also extends its application to entertainment. For example, Full Swing creates golf simulators for commercial and residential use as well as for entertainment venues. Golf consumers who use systems like Full Swing can view information on swing dynamics and golf ball flight. While this data can be useful for instruction and club fitting, it can also create simulated rounds of golf at some of the world's most prestigious golf courses through the process of gamification.

These technologies allow the consumer to be more involved in their own personal development through data analytics that can produce objective measures to which they would otherwise not have had access. All this data can be overwhelming to golfers interested in utilizing these objective measures to improve performance. As data analytics in golf continues to gain traction, there has been a pressing need to educate those who teach and coach the game to understand how to best apply this information in a coachable setting.

With more ways to play the sport and an increase in participation, the need for professional teaching and coaching continues to grow and evolve. The Professional Golfer's Association (PGA) of America, with 30,000 members, is recognized as the largest working sport management association in the world. The PGA commits to lifelong learning opportunities for its members through the PGA Life Learning Model, developed to encourage members to continue to grow as professionals while adding value to the marketplace. As a result, the PGA identified three distinct career paths: Teaching and Coaching, Golf Operations, and Executive Management. Each path is supported by online certifications that are available to PGA members to continue their education/professional development. These certifications allow for a professional to select one of three career paths to progress. These career path certifications are supported through partnerships with higher education and established allied golf associations. For example, the PGA Teaching and Coaching certification is supported through a partnership with PennState, specifically a golf biomechanics course delivered through The Suzy and Jim Broadhurst Golf Teaching and Research Center. The Golf Operations certification is supported through a partnership with the United States Golf Association. Further, the Executive Management certification is supported through a partnership with the UNLV College of Hospitality. Members who complete these certifications benefit by constantly providing themselves the opportunity to gain more knowledge and, hopefully, improve their own business (instruction, tournaments, events, club engagement) within the industry (PGA, n.d.).

Another certification offered by the PGA focuses specifically on coaching and is offered through the PGA Coach program. This certification provides golf instructors with the tools to learn how to expand their business, generate new interest, and retain the players they currently serve. The PGA Coach program also dives deeper into the American Development Model. This model has been used on a variety of platforms with the United States Olympic Committee, which encourages athletes to participate in more than one sport. This approach allows for developing greater skills, positive movement, and long-term health in athletes. This model also focuses on the importance of enjoyment. The certification provides an instructor with the knowledge and skills to shape their players through learning and improving their game, competing in tournaments, and becoming competitive in the field. The goal of this approach is to promote progress among players of different age categories and skill levels (PGA Coach, n.d.)

We see evidence of the workforce in golf becoming more specialized through the popularity and offerings of golf biomechanics certifications. For example, the Titleist Performance Institute (TPI) created a set of certifications that captivate fitness professionals, golf professionals/instructors, and medical professionals. The online certifications break down the body into sections using biomechanics. The certifications are offered in the following categories: Level 1 (broad overview); Level 2, offering insight into medical, junior, fitness, power, and golf levels; and Level 3, which elaborates on the previous level. Each course is tailored to target a specific area to enhance the performance of the player (TPI, n.d.).

Biomechanics in TPI is used to target, and improve, the movement of one area of the body. The TPI certifications are unique in that these involve the understanding of both golf-related biomechanics and fitness exercises that can increase range of motion and reduce risk of injury (TPI, n.d.).

Dr. Kwon's Golf Biomechanics Instructor Training Program also offers certification for golf instructors (Kwon, n.d.). The online certification offers a review of the fundamentals (Level 1), empirical data (Level 2), and advanced application (Level 3). These courses are offered via Zoom and allow professionals to expand their knowledge in biomechanics and obtain a greater understanding of a golf swing through a kinematic sequence. The curriculum supports the instructor's ability to examine common mistakes, errors, or inconsistencies in the player's swing and propose necessary modifications for improvement.

2.3 THE ROLE OF TECHNOLOGY IN GOLF PERFORMANCE OUTCOMES

The outcome of primary importance related to golfer performance is where the golf ball goes. A shot outcome can be described utilizing the "strokes gained" metric. On the golf course, this can be determined based upon where the ball finishes and the distance it lies from the golfer's intended target. In an indoor data collection and research environment we can measure the movement of the golf ball and simulate where it finished relative to its target. To capture these measurements, there are two primary types of technologies, a radar-based ball flight and club delivery unit and a camera-based one. Each type of technology can measure the ball speed, launch angle, and spin rate to accurately predict the distance, trajectory, and shape of a golf shot.

To understand what contributed to the flight of the golf ball, it is important to measure the movements of the club. Fortunately, by utilizing the same technologies, it is also possible to measure and calculate the movements of the golf club through the impact area. Some of the primary club delivery variables include club speed, clubface angle, club path, club angle of approach, dynamic loft at impact, and club face impact location.

The golf club's movements are determined based on the golfer's movements. To quantify the body's movements during a golf swing, various technologies provide a variety of capture options and levels of accuracy. Golf biomechanics laboratories, like those found in The Suzy and Jim Broadhurst Golf Teaching and Research Center at PennState and the Dwaine Knight Center at UNLV, primarily use optical motion capture systems. This type of technology is considered the gold standard for motion capture and is verified to be accurate to within 1 mm (Eichelberger et al., 2016). While there are other technologies available in the marketplace that are more accessible to coaches and golfers, research institutions often prefer optical systems for their high level of accuracy and the flexibility of data collected. Systems like this also synchronize with force plates. Researchers, educators, and coaches are then able to evaluate how golfers interact with the ground and understand how ground reaction forces in three dimensions influence the motions of the body.

Depending on the research or performance question being asked, a set of capture protocols are put into place to ensure the consistent and accurate capture of golfer kinematics, kinetics, and both club delivery and flight data. To make the environment as similar as possible to outdoor play, golf simulators are used. Participants can evaluate each hole and determine their intended target prior to each shot. Upon the completion of a shot, the golfer will see the shot outcome as it comes to rest in the simulated on-course environment. Strokes-gained calculations can then be determined and paired with the motion capture data for each swing.

The evaluation of data collected in a motion capture session is primarily broken down into the categories of kinematics and kinetics. Kinematics is the description of the motions of the golfer without reference to the forces or torques that produce the motion (Handley et al., 2015). These are the motions of the body that determine the direction the club moves in and the resulting ball flight.

Translational motion is defined as movement in a straight line. An example of a translational motion in the golf swing would be the vertical movement of the pelvis. Rotational motion is the turning about an axis. Golfers must tilt at the waist and rotate their torso closer to the ground. This is the forward tilt of the torso (Figure 2.1), which looks like someone is bowing to the golf ball. In the golf swing, these occur separately and simultaneously. For example, in a golfer's backswing, the pelvis can tilt to the side, so that the right hip rises higher than the left, but the pelvis can also move further away from the target at the same time the tilting occurs.

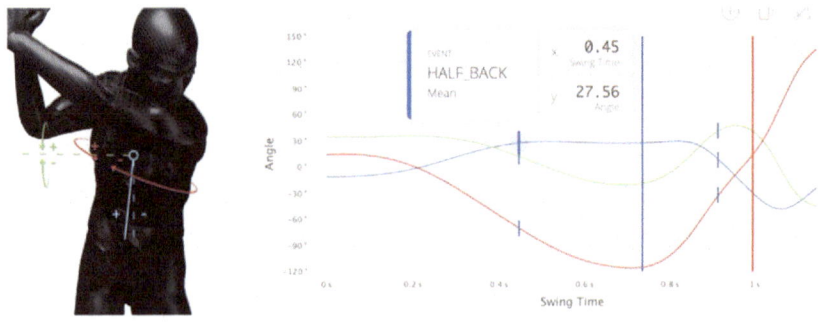

FIGURE 2.1
Example of Torso Rotation Data.

Translational motion can be described and measured in terms of the position, frame of reference, displacement, velocity, and acceleration. Position is the place at which something resides and, in golf biomechanics, is usually expressed in inches, centimeters, or millimeters. The frame of reference is the coordinate system that defines an object's distance in relation to a point and the directions in which we measure its position.

In golf, an example of a translational motion is the sway of the pelvis, or the movement of the center of the pelvis toward or away from the target. Typically, this measurement will begin at zero and then describe the amount and the direction in which the center of the pelvis moved laterally; for example, a golfer's pelvis may begin at 0 inches and move 3 inches away from the target by the top of the backswing. This describes the displacement of the pelvis in the backswing because we are given both the magnitude and the direction that the center of the pelvis translated during that time.

Velocity and acceleration can also be observed when looking at translational motion. Velocity is speed in a defined direction. Looking back at the pelvis sway positional example, the golfer's pelvis moved at 0.1 meters per second (m/s) away from the target during the backswing. This describes the velocity of the pelvis sway because it provides the speed and the direction of the pelvis. Acceleration is how fast something speeds up or slows down in a defined direction. Velocity and acceleration appear remarkably similar; however, velocity is a measure of how much the position changes and acceleration is a measure of how much the velocity changes.

Rotation is defined as the turn about an axis. There is quite a lot of carryover in the terminology from translational motions, and an understanding of those terms will make it quite easy to understand the rotational terminology. Rotational motions can be described as the angle of rotation, axis of rotation, orientation, rotational velocity, and rotational acceleration.

The angle of rotation is the degree an object is rotated about a given point or axis. This is typically expressed in degrees. The axis of rotation is a line that an object rotates about in a circular motion; think about a globe and the earth's axis. Orientation, or the direction that an object is aiming at with respect to another object, is also referred to as the angular/rotational position or angular/rotational displacement. In golf this can be seen when examining the rotation of the pelvis (Figure 2.2). The golfer rotates (turns) their pelvis 45 degrees away from the target by the top of the backswing.

Lastly, there is rotational velocity and rotational acceleration. If there is an understanding of velocity and acceleration, understanding the rotational versions of these terms should be easy. Rotational velocity is the rate at which

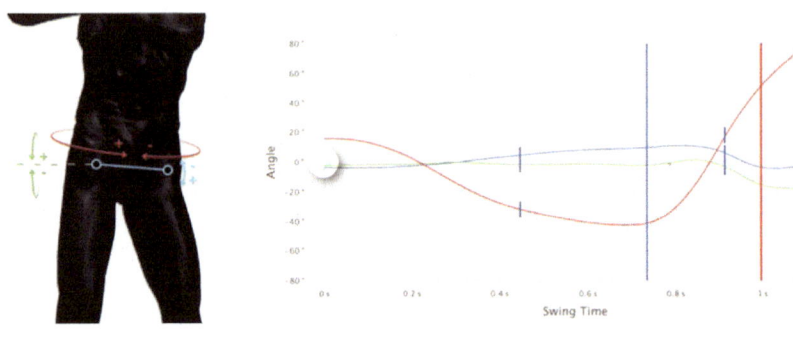

FIGURE 2.2
Example of Pelvis Rotation Data.

an object rotates about one or more axes of rotation. In golf, this is typically expressed in degrees per second (degrees/s) or rotations per minute (rpm). The rotational velocity of the golfer's pelvis in the downswing may be of interest when looking at reasons for slow clubhead speed. It is also quite common to look at the golf ball's spin rate, expressed in rpm, when trying to increase the distance of a player's stroke. Rotational acceleration is how fast the rotational velocity of an object increases or decreases about one or more axes of rotation. Examining a golfer's rotational acceleration and deceleration patterns when looking at a kinematic sequence (rotational velocity) graph can help a coach discover clubhead speed leaks in a golfer's swing.

Along with evaluating a golfer's kinematics, it is imperative to also look at a golfer's kinetics, or the forces that contribute to the motions we see. Just as there are rotational and translational kinematics, there are also rotational and translational kinetics. A golfer moves in three dimensions throughout their swing and also creates forces through their feet interacting with the ground in all three dimensions. These forces, called ground reaction forces, significantly impact a golfer's movement.

To translate and rotate the various parts of a golfer's body, forces must be applied to the ground in both the frontal plane and the horizontal plane. Within the frontal plane, the two main aspects of force considered are medial/lateral and vertical forces. Medial/lateral forces contribute to the translational and rotational movements of a golfer toward and away from the target whereas vertical forces contribute to their upward and downward movements. In the horizontal plane, the anterior/posterior forces, which primarily contribute to golfer rotation relative to the ground, are evaluated.

In addition to the direction of force application, careful study of ground reaction forces includes an evaluation of the timing and the magnitude of the forces (Figure 2.3). A signature order to the peak magnitudes of the forces applied into the ground has been evaluated among elite golfers. This order includes a medial/lateral combined peak force just before the top of the backswing, a lead foot posterior peak as the golfer's lead arm reaches parallel to the ground on the downswing, a lead foot vertical peak near club vertical, and finally a medial/lateral combined peak away from the target just after club parallel in the downswing (Handley et al., 2015). This sequencing of force application helps coordinate the body's movements in a way that supports consistent solid contact with the golf ball and the development of clubhead speed.

With so many ways to analyze the sport of golf, the need for experts to collaborate has become increasingly important. Collaborative research teams are becoming increasingly prevalent in academic and professional communities as the benefits of a diversified skillset have been realized (Illingworth & Chelvanayagam, 2017). While this interprofessional trend emerged in the 1970s (WHO, 2008) in healthcare to improve outcomes for the various stakeholders, that same philosophy extends to other arenas that rely on multiple areas of expertise.

To properly analyze, synthesize, and evaluate the data from the various technologies reporting on a golfer's swing, for example, identifying and recruiting experts in kinesiology, biomechanics, data analytics, sports and innovation, and golf are all warranted and beneficial. It is best to assemble a powerhouse team of experts across disciplines to help flesh out exactly what is going on. Through a set of diverse lenses, issues can be more easily identified and unique solutions to problems may be provided.

The benefits of interdisciplinary collaboration cannot be overstated. First, this type of collaboration enhances the outcomes for the population of interest. For example, if a golfer is looking to improve the distance and accuracy of their drive, it would be beneficial to enlist the assistance of specialists in golf, biomechanics, and kinesiology to harness the information provided from swing analysis. It may also be beneficial to look to dietetics and nutrition, as well as sports medicine, for more physiological solutions to this issue. By enlisting the help of an interdisciplinary team, the evaluation and synthesis of findings become more robust and holistic.

Similarly, if a golf club is seeking ideas for where to invest capital, enlisting the help of marketing, technology, and sports innovation, as well as hospitality and food and beverage specialists, are suggested. The goal for all interdisciplinary teams is to harness the expertise of the various constituents to create unique, meaningful, and customized solutions to real-time problems.

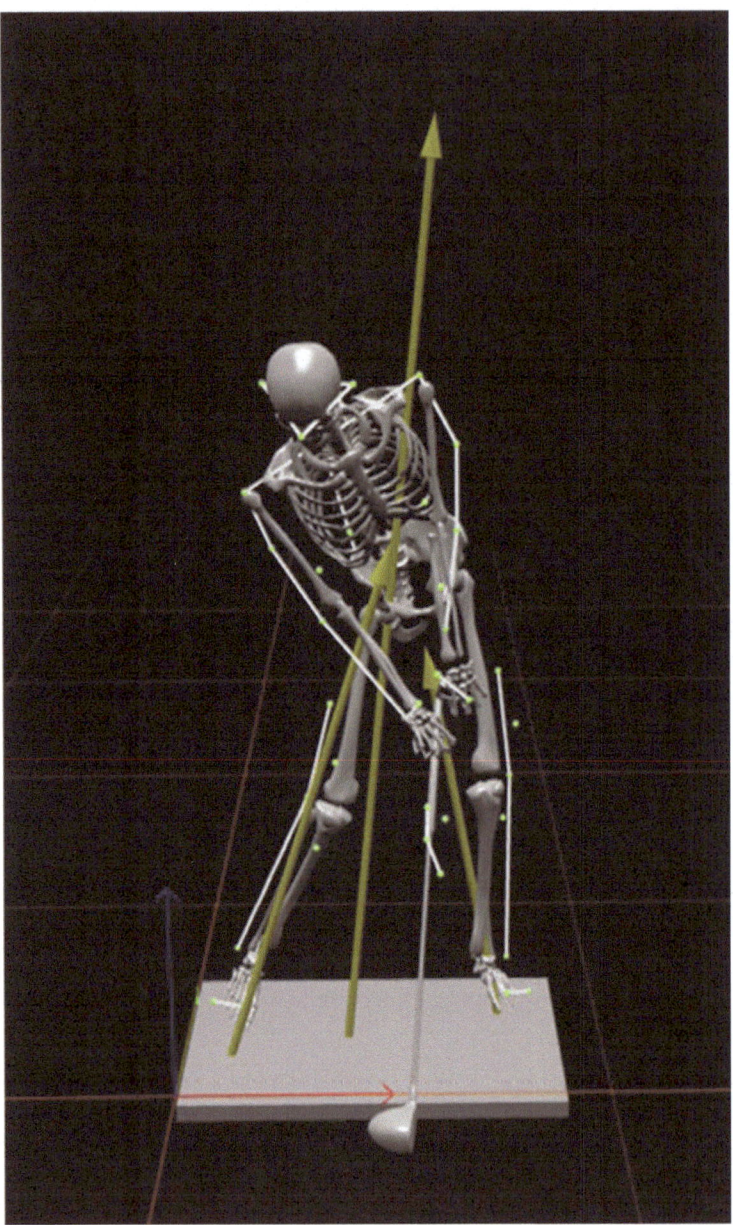

FIGURE 2.3
Example of Golfers Using the Ground Force.

2.4 USE OF TECHNOLOGY AND TECHNOLOGY ACCEPTANCE FOR ELITE ATHLETES

As golf participation has increased, including among younger generations, technology use has become normalized. Technological advancement allows golfers to analyze their performance or swing without direct observation and virtually connect with instructors. During the pandemic, a new lesson platform was created for instructors to train golfers without in-person meetings and publicize their teaching philosophy on social media. This trend created many opportunities for instructors, amateurs, and juniors because it is convenient, useful, and easy. If technology is easy to use, users benefit from proper resources and interaction with other users, according to the technology acceptance model (TAM) (Davis, 1989). With recent technological advancements, it will be inevitable for golfers to use artificial intelligence (AI) technology, specifically in teaching and coaching.

Technology acceptance and use can apply to several types of sports as competitive athletes strive to improve their performance. Golf is not the only sport that players benefit from coaches directly while performing to their ability. Sports ranging from tennis (Figure 2.4) to professional dance can all benefit from the spillovers and applications of technological progress. However, identifying details of errors and developing their intuition based on proper feedback would be necessary. The primary purpose of deriving implications based on findings is to prevent injuries in athletes – by reducing unnecessary behaviors, or establishing the proper sequence of actions – and to maximize their ability to generate ground force reaction or speed of movement.

Elite golfers, who frequently play and practice golf skills to produce outcomes that are consistent, especially in consecutive swing performance, constantly seek small errors in their game and find solutions for enhancing their performance (Kim & Choi, 2022). In general, advanced players and elite instructors are leaders in accepting newly advanced technologies as they foresee their potential implications. Elite golfers and instructors have recently recognized that golf biomechanics analysis tools identify minimal variabilities in body movements that cannot be discerned by the naked eye. The use, findings, and implications of these technologies will analyze patterns in detail, prevent potential injuries, and maximize athletes' abilities.

However, augmented feedback is limited, and as athletes rely while performing activities on intrinsic feedback, self-regulation skills, and coping mechanisms, they tend to trust or be sensitive toward their feelings toward

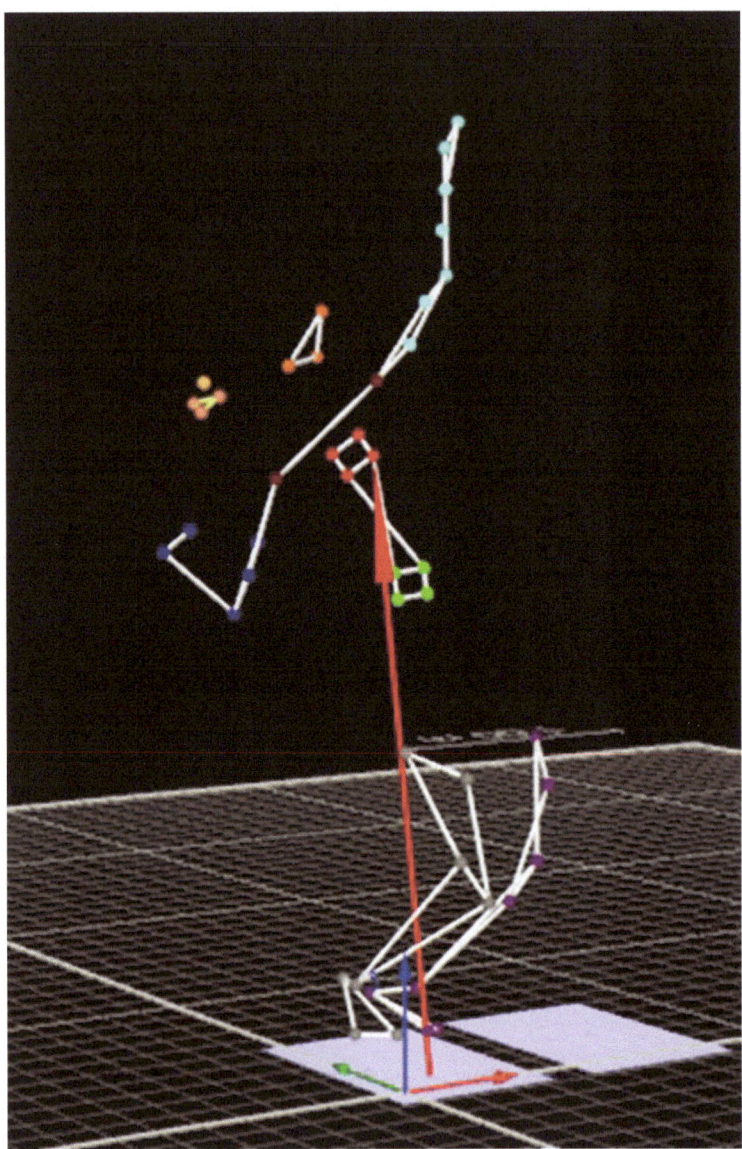

FIGURE 2.4
Example of Tennis Serve.

situations, performance, and emotional stimuli (Gaudreau et al., 2002). Their ability to trust or use their intuition reflects in their decision-making skills, which is strongly related to their commitment level and performance results. However, perception, cognition, and feedback about inputs and outputs are subjective and inconsistent (Mischel & Shoda, 1995), and while analyzing their weaknesses or mistakes athletes often recognize that their perceived feelings are inconsistent or incorrect.

According to the Cognitive Affective Personality System theory (Mischel & Shoda, 1995), individual variability is a natural result of the complexity of human behavior such as social behaviors, emotional information processing, and situation-behavior. For instance, a decision-making process can easily be influenced by social behaviors such as objective comments and situations based on disappointment and excitement. Although individual pattern analysis will constantly include limitations and errors, establishing types of individual patterns would influence individuals' expectations, subjective values, competencies, strategies for success, and self-regulation.

With the technological advancements in recent years, more athletes are interested in reducing the discrepancy between real output versus emotional stimulus (Kerr-Dineen, 2023). Based on Affective Reality Theory (Makowski, 2023), subjective internal cues developed from individual experiences may influence decision-making skills. To enhance the quality of performance, the use of technology for players is critical as it detects real movements and patterns and categorizes results. Those patterns contribute to many practical implications for instructors' teaching methodologies as it enhances the quality of communication regarding technical errors between players and coaches. For this reason, sports athletes and coaches in a variety of fields look out for proper and accurate feedback from the wide use of technology.

Golf biomechanics data, result analysis, and implications will not only strengthen the literature regarding cognitive behaviors such as information processing and decision-making but also recognize the theoretical implications of individuals' acceptance and use of technology (Makowski, 2023; Mischel et al., 1995; Venkatesh & Davis, 2000). This contribution continues to create learning opportunities for instructors and athletes so that their behaviors, perceptions, and patterns can be further explained.

Also, pattern analysis allows instructors and athletes to create or adjust their practice routines. They can enhance, retain, and transfer their skills more effectively based on their goals and personal learning styles with the use of technology, physical features, and expectations. As more scientific data creates patterns and defines human subjective behaviors, instructors will develop their methodologies based on facts rather than their intuitions or perceptions. With their influence, athletes can enhance decision-making abilities and cognitive behavioral patterns.

Elite athletes will benefit from the proper use of technology but implications will strengthen instructional methodologies as well. As instructors and coaches use more logical and scientific data to support their lesson, it enhances the quality of communication between them and players. Players will understand instructors' intentions more efficiently and train themselves using visual demonstrations. Newly introduced technology has always been influencing performance practices as it becomes learning aids.

With the use of biomechanics technology, players now easily visualize their body movements – such as sequence of movements and movement directions – and understand outputs such as force and dynamic balance. In addition, as more data is collected to establish pattern analysis, instructors can explain the impact of individual physical characteristics and abilities to create speed.

The benefits of using biomechanic analytic tools are no secret to other sports professionals. For example, Qualisys offers program modules for running, cricket, baseball, and other sports. The primary purpose of using this analytic tool is similar across sports: professionals are interested in increasing their speed or force by idealizing the sequence of body movements and preventing injuries by detecting unnecessary moves.

Many movement patterns will be produced as more players and instructors accept this technology. Those patterns will explain the personalized movements and their effect to maximize the force or speed. In addition, finding the level of significance in multiple relationships among body portions will allow players to focus on specific body movements for their personal goals. As a result, some implications can be generalized to individuals who share the same goal.

Also, as this technology application is further developed, it might influence the sport's reliance on subjective grading measurement. Performers in dancing, diving, figure skating, and gymnastics might be able to identify their body movements as numerical values that will influence their practice, teaching methodologies, and injury prevention routines.

This technology benefits elite performance and produces multiple solutions for amateurs and beginners. With current limited resources and clear effectiveness to elite performers, the team uses a top-down approach, but certainly implications are not limited to them. Three-dimensional motions and visualization will enhance the quality of communication between golfers and instructors. They can also use the technology as a learning aid. Furthermore, as participation continues to increase, one of the best practices would be to offer solutions to the large population of golfers who have minor or major disabilities so that they can maximize their ability while enjoying the game of golf.

2.5 GOLF ANALYTICS: STROKES GAINED

As in most other sports, data has revolutionized golf, and one of the most important data advances was the introduction in 2001 of PGA's Shotlink system, which tracks beginning and end stroke location (Burke, 2012). The system has since evolved with Shotlink+, which now tracks trajectory, clubhead speed, and launch angle (Barrett, 2019). This rich data allows for not only more accurate stats, but entirely new stats. Here we introduce "strokes gained" (Broadie, 2014), which is based upon average strokes to hole out at any distance and any lie on the course.

Leveraging Shotlink data, Mark Broadie released a seminal paper (Broadie, 2012) analyzing 8 million shots by professional golfers whose findings included aggregated average hole-out data at various distances and lies. Using this data, we estimated benchmark functions using generalized additive models (GAM) and rendered them in Figure 2.5. The color-coded curves, where each curve is on a different lie on the course, show how many strokes on average an PGA professional is expected to make to hole out from different distances in yards. Any position on the hole can be compared to any other position using these benchmark function plots. Three sets of reference lines were created to allow for comparing the differences in distances for the same number of strokes when the ball is on different lies. For example, starting from the fairway, 4 strokes are worth 370 yards, whereas starting from the rough, 4 strokes are worth only 330 yards. Looking at 3 strokes, 50 yards in the sand is worth the same as eighty yards in the rough, or 165 yards on the fairway! This has major implications for choosing accuracy over distance based upon the distance from the pin. Another way of looking at this is the number of strokes required to hole out from the same distance at different lie locations. For example, at 200 yards on the fairway, the average pro golfer will hole out in 3.2 strokes, whereas in the sand it will require an additional 0.4 strokes, for a total of 3.6 strokes.

We can also apply a similar analytical approach to putts. In 2011, Mark Broadie released a paper that analyzed 500,000 putts by professional golfers (Broadie, 2011). Just as we derived the benchmark functions in Figure 2.5, we utilized published aggregate data from Broadie's 2011 paper to create a GAM

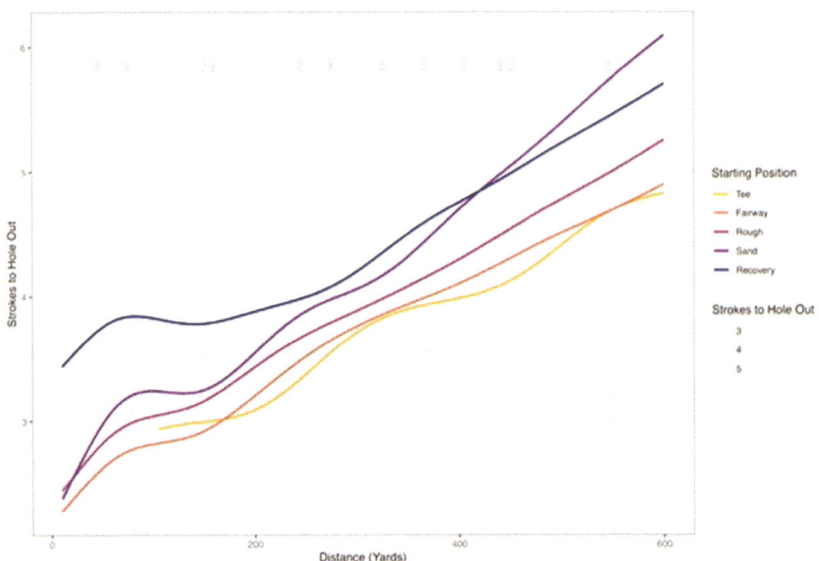

FIGURE 2.5

Benchmark Functions from Various Lies. (Data from Mark Broadie's (2012) analysis of eight million professional golfer shots.)

to estimate the putting benchmark function, which is rendered in Figure 2.6. Note that while Figure 2.5's benchmark functions are in yards, Figure 2.6's benchmark function is in feet to provide more precision.

The benchmark functions in Figures 2.5 and 2.6 can be used to calculate strokes gained, which was originally introduced as Shot Value by Mark Broadie's original work analyzing amateur players (Broadie, 2008). Before the strokes gained metric was introduced, each type of shot in golf was measured in different units –driving yards, greens in regulations (GIR), or number of putts – which made it exceedingly difficult, or impossible, to compare shots or players. The value of strokes gained is that it is fractional, and it uses the same metric across all shot types, enabling direct comparisons between them. The PGA uses four types of stroke gained: "off-the-tee (OTT)," "approach," "around-the-green," and "putting" (*Golf Stat and Records | PGA TOUR*, 2024). "Strokes gained: OTT" only includes tee shots for par-4 and par-5 holes. "Strokes gained: approach" includes all shots beyond 30 yards, excluding tee shots for par-4 and par-5 holes. "Strokes gained: around-the-green" include all shots within 30 yards except for those on the green. "Strokes gained: putting" only include those on the green. All 4 types can be added together to find "strokes gained: total," which is the number of strokes a player gained

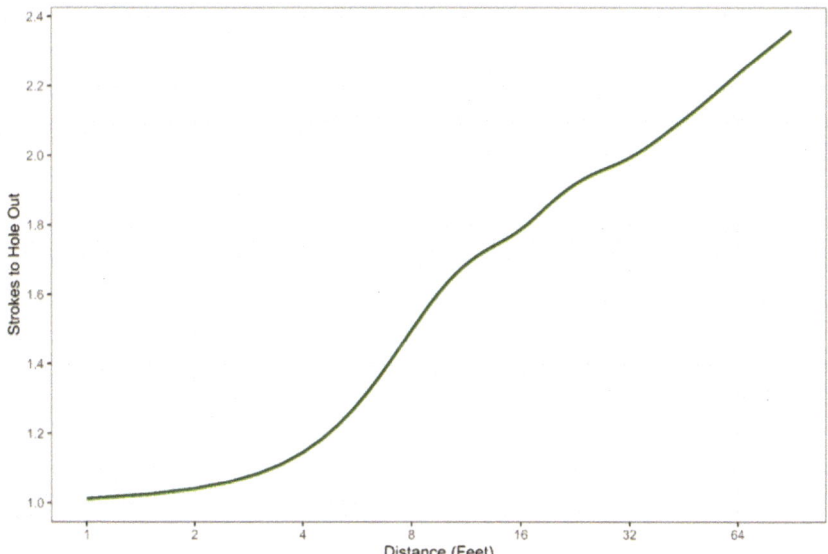

FIGURE 2.6
Benchmark Function from Putting. (Data from Mark Broadie's (2011) analysis of 500,000 professional golfer putting shots.)

or lost on a hole compared to an average professional player. For instance, if on a particular hole the average professional takes 4 strokes to hole out, but a specific player does it in 3, that player gains a stroke. However, we can also add fractional strokes, such as if on a hole the average professional takes 3.25 strokes to hole out, and a specific player does it in four, then that player loses 0.75 strokes.

To demonstrate how to calculate the different types of strokes gained, we will calculate strokes gained for two professional golfers (Table 2.1) at the same random five-par hole—Zac Blaire, who is a master on the fairway, but somewhat average off the tee, and Tony Finau, who is known for his very long drives, but struggles with precision.

For this hole, both golfers hole out in four strokes. According to the off-the-tee benchmark function in Table 2.1, the average strokes at 589 yards is 4.81, therefore both of their strokes gained: total is calculated as 4.81 – 4 = + 0.81. However, the story does not end here—the benefit of strokes gained lies in its ability to facilitate comparisons among players across several types of shots throughout the hole, all measured in fractions of a stroke.

Starting from the tee, Zac Blaire hits the ball 269 yards to the fairway, with 319 yards to go. The starting position's expected strokes is 4.81, and the end

TABLE 2.1

Strokes Gained for Two Professional Golfers

Shot	Start Distance	Start Lie	Distance	End Distance	End Lie	Start xStrokes	End xStrokes	SG
Zac Blaire								
1	589 yd	Tee	269 yd	319 yd	Fairway	4.81	3.83	-0.02
2	319 yd	Fairway	257 yd	62 yd	Fairway	3.83	2.70	0.13
3	62 yd	Fairway	64 yd	5 ft	Green	2.70	1.22	0.48
4	5 ft	Green	5 ft	0 ft	In the hole	1.22	0.00	0.22
								0.81
Tony Finau								
1	589 yd	Tee	321 yd	268 yd	Fairway	4.81	3.62	0.19
2	268 yd	Fairway	279 yd	37 yd	Rough	3.62	2.72	-0.10
3	37 yd	Rough	41 yd	16 ft	Green	2.72	1.79	-0.07
4	16 ft	Green	16 ft	0 ft	In the hole	1.79	0.00	0.79
								0.81

position is 3.83. To calculate the strokes gained: OTT we subtract the end position from the start position and subtract one to account for the current swing. Therefore, strokes gained: OTT = 4.81 – 3.83 – 1= -0.02. Since this is close to zero, Blaire is average off the tee for this hole. From there, he hits the ball 257 yards to 62 yards from the pin, again, on the fairway. Since he is still on the fairway, and beyond thirty yards, this will be a measure of strokes gained: approach. Using the benchmark function, we find that the expected strokes to hole out on the fairway from start position of 319 yards equals 3.83 strokes and the expected strokes to hole out on the fairway from the end position of 62 yards equals 2.70 yards, therefore SG: approach = 3.83-2.70-1 = 0.13 strokes. Blaire's third shot is sixty-four yards to the green, which lands five feet away from the pin. The start position's expected strokes, which is sixty-four yards on the fairway, is 2.70 strokes, while the end position expected strokes is 1.22 strokes from the benchmark function in figure J2. Since the start position was beyond 30 yards, it is still considered a SG: approach, therefore SG: approach = 2.70 – 1.22 – 1 = 0.48. Finally, SG: putting is calculated as the average number of strokes at the start position on the green minus the number of strokes required to hole out once on the green, therefore SG: putting = 1.22 – 1 = 0.22. Here are the three recorded categories for Blaire, SG: OTT = -0.02, SG: approach = 0.13 + 0.48 = 0.61, and SG: putting = 0.22.

Tony Finau starts off with a long 321-yard drive that ends up 268 yards from the pin. At this distance, the expected number of strokes to hole out is 3.62, so his SG: OTT = 4.81 – 3.62 – 1 = +0.19. His fairway shot flies 279 yards, but lands in the rough 37 yards from the hole. At this distance, the average pro golfer will need 2.72 strokes to hole out, so Finau's strokes gained: approach = 3.62 – 2.72 – 1 = -0.10. From the rough, he lands on the green at 16 feet from the hole, which on average would take professional golfers 2.72 holes to sink. Therefore, his strokes gained: approach from this position = 2.72 – 1.79 – 1 = -0.07. Finally, on the green he sinks a 16-foot putt, which takes an average professional golfer 1.79 strokes to hole out, so he gains 1.79 – 1 = +0.79. So, for Finau, SG: OTT = 0.19, SG: approach = -0.10 + -0.07 = -0.17, and SG: putting = 0.79.

While comparing SG: total, there is no difference between these two golfers for this hole (0.81), however looking at the types of shots, we see an entirely different picture. For Finau, his SG: OTT and SG: putting were far superior to Blaire, who walloped Finau in the SG: approach game. While a single hole is not enough to suggest any trends, over a few tournaments or seasons, a full picture starts to emerge of a player's game. This information can lead to finding areas of improvement, along with understanding how that improvement will affect the player's overall game. Tradeoffs can also be determined, for instance it has been determined through strokes gained analysis that driving distance is more important than driving accuracy when it comes to scoring (Broadie, 2014).

2.6 RESEARCH IN ACTION: DATA ANALYTICS AND MACHINE LEARNING APPLICATIONS IN GOLF

The collaborative research team has collected over 50 cases using golf biomechanics technology in the last 5 years since the Institutional Review Board (IRB) submission of our Elite Golfers Performance Evaluation to three institutions: UNLV, Penn State University, and Syracuse. Study participants include male and female professional tour players in addition to active and former collegiate players. As elite athletes make fewer mistakes and pay more attention to small errors for performance enhancement, this population is suitable for exploratory research regarding the implications for technology use, pattern analysis, and teaching.

A target sample criterion was set based on participants' playing ability. Participants are elite right-handed golfers who have less than 12 golf handicaps, which represent the average scores. Participants were randomly selected by National Collegiate Athletic Association (NCAA) Division I coaches and golf instructors. There was variability of individual features such as gender, expectations based on their game status, and body mass index. This data allowed investigators to detect some different patterns as it can be categorized by those features. Their height ranges between 53 inches to 73 inches, and weight varies from 130 lb to 210 lb. As the data collection continues, those features can be expanded to a variety of tour status, distinct levels of collegiate golfers, and age. To analyze these players, we use an assortment of machine learning tools.

Numerous machine learning algorithms are well suited for analyzing golf data. The primary tool that our team uses is ordinary least square (OLS) linear regression, which allows us to determine the relationship between one or more independent variables and a dependent variable. For example, we can explore the relationship between driving distance, which is an independent variable, and strokes per round, which is the dependent variable. Mark Broadie found, by using OLS linear regression, that the marginal effect of adding an additional 20 yards of driving distance for a PGA pro equates to an additional ¾ strokes per round (Broadie, 2014). Another example that our team has been investigating is estimating the marginal effect that golf swing variance (consistency) has on drive distance and accuracy. In our preliminary study involving professional and collegiate athletes, we observed that transitioning from a higher to a lower swing variance ranking among our subjects resulted in an average gain of +0.868 strokes gained per round. The relationship between swing variance and strokes gained per swing is illustrated in Figure 2.7. Each data point represents a subject, comparing their mean average swing variance to their mean average strokes gained. The plot clearly shows that as swing variance decreases, indicating a more consistent swing, strokes gained increases. Our findings may prove useful for coaches to discover novel methods of improvement in golfers.

Another tool that we use is a GAM which, unlike an OLS linear regression model, can measure nonlinear relationships. This is because GAMs can include splines, which are piecewise-defined polynomial functions that smoothly connect to each other (Hastie & Tibshirani, 1999). With splines, smooth boundaries can be correctly modeled whereas with OLS, higher order polynomial parameters are required, which have many drawbacks, including affecting global areas outside of the localized boundaries. We have used GAMs to estimate complex curves such as swings or benchmark functions. Our swing models were used to measure variance, as discussed above, and

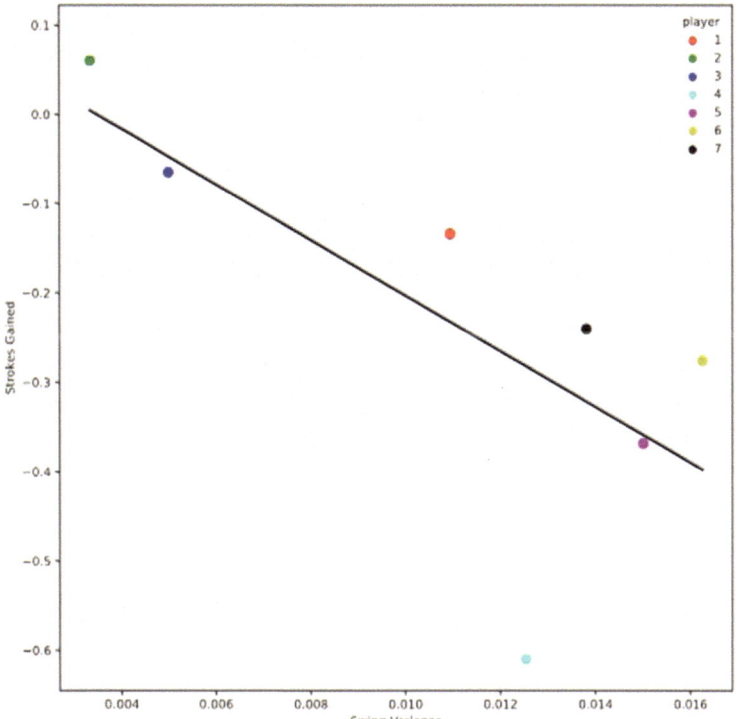

FIGURE 2.7
Relationship of Variance and Strokes Gained.

our benchmark functions are used to estimate expected strokes to hole out, as discussed earlier in the chapter.

When tracking golf swings, we typically capture 9 biomechanical time series variables for each participant: pelvis displacement, torso displacement, left ground reactionary force (GRF), left center of pressure (COP), right GRF, right COP, pelvis angle, torso angle, and center of mass (COM) displacement, with each measured in the X, Y, and Z dimensions. This gives us 27 dimensions worth of data, captured at 340 times per second, which is a tremendous amount of data to model. To manage this amount of data, we are able to employ principal component analysis (PCA), which transforms high-dimension data into low-dimension data, while at the same time maximizing variance and minimizing information loss (Jolliffe & Cadima, 2016). We have used this to successfully reduce a swing from 27 dimensions to a single dimension, while still retaining enough information to model the swing using a GAM. Another use of PCA can be found in a study (Morrison et al., 2018) that isolates the effect of any deviations of the club from the swing plane. The findings of this study suggested that a swing with less deviation from the swing plane is associated with a less variability of the clubface impact location, which may result in more consistent drives. This may also allow golf coaches to increase the precision of striking the ball by simplifying swings to follow the swing plane (Morrison et al., 2018).

A final machine learning model that we commonly employ is the regression tree. This allows us to visually infer how the contributing factors produce a final prediction. For instance, when using the 27 dimensions of biomechanical swing tracking data to predict the distance of a swing, a regression tree can highlight which of these dimensions are most important in determining the length of this swing and the extent these dimensions affect the final yardage. Additionally, there are more advanced algorithms that are based upon ensembles of trees, such as XGBoost or RandomForests. While these algorithms tend to be more accurate than single trees, inference is more difficult due to their complexities.

In conclusion, machine learning tools are incredibly important in analyzing golf data. The amount of golf data is exploding, and now that flight trajectory and biomechanical tracking data are captured in addition to start and end location of swings, more sophisticated machine learning techniques are required to make sense of the data. The combination of golf data and machine learning is revolutionizing the sport as insights are now available to not only analysts but also athletes, coaches, and fans.

2.7 CONCLUSIONS

This chapter presented readers with a clear understanding of the current and future economic impact of the sport of golf. The multibillion-dollar influence of the sport coupled with the record number of people engaging with the sport in on- and off-course modalities warrants further examination. The proliferation of technology, from social media to statistical and gaming apps to simulators and swing analysis tools, has played a pivotal role in enhancing and increasing awareness and participation in golf.

Moreover, technology is now being leveraged to complement professional teaching and coaching. These tools not only facilitate a data-driven, analytical approach to feedback on players' swings but also allow coaches to identify key indicators that allow elite golfers to perform optimally. The use of biomechanics enables these players to visualize their body movements through

3-D motion capture to better understand their sequence of movements and movement directions as well as the force they can generate and their balance. Over time, they are also able to pinpoint patterns in their swings and better understand how their own body composition can be used most effectively to generate force, create speed, and improve club delivery and ball flight.

Ultimately, the application of data analytics and machine learning applications in golf have led to collaborative, interdisciplinary research teams that seek to harness the power of big data. Experts in golf, sport management, kinesiology, nutrition and dietetics, and data analytics will continue to collect data from elite athletes and myriad other types of golfers to help advance our understanding of how we play the game. The goal of all of this is to use data to identify how we can continue to improve the landscape of golf today and increase participation, performance, and enjoyment into the future. After all, golf is more than just a stick and a ball.

REFERENCES

Barrett, D. (2019, June). *How ShotLink+ is Transforming Golf Data*. PGA TOUR, June-November 2019.

Broadie, M. (2008). *Assessing Golfer Performance Using Golfmetrics*. Science and Golf V: Proceedings of the 2008 World Scientific Congress of Golf, 9.

Broadie, M. (2011). *Putts Gained: Measuring Putting on the PGA TOUR*. https://api.semantic scholar.org/CorpusID:18497868

Broadie, M. (2012). Assessing Golfer Performance on the PGA TOUR. *Interfaces*, 42(2), 146–165. https://doi.org/10.1287/inte.1120.0626

Broadie, M. (2014). *Every Shot Counts: Using the Revolutionary Strokes Gained Approach to Improve Your Golf Performance and Strategy*. Gotham.

Burke, M. (2012, April 5). *ShotLink Is Making Golf Easier for Hacks and Harder for Pros*. Forbes.

Cain, C., & Cain, L. (2022). *Golf's Rebirth: Rapidly Evolving Applications in Hospitality and Sport Management*. Kendall Hunt.

Davis, F. D. (1989). Perceived usefulness, perceived ease of use, and user acceptance of information technology. *MIS Quarterly, 13*(3), 319–339.

Eichelberger, P., Ferraro, M., Minder, U., Denton, T., Blasimann, A., Krause, F., & Baur, H. (2016). Analysis of accuracy in optical motion capture – A protocol for laboratory setup evaluation. *Journal of Biomechanics, 49*(10), 2085–2088. https://doi.org/https://doi.org/10.1016/j.jbiomech.2016.05.007

Gaudreau, P., Blondin, J. P., & Lapierre, A. M. (2002). Athletes' coping during a competition: relationship of coping strategies with positive affect, negative affect, and performance-goal discrepancy. *Psychology of Sport and Exercise, 3*, 125–150.

Golf Stat and Records | PGA TOUR. (2024). www.pgatour.com/stats

Handley, E., Davis, D., Masters, S., Merrell, D., & Duffey, M. (2015). *The Biomechanics of Golf. Introduction to 3D Motion Analysis*. https://golf.psu.edu/

Hastie, T., & Tibshirani, R. (1999). *Generalized Additive Models*. Chapman & Hall/CRC.

Illingworth, P., & Chelvanayagam, S. (2017). The benefits of interprofessional education 10 years on. *British Journal of Nursing, 26*(14), 813–818.

Jolliffe, I. T., & Cadima, J. (2016). Principal component analysis: A review and recent developments. *Philosophical Transactions of the Royal Society A: Mathematical, Physical and Engineering Sciences, 374*(2065), 20150202. https://doi.org/10.1098/rsta.2015.0202

Kerr-Dineen, L. (2023). Justin Thomas is grinding on his golf swing – Let's break down the video. *Golf Digest*. Retrieved from www.australiangolfdigest.com.au/justin-thomas-2023-ryder-cup-golf-swing-drill/

Kim, S. Y., & Choi, C. (2022). Difference in stress, stress-coping behavior, and quality of life based on the performance of Korean Ladies Professional Golf Association Tour Players. *International Journal of Environmental Research and Public Health, 19,* 6623.

Kwon, Y.-H. (n.d.). Dr. Kwon's golf biomechanics instructor training program certification courses. Retrieved from www.drkwongolf.info/courses.html

Makowski, D. (2023). How do we know what is real? The "Affective Reality Theory". Retrieved from https://dominiquemakowski.github.io/post/2023-04-11-affectivereality/

Mischel, W., & Shoda, Y. (1995). A Cognitive-affective system theory of personality: Reconceptualizing situations, dispositions, dynamics, and invariance in personality structure. *Psychological Review, 102*(2), 246–268.

Morrison, A., McGrath, D., & Wallace, E. S. (2018). Analysis of the delivery plane in the golf swing using principal components. *Proceedings of the Institution of Mechanical Engineers, Part P: Journal of Sports Engineering and Technology, 232*(4), 295–304. https://doi.org/10.1177/1754337117751729

NGF. (2018). Technology and Golf's Best Customers. National Golf Foundation. Retrieved from www.ngf.org/product-tag/technology/

NGF. (2023a). The Graffis Report Golf Industry 2023 Year in Review. National Golf Foundation. Retrieved from www.ngf.org/product/the-graffis-report-2024/

NGF. (2023b). Perceptions of Golf. National Golf Foundation. Retrieved from www.ngf.org/perceptions-of-golf/

NGF. (2023c). Off-Course to On-Course: Golf's New Engagement and Conversion Pathway. National Golf Foundation. Retrieved from www.ngf.org/product-tag/off-course-golfers/

NGF. (2023d). Simulator Golf Sees Real Surge. National Golf Foundation. Retrieved from www.ngf.org/simulator-golf-sees-real-surge/

NGF. (2023e). Golf Participation in the U.S. National Golf Foundation. Retrieved from www.ngf.org/golf-industry-research/

NGF. (2023f). Golf Economic Impact Report 2023. National Golf Foundation. Retrieved from www.ngf.org/product/golf-economic-impact-report-2023/

PGA. (n.d.). PGA of America Lifelong Learning. PGA of America. Retrieved from https://southcentral.pga.com/lifelong-learning/

PGA Coach. (n.d.). Golf's American Development Model. PGA Coach. Retrieved from https://pga.coach/Golf%27s_American_Development_Model.pdf

TPI. (n.d.). Certification. MyTPI. Retrieved from www.mytpi.com/certification

Venkatesh, V., & Davis, F. D. (2000). A theoretical extension of the technology acceptance model: Four longitudinal field studies. *Management Science, 46*(2), 186–204.

World Health Organization. (2008). *Integrated Health Services*. What and Why? Technical Brief No.1, May 2008. WHO Geneva. https://terrance.who.int/mediacentre/data/sage/SAGE_Docs_Ppt_Apr2014/10_session_child_health_services/Apr2014_session10_integrated_health_services.pdf

3

Analytics Democratization: How the NFL Fosters a Pipeline of Future Analysts through Digital Data Accessibility

Bradley J. Congelio

3.1 INTRODUCTION

In a 2018 article for *The Ringer*, Kevin Clark explained that the analytics movement in the National Football League (NFL) is currently happening right in front of us in real time. Unlike the prominent "moneyball" movement in Major League Baseball (MLB) or the data-centric approach in the National Basketball Association (NBA) that killed the mid-range shot, the NFL is navigating its own analytics revolution in a subtle yet significant fashion, harnessing a movement that is uniquely driven by an influx of publicly accessible game data. This data, disseminated through computer programming packages such as the {nflverse} or companies like Pro Football Focus (PFF) and Sports Info Solutions (SIS), has democratized NFL analytics, thus nurturing a robust community of amateur analysts. Using computer programming languages such as Python and R, these fans of the game have created and shared exploratory analysis and models alike, thereby introducing innovative approaches to understanding and dissecting the game of football. Recognizing the value within this emergent community, the NFL hosted the inaugural Big Data Bowl in 2019. Since this inaugural contest, more than 50 participants have gone on to analytics roles with professional teams. Moreover, numerous winning entries have been adopted by the NFL as official league metrics for use on their website and television broadcasts. This chapter endeavors to elucidate how digital transformations, manifested through continually growing amounts of accessible football data, have

DOI: 10.1201/9781032665191-3

(1) lowered the barrier of entry for individuals aspiring to learn computer programming and sports analytics and (2) empowered the NFL to leverage this amateur analytics movement to continue discovering and implementing fresh analytics insights, methodologies, and models. This chapter explores this mutually beneficial ecosystem where aspiring analysts gain a platform to refine and showcase their skills while the NFL avails itself from a wider spectrum of analytics perspectives.

In 2014, Doug Pederson – then the head coach of the NFL's Philadelphia Eagles – confessed that his team eschewed long-held league tradition and fully embraced the inclusion of analytics. Pederson explained that all decisions made by the Eagles organization – from game planning to draft strategy – were informed by hard data and analytics. Philadelphia's early adoption of analytics was spearheaded by Joe Douglas and Alec Halaby – the latter being described as a "31-year-old Harvard grad with a job description" that had an emphasis on "integrating traditional and analytical methods in football decision-making" (Awbrey, 2020). Reporting directly to Howie Roseman, the team's Vice President, the duo blended traditional and analytical methods that were often only seen in other leagues, such as the NBA and MLB (Rosenthal, 2018). Pederson believed in and trusted the team's analytics approach so much that a direct line of communication was created between the two during games, with the analytics department providing the head coach with math-based recommendations for any scenario Pederson requested (Awbrey, 2020).

Pederson's approach to blending traditional and analytical approaches to football was a significant factor in the Eagles winning the Super Bowl at the end of the 2017 season. Perhaps the most visible – and easily understood – impact of the organization's analytical approach was Pederson's record-breaking aggressiveness on 4th downs. The Eagles went for it on 4th down 26 times during the season and converted on 17 of the attempts, for a success rate of 65.4 percent. Such an aggressive approach on 4th downs bucked traditional coaching wisdom in the NFL and, as Heifetz argued, "changed the language of football." Moreover, because the NFL is a "copycat league," teams immediately began to carbon-copy Philadelphia's approach to folding traditional football strategy with a new-age analytics approach (Fortier, 2020; Heifetz, 2019).

The impact of this increased adoption of analytics was immediate, as there was a staggering 96.3-percent increase in the number of 4th down attempts from 2000 and 2021. This increase in 4th down attempts is further bolstered by analytics. For example, during week one of both the 2020 and 2021 NFL seasons, *not* going for it on 4th down "cost teams a cumulative 170 percentage

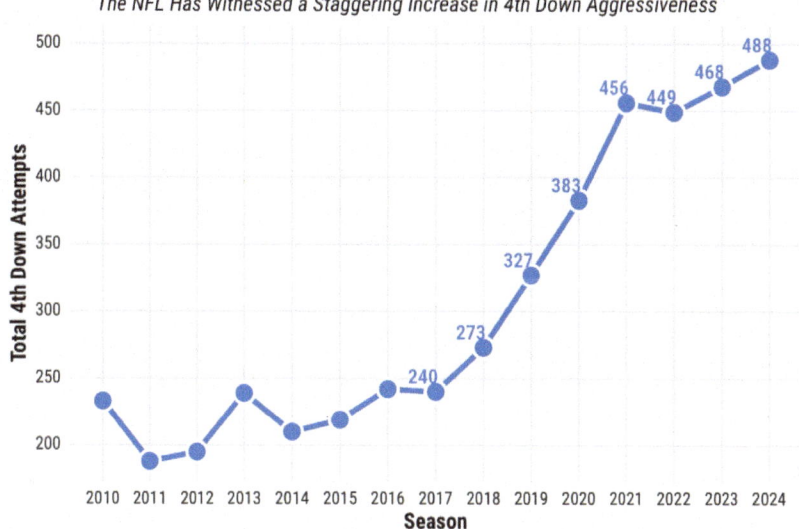

FIGURE 3.1
The NFL has witnessed a staggering increase in the number of 4th down attempts since the 2017 season.

points of win probability" (Bushnell, 2021). Figure 3.1 shows the rapid increase in 4th down aggressiveness starting in the 2017 NFL season.

Kevin Clark was an early harbinger of how the Eagles' 2017 season was altering the decision-making process, noting in a 2018 article in *The Ringer* that, despite not being as obvious as the sabermetrics movement in baseball, the analytics movement in the NFL was currently taking place in front of fans in real time (Clark, 2018). In the years since the publishing of his article, it has become hard to ignore the analytics movement in the NFL. Yet, there is still much growth to happen in the marriage between the NFL and advanced metrics. For example, there is no denying that the sabermetrics movement drastically "altered baseball's DNA" (Heifetz, 2019) and that the movement in the NBA essentially killed the midrange shot (Partnow, 2022).

Compared to both the NBA and MLB, the NFL is playing catch-up in using analytics to drive changes that are equivalent to the death of the midrange shot or the plethora of additional tactics and changes to baseball because of sabermetrics. Joe Banner, the President of the Philadelphia Eagles from 2001 to 2012 and then the Chief Executive Officer of the Browns from 2012 to 2013, explained that some of the hesitation to fully embrace analytics in NFL game planning was a result of the game being "very much driven by conventional wisdom to an extreme degree" (Fortier, 2020). Perhaps nobody encapsulates this better than Pittsburgh Steelers Head Coach Mike Tomlin who, when asked about his position on analytics during the 2015 season, explained:

> I think that's why you play the game. You can take analytics to baseball and things like that, but football is always going to be football. I [have] a lot of respect for analytics and numbers, but I'm not going to make judgments based on those numbers. The game is the game. It's an emotional one played by emotional and driven men. That's an element of the game you can't measure. Often times, decisions such as that weigh heavily into the equation.
>
> *Kozora, 2015*

Despite some coaches, such as Tomlin, that continue to resist fully embracing analytics, the thirst for new knowledge and advantages in the NFL is no less than in any other league. While the NBA and MLB can certainly serve as a roadmap to where analytics may take the NFL, the league is still very much in the "first frontier of what will likely be sweeping changes over the next two decades" (Heifetz, 2019). Because of the modernity of this relationship between long-held football dogmas and analytics, nobody can be quite sure what other impacts it will have on the gamesmanship of football.

However, unlike the prominent "moneyball" movement in MLB or the data-centric approach in the NBA that made the midrange shot less prominent, the NFL is navigating its own analytics revolution in a subtle yet significant fashion by harnessing a movement that is uniquely driven by an inflex of publicly accessible game data. This data, disseminated through computer programming packages such as the {nflverse} or companies like Pro Football Focus (PFF) and Sports Info Solutions (SIS), has democratized NFL analytics, thus nurturing a robust community of amateur analysts. Using computer programming languages such as R and Python, these fans of the game created and shared exploratory analysis and models alike, thereby introducing innovative approaches to understanding and dissecting the game of football. Uniquely, the NFL has recognized the value in this emergent analytics community and, rather than attempting to limit the amount of league data that is publicly available, leaned into the movement by providing continued support, including allowing the continued collection of play-by-play data by the {nflverse} family of R packages and the creation of the Big Data Bowl wherein the league releases data from its proprietary tracking data.

This chapter aims to elucidate how this mutually beneficial ecosystem, manifested by the continually growing amount of accessible football data, has (1) lowered the barrier of entry for individuals aspiring to learn computer programming and sports analytics and (2) empowered the NFL to leverage the amateur analytics community to continue discovering and implementing fresh analytics, insights, and models.

3.2 LOWERED BARRIER OF ENTRY FOR NFL ANALYTICS

On April 27, 2020, Ben Baldwin hit send on a Tweet to announce the release of {nflfastR}, an R package designed to allow easy access to robust NFL play-by-play data (Computer Cowboy, 2020). The {nflfastR} package was inspired by the {nflscrapR} project, which was the existing package to retrieve NFL data at the time of {nflfastR's} release. The {nflscrapR} package was created by the Carnegie Mellon University student and professor duo of Maksim Horowitz and Sam Ventura as part of their research into properly evaluating NFL players. In what is now a seminal paper in the field of football analytics and research, Yurko, Ventura, and Horowitz (2018) introduced a novel logistic regression approach to estimate each play's expected points (EP) in order to calculate the individual win probability (WP) for each using a generalized additive model. However – as noted by the authors – the NFL "lacks comprehensive statistical rating for player evaluation that are both reproducible and easily interpretable in terms of game outcomes." Importantly, any model that did currently exist at the time relied on data that was wholly proprietary and not accessible to the public. Thus, the authors of the paper created {nflscrapR}.

In short, the package used individual 10-digit game identification numbers to connect to the NFL's application programming interface (API). The data was scraped in raw JavaScript Object Notation (JSON) and organized into three groups: the individual game outcomes, the player statistics for each game, and the play-by-play information for each specific game ID. With the creation of {nflscrapR}, play-by-play data dating back to the 2009 NFL season could be collected and used to create, train, and test the EP and WP models as outlined in the paper. Following Horowitz's graduation – and hiring by the NBA's Atlanta Hawks – the responsibility for the continued development of the {nflscrapR} project was handed to Yurko. Despite his continued work on the package, the {nflscrapR} project ended when the specific JSON feed used to gather the data was changed at the endpoint by the NFL. Yurko marked the end of the {nflscrapR} era with a Tweet on September 14, 2020 and informed that those still seeking NFL data would use the {nflfastR} package (nflscrapR, 2020).

Since, the {nflfastR} package served as the impetus for further package development, including {nflseedR}, {nfl4th}, {nflplotR}, and {nflreadr}. The {nflseedR} package allows for the simulation of NFL seasons by utilizing user-created models or, by default, can run "thousands of Monte Carlo style simulations of the NFL regular season" in lieu of a custom modeling specification (Sharpe & Carl, 2024). The {nflplotR} package is auxiliary in nature in that it provides "functions and geoms that help visualization of NFL related analysis" (Carl, 2024). The {nfl4th} package builds upon the knowledge that an NFL head coach has three choices on any given 4th down: attempt a field goal, punt to the opposing team, or attempt to gain enough yardage to get a new set of downs. In short, the {nfl4th} package houses a pretrained model and provides a recommendation based on the win probability added for each of the choices. Using {nflfastR's} ability to collect play-by-play data in near real time, the {nfl4th} package is set to automatically run the model on every 4th down scenario, place the information into a {gt} table, and then Tweet the information in near real time (Baldwin, 2020). Figure 3.2 shows an example Tweet created by Ben Baldwin's 4th down decision model wherein the Seattle Seahawks made the right decision to "got for it" based on the small difference in win percentage added between going for it and attempting a field goal.

However, despite the popularity of the {nfl4th} package on social media, the most widely used package is {nflreadr}, which provides the ability to download data easily and efficiently from all the various repositories belonging to the {nflverse} family of packages. Because of the coalescing between {nflreadr}

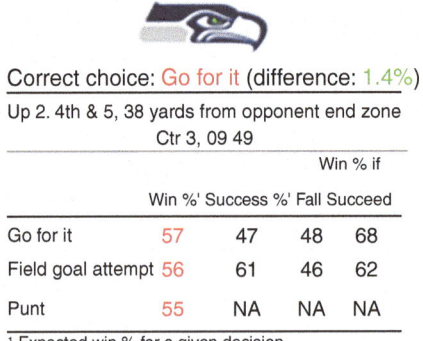

Correct choice: Go for it (difference: 1.4%)

Up 2. 4th & 5, 38 yards from opponent end zone
Ctr 3, 09 49

			Win % if	
	Win %[1]	Success %[1]	Fall	Succeed
Go for it	57	47	48	68
Field goal attempt	56	61	46	62
Punt	55	NA	NA	NA

[1] Expected win % for a given decision
[2] Likelihood of converting on 4th down or of making field goal

FIGURE 3.2

An Example Output from the {nfl4th} Package.

and {nflfastR}, many of the newly developed functions within the {nflverse} are only available when calling functions using 'nflreadr::`. While {nflfastR} did serve as the starting point of the amateur NFL analytics movement, after taking the place of {nflscrapR}, the {nflreadr} package has superseded it in that the package now serves as the "catchall" for all the various bits and pieces of {nflverse} data (Congelio, 2023).

The {nflreadr} package is also responsible for the democratization of NFL data and lowering the barrier of entry for amateur analysts. Included in the play-by-play data that is easily retrievable by the end user are pre-calculated metrics for EP, WP, and Completion Probability (CP). The Expected Points Model estimates the points a team is expected to score from any point on the field at any given time. The Win Probability Model calculates the likelihood of winning the game based on the current game state. The Completion Probability Model predicts the probability of a completed pass. All the machine learning for the models is conducted via XGBoost.

The use of the data included with {nflreadr} manifests in many ways, of which only a few can be outlined in this chapter. For example, it was used to create a Draft Surplus Value model by using historical draft data and assigning values to draft picks based on both expected player performance and career outcomes. The model considers factors like draft round, player position, and team needs, utilizing machine learning to provide more accurate and dynamic valuations compared to traditional models (Schuckers, 2011).

Gurshish Bagga (2023) used the data in {nflreadr} to examine the significant role that penalties play in influencing the outcomes of NFL games. The study utilized a combination of linear regression, logistic regression, and random forest algorithms to analyze how offensive and defensive penalties impact score differentials and drive success rates. Specifically, Bagga used play-by-play data between the 2011 and 2022 seasons to determine that the random forests models better captured the nonlinear interactions of those factors at play in any given offensive drive. While it is not surprising to learn that both offensive and defensive penalties alter the flow and outcomes of games, Bagga's approach allowed for the first nuanced understanding of the impact using a machine learning process.

In some cases, the work being done using {nflreadr} directly conflicts with the package's data and/or approach. Brill, Yurko, and Wyner (2023) examined the complexities and uncertainties inherent in the statistical models used for 4th down decision-making. The standard approach to these decisions typically involves maximizing estimated win probabilities derived from machine learning models trained on the historical play-by-play data, as is the case with the decision model used in {nfl4th}. However, the trio argues that these models are often overfitted and have high variance due to the highly correlated nature of football data. To address this, the authors proposed using bootstrapping techniques to incorporate uncertainty quantification into the decision-making process. This method allows for the inclusion of variance and uncertainty in the win probability estimates. The findings suggest that the uncertainty in these estimates is significantly greater than what is often acknowledged by sports analysts and, as a result, many 4th down decisions are not as clear-cut as they may seem. The work in the paper emphasizes the need for a more nuanced approach to 4th down decision-making that considers the uncertainties that are inherent in the data. Elsewhere, Benjamin Stern (2023) investigated the elements of pass protection and the pass rush using the publicly available data in {nflreadr}. The findings of his blitz prediction model, built using tree-based models, found that while machine learning can identify certain patterns in a blitzing scheme, defensive coordinators maintain a level of unpredictability. Regarding pressure, a model based on a convolutional neural network (CNN) was developed that measured the increasing, or decreasing, pressure continuously as the play developed.

In other cases, users have created packages that build further upon the foundation laid by the {nflverse} family. For example, {NFLSimulatorR} is a package designed to simulate NFL plays and drives using historical play-by-play data. The package allows for the evaluation of in-game strategies and potential rule changes through robust statistical methods. The package employs a sampling procedure that draws from past NFL season data to generate simulations. A more notable application of the package is the analysis of 4th down decision-making strategies. The package provides several sub-strategies, including "always going for it", "never going for it", and "making decisions based on the yardage required for a first down." These strategies are compared by simulating drives and examining outcomes such as scoring probabilities, thus offering a data-driven approach to traditionally heuristic coaching decisions. In addition to 4th down strategies, the package also explores the frequency of passing versus running plays, providing a comprehensive tool for amateur analysts (Williams et al., 2023).

Not all the work being done with the data available in the {nflverse} family of packages is confined to academic papers. Importantly, much public-facing work is completed and shared widely on Twitter. For example, Sam Hoppen, a data scientist at FantasyPros.com, uses the personnel information from {nflreadr} to compile each team's pass rate above/below expectation based on personnel package for each week of the NFL season (Hoppen, 2022). Using a principal component analysis (PCA) model to determine the coverage and market efficiency with team constraints, Steve Patton ranks the performance of both offensive and defensive coordinators on a weekly basis (Patton, 2024). Kevin Cole, previously of Pro Football Focus, introduced an updated NFL Plus-Minus metric to address the difficulty in player valuation, particularly for non-quarterbacks. For example, using statistics and player participation data from {nflreadr}, Cole clustered statistically similar wide receivers via K-means using routes per game, slot rate, yards per route run, touchdowns as a percentage of routes, first-down percentage, deep rate, and yards per season. Through this method, Cole can account for on/off splits that make it "difficult to pinpoint the effect of one player on the field." By clustering similar receivers together, Cole is growing the sample size for each group to "minimize the noise and boost signal" (Cole, 2023). Figure 3.3 shows the pass rate over expected for each team based on offense personnel on the field.

Despite this outstanding public-facing analytics work, the NFL has the authority – and ability – to stop the flow of data to the {nflverse} family of packages. However, it can be argued that the league recognizes the significant value these tools bring to the football analytics community. By allowing these packages to continue to operate, the NFL encourages the development of new metrics and analytical insights, fostering innovation and deeper engagement with the sport. In fact, the NFL actively leans into this collaborative approach by incorporating the {nflverse} family of packages into its annual Big Data

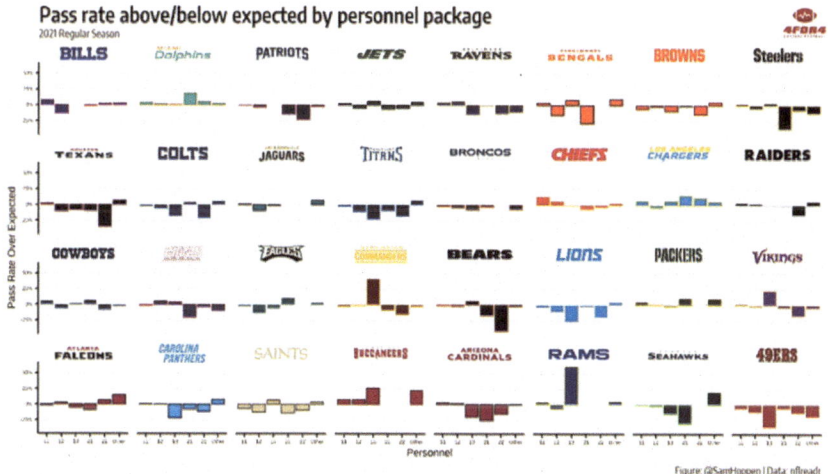

FIGURE 3.3
Sam Hoppen's Pass Rate Above/Below Expected.

Bowl competition, outlining in the contest rules that use of data from the packages is both welcomed and encouraged.

3.3 NFL LEVERAGING THE AMATEUR ANALYTICS COMMUNITY

On December 19, 2018, the NFL announced the inaugural Big Data Bowl, described as a "football analytics competition open to college students and professionals" where each competitor is given the "opportunity to utilize historical data sets of the same player tracking data used by teams and suggest innovations about how football is played and coached" (*NFL Announces Inaugural Big Data Bowl*, 2018). The player tracking data collected by the NFL is largely considered the "holy grail" of analytics information, as the technology collects position, direction, acceleration, deceleration, and speed of each player on the field every 1/10th of a second. The data is accurate "within six inches" whereas the GPS iin your car, for example, is accurate to 39 inches (Rodrigue, 2024). The selected finalists for each Big Data Bowl are brought to the NFL Combine, where the winning team earns $25,000 in prize money. Moreover, as explained by Mike Lopez – the NFL Director of Football Data and Analytics – each team is attempting to be the first "in the history of the world to ever answer" the prompt question by the NFL with the use of tracking data. From the NFL's standpoint, the presentation of the research at the Combine allows NFL team executives the unique chance to meet firsthand the "next wave of talented analysts who can make sense of complex player-tracking data" (Baldwin, 2021). Table 3.1 shows the general prompt that was provided by the competition organizers and what metric was created by the winning submission.

Each annual iteration of the Big Data Bowl presents a prompt that entrants must analyze using player-tracking data. In 2020, competitors were challenged to determine how many yards a running back was likely to gain at the point of handoff. Using tracking data from the final five weeks of the 2019 NFL season, over 2,000 entries were submitted. The winning entry came from Phillip Singer, a Ph.D. in computer science, and Dmitry Gordeev, a graduate in applied mathematics and data from Moscow State University. Both employed by the UNIQA Insurance Group, the duo had previously won six Kaggle gold medals yet had limited knowledge of the NFL. Their

TABLE 3.1

The Annual Prompt Provided by the Organizers of the Big Data Bowl and the Corresponding Outcome from the Winning Submission

BDB Year	General Prompt	Winning Outcome
2020	Rushing Plays at Time of Handoff	Expected Rushing Yards
2021	Analysis of Coverage & Pass Defense	Coverage Classification
2022	Special Teams Play	Expected Return Yards
2023	Pass Rush & Offensive Line Performance	O-line Pressure Probability
2024	Snap to Tackle	Tackle Probability

winning entry utilized a CNN to predict the expected yards a running back should gain at any given handoff. Figure 3.4 shows a graphical schema of the convolutional neural network that was used to create the rushing yards over expected model that won the Big Data Bowl.

The neural network was constructed using five inputs from the tracking data: the location of each defender on the field, the distance between each defender and the ball carrier, the "closing speed" of each defender to the ball carrier, the distance between each defensive player and offensive player on the field, and the speed between each defensive and offensive player. The completed model was nearly perfectly calibrated, with the predicted number of yards closely matching the actual yardage from the training dataset.

By July 2020, the NFL officially introduced Expected Rushing Yards as a statistic. Additionally, the NFL utilized the CNN model developed by Singer and Gordeev to create further "expected metrics", including (1) Expected Rushing Yards, (2) Rushing Yards Over Expected, (3) Rushing Yards Over Expected per Attempt, (4) Rush Percentage Over Expected, (5) First Down Probability, and (6) Touchdown Probability. The league's existing model for Expected Yards After Catch was also recalibrated using the CNN developed by Singer and Gordeev (*Next Gen Stats: Intro to Expected Rushing Yards*, 2020). All these metrics are regularly featured on Sunday Night Football broadcasts.

The 2021 Big Data Bowl was won by Wei Peng, Marc Richards, Sam Walczak, and Jack Werner. The team's model was built off the concept that the current defensive coverage metrics were "only calculated on plays where the defender's assigned offensive player" was the one targeted (Peng et al., 2021). The authors argued that this was a flawed concept in that a receiver's lack of participation in any given play was likely the result of strong defensive coverage. The group's model – built using K-Means clustering and Sequential Modeling (IO-HMM) – grouped each play into the correct defensive coverage

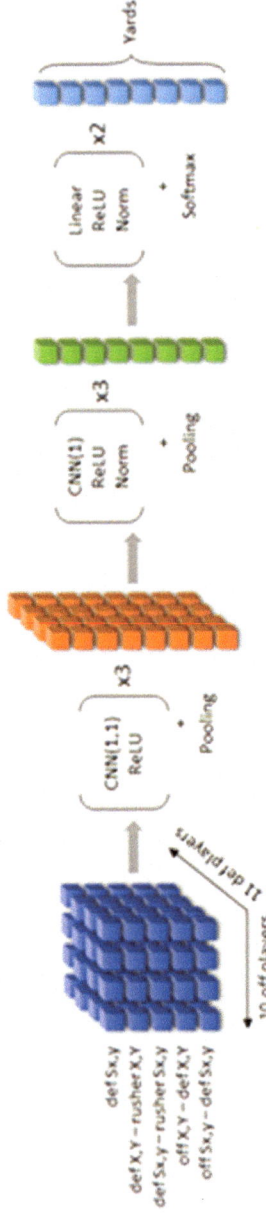

FIGURE 3.4

The CNN Used to Win the 2020 Big Data Bowl.

assignments and, importantly, allowed for the prediction of metrics based on the distance between all the defenders and receivers on the field. Richards was hired by the Kansas City Chiefs as a Football Research Analyst in 2022.

The 2022 Big Data Bowl shifted to examine special teams play. A group of graduate students from Simon Fraser University in Canada – Robyn Ritchie, Brendan Kumagai, Ryker Moreau, and Elijah Cavan – were named winners after designing a model that could (1) "determine the punt returner's optimal path instantaneously" as the play progressed and (2) "evaluate returns and predicted expected yards remaining for each punt return at every frame" (Ritchie et al., 2022). The project was created using a Random Forest Conditional Density Estimate Model, which is the non-parametric regression technique of a random forest fitted for the inclusion of conditional probability distributions (Pospisil & Lee, 2018). The group's model played a role in developing expected return yards as an official metric by the NFL and Amazon Web Services (*AWS and NFL Launch Next Gen Stat 'Expected Return Yards' The newest advanced ML-powered stat from AWS and the NFL tackles the hidden dynamics of punt and kickoff returns*, n.d.).

Hassaan Inayatali, Aaron White, and Daniel Hocevar from the University of Toronto won the 2023 Big Data Bowl which focused on the play and performance of offensive and defensive linemen. The aim of the project was to "isolate the performances of offensive/defensive lines from that of the QB" and to "determine the surplus pressure a defensive linemen provides relative to that of their teammates" (Inayatali et al., 2023). To determine a player's "continuous pocket pressure" the team developed a bivariate normal distribution model while a Kaplan-Meier estimator was used to evaluate the ability of an offensive and defensive lines to resist or create pressure.

The 2024 Big Data Bowl was won by Matthew Chang, Katherine Dai, Daniel Jiang, and Harvey Cheng. The winning project argued that the "traditional metrics" of missed tackles provided only a "surface-level understanding of a defender's tacking skill" (Chang et al., 2024). The group introduced four new metrics: tackle probability, tackle opportunity, missed tackle opportunity, and converted tackle opportunity. The model was built using an XGBoost binary classifier with nine features, including the forward Voronoi area and a unique approach to classifying a team's individual influence. Specifically, the team's influence was generated using a 2D Gaussian function, which was then translated and scaled using the provided location, speed, and direction from the data.

However, it is not just the winners of each competition that garner interest from NFL teams. For the 2020 Big Data Bowl, Alex Stern – then a student at the University of Virginia studying quantitative statistics and computer science – submitted an entry that determined the specific amount of open field each offensive linemen created on a running play and then standardized the information to provide a grade for each blocker (Reid, 2020). In July of 2021, Stern was hired by the Los Angeles Chargers as a Research Analyst. Another 2020 Big Data Bowl participant, Caio Brighenti – then a student at Colgate University – developed an algorithm that computed each team's control of the field at the point of handoff to determine the most likely outcome of the rushing attempt. As a result, Brigneti determined that the "expected point of intersection" with the field's line of scrimmage was the most important factor in predicting the total rushing yards gained (*2020 Big Data Bowl Recap*, 2020). Almost immediately after the competition, in June of 2020, Brigneti was hired by the Detroit Lions as a Football Analytics Assistant. He was promoted to an Analyst of Football Information in March 2021 and again to Manager of Football Information in June 2023 (Bianchi, 2023). A Grand Finalist in the 2020 Big Data Bowl, Matt Ploenzke – from Harvard University – submitted an entry that highlighted the impact of a running back's downfield acceleration in correlation with defensive blocking and spacing. Ploenzke was hired by the San Francisco 49ers in July 2020 as a Football Research Analyst. By July of 2023, he was the Director of Research and Development where he develops "player valuation metrics using advanced statistical techniques" and "provides interpretations of these metrics to aid in roster acquisitions" (*San Francisco 49ers*, n.d.).

After competing in the 2021 Big Data Bowl, Meyappan Subbaiah was hired by the sports-focused Zelus Analytics. In November of 2022, he was hired by the NFL as a Data Scientist. Zack Drapkin, a finalist in the 2021 Big Data Bowl and an honorable mention in the 2022 version, was hired by the Philadelphia Eagles as a Quantitative Analyst in March 2022 before being promoted to a Senior Quantitative Analyst in May of 2024 (Basiouny, n.d.). Joe Andruzzi, a finalist in the 2021 Big Data Bowl and the Sports Info Solutions Football Analytics Challenge, was hired by the Arizona Cardinals in January of 2022. Ella Summer – whose submitted model was able to "isolate individual defender effects on target and completion probability" – was hired as a Football Analytics Staff Assistant by the Miami Dolphins in September 2021 before being promoted to the Head Football Analyst in May 2022.

Dominic Borsani, a 2023 finalist in the Big Data Bowl Coaching Track, was hired by the Cleveland Browns in April of 2023 as a Football Research Analyst. Borsani's entry built two predictive models aimed at assisting defensive coaches during the game planning process – the first predicted which direction the offensive line's center would turn to block while the second made predictions on which defensive players were likely to blitz during any given play. Shane Hauck's 2024 Big Data Bowl submission focused on "setting the edge" and its overall impact on designed zone run plays. While working with the coaching staff at Carnegie Mellon University, the final submission included the creation of a "Edge Intensity Rating to evaluate the real-time effectiveness of edge-setting" (*No Edge No Chance: The Impact of Setting the Edge on Zone Running Plays*, n.d.). He was hired by the Dallas Cowboys as a Strategic Football Fellow in May of 2024 (Chavanelle, 2024).

Several participants in the NFL Big Data Bowl have leveraged their success to secure roles in professional sports leagues outside of the NFL. Dani Chu, a finalist in the 2021 Big Data Bowl, became a Senior Quantitative Analyst for the Seattle Kraken in the NFL. Likewise, Jill Reiner, also a 2021 finalist, joined the Toronto Maple Leafs as an Analyst for Research and Development. James Venzor, yet another 2021 finalist, transitioned to the MLB as a Data Scientist for the Cleveland Guardians. Most recently, Hassaan Inayatail, a finalist in the 2024 Big Data Bowl, was hired as a Data Scientist by the Chicago Blackhawks. These examples underscore the cross-disciplinary impact of the NFL's Big Data Bowl and further highlight how expertise in using NFL tracking data can open doors across various professional sport leagues.

3.4 CONCLUSION

The democratization of analytics in the NFL has transformed the relationship between the league and analysts. By making extensive data publicly accessible, both through {nflreadr] and the Big Data Bowl, the NFL created unique ways to accelerate the integration and acceptance of advanced metrics into the sport. The Big Data Bowl ultimately serves as the core bridge between mingling traditional football strategies and modern, data-driven approaches.

From the first Big Data Bowl in 2019, it has become clear that the NFL's commitment to open data and collaborative innovation is reshaping the game. The competition has provided a platform for budding analysts to show-case their talents, often leading to professional opportunities both within and outside of the NFL. Participants like Dani Chu, Jill Reiner, James Venzor, and Hassaan Inayatail have demonstrated that the skills and insights needed for success in the Big Data Bowl are highly transferable and valued across various professional sports leagues. This phenomenon not only enhances the analytical capabilities within the NFL but also enriches the entire sport industry by cross-pollinating ideas and methodologies. As well, the continuous development and refinement of analytics tools – from those amateur analysts using {nflreadr} data to those using CNN models to created expected metrics – illustrate the NFL's proactive stance in leveraging analytical advancements. These innovations are now a vital part of the league's official statistics and national television broadcasts, enhancing the viewing experience for fans and providing deeper insights into the game.

This chapter has explored how digital transformations, manifested through accessible football data, have lowered the barrier of entry for individuals aspiring to learn computer programming and sports analytics. This democratization has empowered a new generation of analysts, providing them with the tools and opportunities to contribute meaningfully to the field. The NFL, in turn, has benefited from this influx of fresh perspectives, leading to innovative strategies and improved performance metrics. This mutually beneficial ecosystem created by the NFL's open-data initiatives and the Big Data Bowl exemplifies a forward-thinking approach that other leagues and organizations should, and could, emulate.

The NFL's approach to analytics has not only revolutionized football but has also set a precedent for other sports. The democratization of data, the success of the Big Data Bowl, and the integration of advanced metrics into mainstream analysis highlight the transformative power of open data and collaborative innovation. As the NFL continues to embrace and expand its analytics capabilities, it paves the way for a future where the game is continually enhanced by the insights and contributions of a global community of amateur and professional analysts alike.

BIBLIOGRAPHY

Awbrey, J. (2020, June 9). *The future of NFL data analytics*. Samford University. Retrieved from www.samford.edu/sports-analytics/fans/2020/The-Future-of-NFL-Data-Analytics

AWS and NFL Launch Next Gen Stat 'Expected Return Yards' The newest advanced ML-powered stat from AWS and the NFL tackles the hidden dynamics of punt and kickoff returns. (n.d.). Amazon Web Services. Retrieved from https://aws.amazon.com/sports/nfl/nfl-expected-return-yards/

Bagga, G. (2023). *Impact of penalties on score differentials and drive outcomes in the NFL* (Y. Lu, Ed.) [Master of Science, Simon Fraser University]. https://summit.sfu.ca/_flysystem/fedora/2024-02/etd22841.pdf

Baldwin, B. (2020, October 28). *NFL fourth-down decisions: The math behind the league's new aggressiveness*. Retrieved from https://theathletic.com/2144214/2020/10/28/nfl-fourth-down-decisions-the-math-behind-the-leagues-new-aggressiveness/

Baldwin, B. (2021, March 23). 'I'd have to kill you if I told you': Big Data Bowl offers peek inside NFL teams' use of analytics. *New York Times*. Retrieved from www.nytimes.com/athletic/2444020/2021/03/23/id-have-to-kill-you-if-i-told-you-big-data-bowl-offers-peek-inside-nfl-teams-use-of-analytics/

Basiouny, A. (n.d.). *Soaring with the Eagles: Wharton student lands data job with NFL*. Retrieved May 29, 2024, from https://analytics.wharton.upenn.edu/news/soaring-with-the-eagles-wharton-student-lands-data-job-with-nfl/

Bianchi, N. (2023, July 10). Lions name new manager of football information. *The Detroit News*. Retrieved from www.detroitnews.com/story/sports/nfl/lions/2023/07/10/detroit-lions-name-new-manager-of-football-information/70399583007/

Brill, R. S., Yurko, R., & Wyner, A. J. (2023). Analytics, have some humility: a statistical view of fourth-down decision making. *arXiv [stat.AP]*. arXiv. Retrieved from http://arxiv.org/abs/2311.03490

Bushnell, H. (2021, September 15). *NFL teams are taking 4th-down risks more than ever — but still not often enough*. Yahoo Sports. Retrieved from https://sports.yahoo.com/nfl-teams-are-taking-4th-down-risks-more-than-ever-but-still-not-often-enough-163650973.html?guccounter=1

Carl, S. (2024). *nflplotR: NFL Logo Plots in ggplot2 and gt*. Retrieved from https://cran.r-project.org/web/packages/nflplotR/nflplotR.pdf

Chang, M., Dai, K., Jiang, D., & Cheng, H. (2024, February 2). *Uncovering missed tackle opportunities*. Kaggle. Retrieved from www.kaggle.com/code/matthewpchang/uncovering-missed-tackle-opportunities/

Chavanelle, N. (2024, May 17). *Dallas Cowboys make two new hires ahead of OTAs*. Yardbarker. Retrieved from www.yardbarker.com/nfl/articles/dallas_cowboys_make_two_new_hires_ahead_of_otas/s1_17236_40373577

Clark, K. (2018, December 19). *The NFL's analytics revolution has arrived*. Retrieved from www.theringer.com/nfl/2018/12/19/18148153/nfl-analytics-revolution

Cole, K. (2023, February 7). *(Re)Introducing NFL Plus/Minus, a superior player valuation metric*. Unexpected Points. Retrieved from https://unexpectedpoints.substack.com/p/reintroducing-nfl-plusminus-a-superior

Computer Cowboy [benbbaldwin]. (2020, April 27). *INTRODUCING: @nflfastR, an R package for scraping NFL data faster*. Twitter. Retrieved from https://twitter.com/benbbaldwin/status/1254846456390975494

Congelio, B. (2023). *Introduction to NFL Analytics with R*. CRC Press.

Fortier, S. (2020, January 16). The NFL's analytics movement has finally reached the sport's mainstream. *The Washington Post*. Retrieved from www.washingtonpost.com/sports/2020/01/16/nfls-analytics-movement-has-finally-reached-sports-mainstream/

Heifetz, D. (2019, August 15). *We salute you, founding fathers of the NFL's analytics movement*. The Ringer. Retrieved from www.theringer.com/nfl-preview/2019/8/15/20806241/nfl-analytics-pro-football-focus

Hoppen, S. (2022). *More fun with personnel packages from #nflreadr, this time looking at team pass rate over expectation by offensive personnel! The #Commanders, #Buccaneers, and #Rams all pass more than expected out of heavy 13 personnel #nflverse*. Retrieved from https://x.com/SamHoppen/status/1557024382643568640

Inayatali, H., White, A., & Hocevar, D. (2023, January 7). *Between the lines: How do we measure pressure?* Kaggle. Retrieved from www.kaggle.com/code/hassaaninayatali/between-the-lines-how-do-we-measure-pressure

Kozora, A. (2015, September 22). *Tomlin prefers "feel" over analytics*. Retrieved from https://steelersdepot.com/2015/09/tomlin-prefers-feel-over-analytics/

NFL. (2018, December 19). *NFL announces inaugural Big Data Bowl*. Retrieved from www.nfl. com/news/nfl-announces-inaugural-nfl-big-data-bowl-0ap3000001001967

NFL. (2020, July 20). *Next Gen Stats: Intro to expected rushing yards*. Retrieved from www.nfl. com/news/next-gen-stats-intro-to-expected-rushing-yards

NFL Operations. (2020, February 27). 2020 Big Data Bowl Recap. Retrieved from https://ope rations.nfl.com/gameday/analytics/stats-articles/2020-big-data-bowl-recap/

nflscrapR [nflscrapR]. (2020, September 14). *Please use @nflfastR from here on out – and send all of your questions and issues to @benbbaldwin @mrcaseb*. Twitter. Retrieved from https://x.com/nflscrapR/status/1305586160262152193

No Edge No Chance: The Impact of Setting the Edge on Zone Running Plays. (n.d.). Hauck, Shane. Retrieved May 29, 2024, from www.kaggle.com/code/devinbasley26/no-edge-no-chance

Partnow, S. (2022). *The midrange theory: Basketball's evolution in the age of analytics* (Reprint edition). Triumph Books.

Patton, S. (2024). *The AFC Championship game will feature two top 10 defensive play callers in Macdonald and Spagnuolo. Half of the defensive coaches with a score below zero have either been dismissed or mutually parted ways*. Retrieved from https://x.com/PattonAn alytics/status/1750602083315663253

Peng, W., Richards, M., Walczak, S., & Werner, J. (2021, January 7). *A defensive player coverage evaluation framework*. Kaggle. Retrieved from www.kaggle.com/code/model284/a-defensive-player-coverage-evaluation-framework

Pospisil, T., & Lee, A. B. (2018). RFCDE: Random Forests for Conditional Density Estimation. *ArXiv [Stat.ML]*. arXiv. Retrieved from https://arxiv.org/abs/1804.05753

Reid, W. (2020, October 13). *A data science student's algorithm has the NFL's full attention*. UVA Today. Retrieved from https://news.virginia.edu/content/data-science-students-algorithm-has-nfls-full-attention

Ritchie, R., Kumagai, B., Moreau, R., & Cavan, E. (2022, January 6). *Punt returns: Using the Math to find the path*. Kaggle. Retrieved from www.kaggle.com/code/robynritchie/punt-returns-using-the-math-to-find-the-path

Rodrigue, J. (2024, February 3). What is player movement tracking technology and how do NFL teams use it? *New York Times*. Retrieved from www.nytimes.com/athletic/5236 255/2024/02/03/nfl-player-tracking-system-speed-prospects/

Rosenthal, G. (2018, January 31). *Super Bowl LII: How the 2017 Philadelphia Eagles were built*. NFL. Retrieved from www.nfl.com/news/super-bowl-lii-how-the-2017-philadelphia-eagles-were-built-0ap3000000912753

San Francisco 49ers. (n.d.). Matt Ploenzke – Front office roster. Retrieved May 29, 2024, from www.49ers.com/team/front-office-roster/matt-ploenzke

Schuckers, M. (2011). An alternative to the NFL draft pick value chart based upon player performance. *Journal of Quantitative Analysis in Sports*, 7(2). https://doi.org/10.2202/1559-0410.1329

Sharpe, L., & Carl, S. (2024). *nflseedR: Functions to efficiently simulate and evaluate NFL seaons*. Retrieved from https://nflseedr.com

Stern, B. (2023). *Bringing the heat: Predicting the pass rush and quantifying pressure in NFL football* [Bachelor of Arts, Harvard College]. Retrieved from https://dash.harvard. edu/bitstream/handle/1/37378285/Ben%20Stern%20Senior%20Thesis%20%281%29. pdf?sequence=1&isAllowed=y

Williams, B., Palmquist, W., & Elmore, R. (2023). Simulation-based decision making in the NFL using NFLSimulatoR. *Annals of Operations Research*, *325*(1), 731–742.

Yurko, R., Ventura, S., & Horowitz, M. (2018). nflWAR: A reproducible method for offensive player evaluation in football. *arXiv [stat.AP]*. arXiv. Retrieved from http://arxiv.org/abs/1802.00998

4

Surveying Various Information Systems Theories Used in the Context of AI and IoT in Sports

Mukesh Chaware and Sreejith Alathur

4.1 INTRODUCTION

The 2011 movie *Moneyball* based on the Michael Lewis book bearing the same name, depicts the true story of how Oakland A's general manager Billy Beane revamped the squad following the departure of three key players to wealthier teams and transformed the A's. Portrayed by Brad Pitt, Beane leveraged the analytics of past games, instead of large sums of money, to recruit potential players undervalued by others. In the latter part of 2002, the Oakland A's won 20 games, a new record in those times, with an overall expenditure of $41 million, by employing Beane's Moneyball strategy, while the Yankees had a $125 million expenditure that season. All of this drew much needed attention into the backend role of data analytics, prediction, and optimization in sports.

Around the same time, another book, *Buzz* (Salzman et al., 2003), was published. It briefly touched upon the inherent human affinity for trends and how the associated dynamics are changing with the unbridled explosion of information through the internet and advertising-induced marketing buzz. The advent of artificial intelligence (AI) and the Internet of Things (IoT) has also given rise to many such trends. Gartner[1] has made specific mention of certain AI trends in their recent annual Hype Cycle (refer Figure 4.1) and Priority Matrix (refer Figure 4.2) for Emerging Technologies (Chandrasekaran & Davis, 2023).

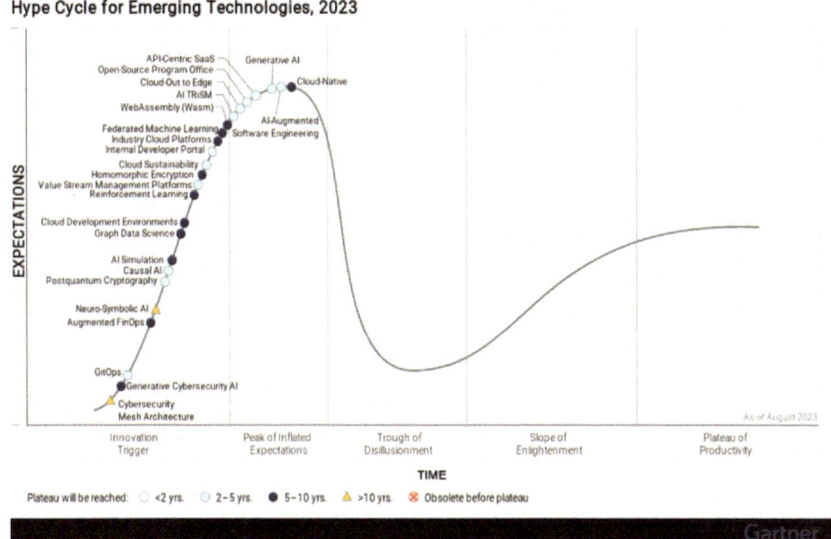

FIGURE 4.1
GARTNER-2023 Hype Cycle for Emerging Technologies. (Chandrasekaran & Davis, 2023.)

Gartner

Priority Matrix for Emerging Technologies, 2023

Benefit	Years to Mainstream Adoption			
↓	Less Than 2 Years ↓	2–5 Years ↓	5–10 Years ↓	More Than 10 Years ↓
Transformational		AI-Augmented Software Engineering Generative AI	Augmented FinOps Generative Cybersecurity AI Homomorphic Encryption Industry Cloud Platforms WebAssembly (Wasm)	Cybersecurity Mesh Architecture
High		AI TRISM API-Centric SaaS Causal AI Cloud-Out to Edge Cloud Sustainability GitOps Internal Developer Portal Open-Source Program Office Postquantum Cryptography Value Stream Management Platforms	AI Simulation Cloud Development Environments Cloud-Native Federated Machine Learning Graph Data Science Reinforcement Learning	Neuro-Symbolic AI
Moderate				
Low				

FIGURE 4.2
GARTNER-2023 Priority Matrix for Emerging Technologies. (Chandrasekaran & Davis, 2023.)

Gartner predicts that the disruptive technologies mentioned in the Hype Cycle will impact business and society until 2033. Chief technology officers (CTO) and other technology innovation leaders can utilize Hype Cycle to evaluate emerging AI technologies with transformative potential for their business and technology capabilities. This analysis can help strategize for competitive advantage and market growth by exploring different use cases. Gartner recommends using the Priority Matrix to align the generalized benefit rating of each technology with the time needed for it to become widely adopted. Note that the benefit rating reflects the technology's potential and may differ depending on the industry and organization.

4.1.1 Background and Significance

A section of these trends and technology patterns can evolve significantly and have a transformative influence as they progress from being a passing fad to becoming widely accepted. The sports arena has transformed significantly due to the emergence of AI and IoT. The integration of AI with IoT in several industries, including sports, has given rise to a new field called 'Artificial Intelligence of Things' (AIoT), which is yielding novel outcomes. AIoT has the potential to transform the functioning of sports organizations, athlete training, and fan engagement. AIoT has led to increased productivity, smoother transitions, and innovative technology applications that were previously non-existent. However, in the actual implementation scenarios of the sports industry, there could be the usage of only AI, or only IoT, or both AI and IoT, and in the remainder of this chapter we use the term 'AI-IoT-tech' to collectively denote the same.

4.1.2 Purpose and Scope

Combining the AI and IoT technologies in sports could lead to unforeseen alterations in sports ecosystems and human interaction dynamics, albeit facing resistance from established norms in the sports sector. It is essential to draw valuable insights from proven information systems (IS) theories to effectively address these difficulties and optimize the usage of AI-IoT-tech in sports. The present study aims to thoroughly examine several IS theories related to 'AI & IoT' (hereafter referred to with the term 'AI-&-IoT-tech') in the sports business and their impacts. It does not employ any specific research approach, such as systematic literature review, qualitative interviews, or surveys, to provide quantifiable results that would support current theory.

We focus on acceptance-oriented IS theories like Theory of Planned Behavior (TPB), the Diffusion of Innovations (DOI) theory, Technology Acceptance Model (TAM), and alike. We haven't conducted any actual studies or gathered empirical survey data or conducted any literature review. We rather focused on the prevailing use of IS theories, frameworks, and models in the sports ecosystem and then went on to check if any of these implementations have already leveraged the strengths of AI or IoT technologies, else we prompt the possible suitability of using AI-IoT-tech in the sports scenario of such existing studies.

4.2 EMERGENCE OF AI-IOT-TECH IN SPORTS ECOSYSTEM

Let us start by understanding things from a layman's perspective. AI pertains to the capacity of any equipment (including computers, mobiles etc.) to carry out tasks requiring intelligence – such as learning, design, critical thinking, and innovative problem-solving – akin to human capabilities (Mogaji et al., 2020). Recent studies indicate that companies count on AI to achieve a market-oriented competitive advantage during their journey of digitalization (Jang et al., 2021).

Sports fraternities are known to frequently employ the term 'AI' colloquially to refer to something that is advanced in technology and data-centric; they need not be visualizing any precise framework or definition in mind. In this study, AI is defined based on the Sense-Model-Plan-Act loop which is also known by the acronym 'SMPA'. While alternative AI concepts exist, such as reactive machines and subsumption architecture, this model offers a solid for understanding the advent of intelligent systems in a dynamic ecosystem like sports (Brooks, 1986). The term 'IoT' is usually used in the context of physical objects which are inter linked like a network, and these objects are referred to as 'things', which are equipped with software, sensors, and other such technologies to connect and thereby share data with other devices and systems via the internet. There are many other specific implementations of the term 'IoT' – including, but not limited to, 'Industrial Internet of Things (IIoT)', 'Industrial Robotics of Things (IRoT)', 'Edge Computing for the Internet of Things (EC-IoT)', 'Web of Things (WoT)', 'Internet of Medical Things (IoMT)', and 'Internet of Vehicles (IoV)'. However, this study simply considers all such extended forms under the single umbrella term 'IoT'.

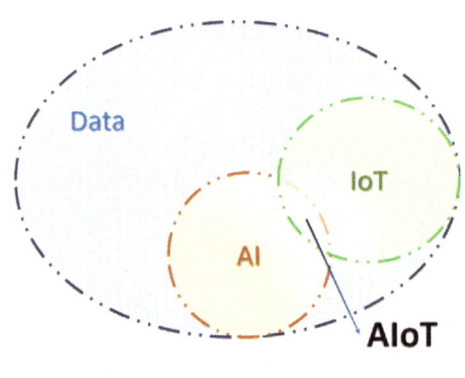

DATA: represents both types of data – real-time data points generated by IoT devices plus the earlier prevailing historical data patterns used to train the AI model

IoT: it enhances efficiency by monitoring and streamlining repeated processes, hence reducing the amount of time required to process them.

AI: the AI algorithms are designed to gather and analyze large quantities of data to produce significant, practical and actionable insights. The data stream coming from IoT devices also gets analyzed to find trends.

AIoT: it synthesizes of raw data with AI-generated insights to effectively deploy data-driven solutions in real time. And takes proactive measures to address the requirements of the end user.

FIGURE 4.3
Schematic Representation of AI + IoT + Data Ecosystem.

AI is predominantly based on software while IoT is predominantly hardware, and their integration has led to the emergence of the composite system called AIoT. This technological convergence through AIoT gets accentuated when one understands how the ecosystem's data gets handled, processed, and enriched, thus transforming various sectors and industries. This is depicted through a simple schematic block diagram (refer Figure 4.3).

4.2.1 The Convergence of IoT and AI

The IoT offers a chance to gather data on all facets of a business's activities continually. Companies worldwide are rapidly utilizing IoT to develop innovative products and services, leading to new business prospects and revenue streams. This change is introducing a new era in the functioning style of a firm and its engagement with customers. The existing collection of various IoT smart devices and AI deployments continuously gather data from multiple sources – including chatbots, location-based advertisements, social media, e-mails, and websites – to create a large volume of digital information, referred to as big data (Yang et al., 2019). Businesses have great opportunities to convert raw IoT data into valuable market insights, and effective data analysis is crucial for accomplishing such an objective. Implementing data monetization techniques in IoT, especially when combined with AI, can result in spawning fresh revenue streams and gaining a competitive edge (Suciu, 2016).

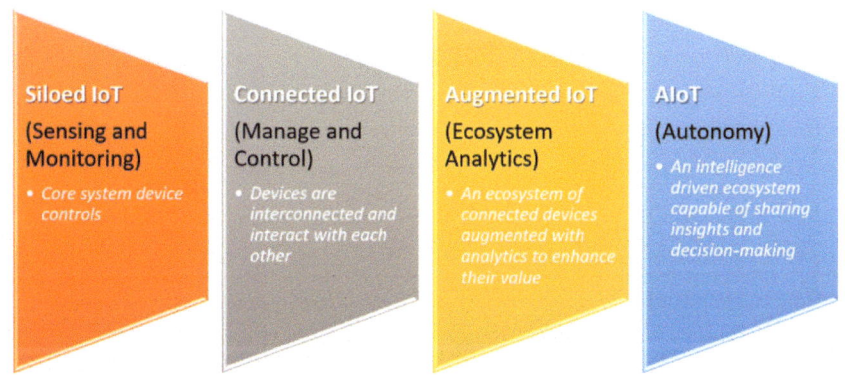

FIGURE 4.4

Block Diagram of Evolution of AIoT – From Smart Devices to Smarter Systems. (Parihar et al., 2023.)

Organizations are looking to analyze their data more thoroughly to discover new methods for enhancing efficiency and competitiveness. Organizations are increasingly utilizing more extensive research methodologies due to recent developments in science and technology, especially AI. For enterprises to maximize the advantages of IoT, they need to combine it with advancing AI technology, allowing 'smart machines' to replicate intelligent actions and make educated judgments with little human involvement. Commercial applications of AIoT focus on combining the predictive and cognitive skills of AI with the connection and pervasive computing potential of IoT, utilizing backend data (refer Figure 4.4) (Parihar et al., 2023).

4.2.2 Introduction to AI-IoT-Tech in Sports

The presence of AI and IoT in the sports industry offers sophisticated technology to analyze data, enhance performance, and reduce the risk of injury. These technologies enable precise monitoring and evaluation of athletes' movements, resulting in improved training methods and strategic decision-making. Further sections will explain how the AI-IoT-tech integration in sports is enhancing athletic performance; impacting sports coaching, biomechanics, and forecasts; and providing novel solutions for improving athletic performance, training, and injury prevention. These technologies are revolutionizing the sports industry by utilizing data collecting and analysis to change how sports are played, coached, and enjoyed.

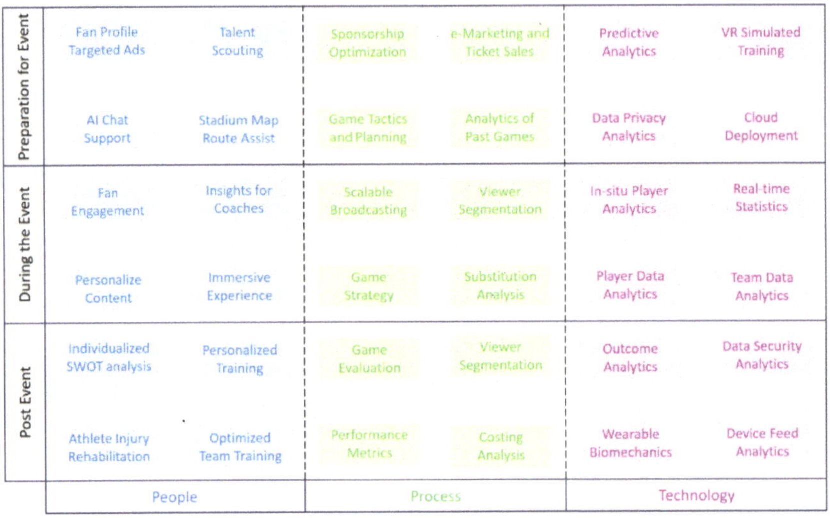

	People		Process		Technology	
Preparation for Event	Fan Profile Targeted Ads	Talent Scouting	Sponsorship Optimization	e-Marketing and Ticket Sales	Predictive Analytics	VR Simulated Training
	AI Chat Support	Stadium Map Route Assist	Game Tactics and Planning	Analytics of Past Games	Data Privacy Analytics	Cloud Deployment
During the Event	Fan Engagement	Insights for Coaches	Scalable Broadcasting	Viewer Segmentation	In-situ Player Analytics	Real-time Statistics
	Personalize Content	Immersive Experience	Game Strategy	Substitution Analysis	Player Data Analytics	Team Data Analytics
Post Event	Individualized SWOT analysis	Personalized Training	Game Evaluation	Viewer Segmentation	Outcome Analytics	Data Security Analytics
	Athlete Injury Rehabilitation	Optimized Team Training	Performance Metrics	Costing Analysis	Wearable Biomechanics	Device Feed Analytics

FIGURE 4.5
PPT Framework-Based Visualization of AIoT in Sports Ecosystem.

4.2.3 Prevailing Presence of AI-IoT-Tech in Sports

The block diagram below (refer Figure 4.5) has been formulated to illustrate the prevailing presence of AI and IoT into the sports ecosystem, focusing on People, Process, and Technology (PPT). The PPT is an approach designed to assist corporations in prioritizing and managing projects and operations. The PPT framework emphasizes the need for synergy among people, process, and technology for effective business functioning, operations, and change management. Any deficiency in one component can affect the entire efficiency and effectiveness if it is not in harmony with the rest. This self-explanatory block diagram has been formulated by deriving ideas from two prior research works wherein they used the PPT framework for a representational view of their study (Chen et al., 2024; Thomas et al., 2023).

4.3 VARIOUS THEORIES IN SPORTS

The existent theories in the sports ecosystem come from multiple domains. A set of high-level domains from which most existent theories in the sports ecosystem have emanated have been depicted in the schematic representation below (refer Figure 4.6).

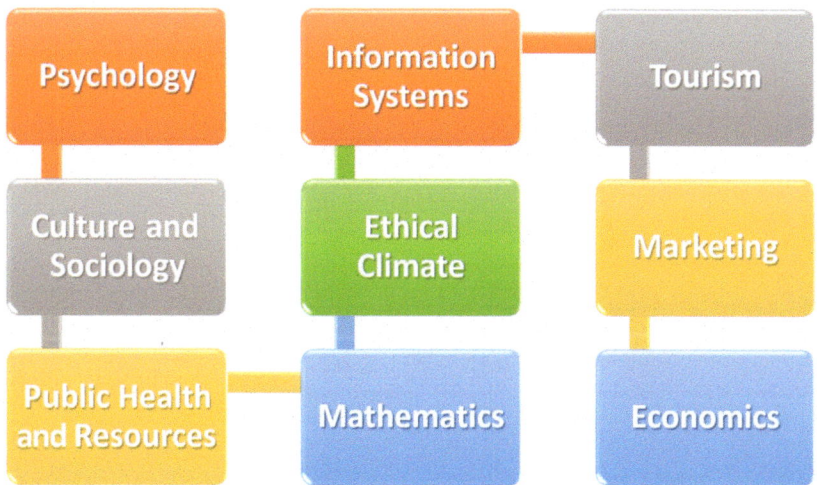

FIGURE 4.6
Theories Emanating from High Level Domains in Sports Ecosystem.

Table 4.1 presents the well-established theories, frameworks, and models related to the psychology domain.

The authors have on purpose created only Table 4.1 showcasing the well-established theories, frameworks, and models related to the psychology domain; and, on similar lines, the remaining domains can be analyzed and tabulated for their share of leading theories. The authors have purposely skipped the construction of tables for the remaining domains, as the focus of this chapter is on IS theories, and instead a generic bulleted list of 'cross-domain' theories has been explained to maintain continuity. The cross-domain theories, frameworks, and models adopt a multidisciplinary approach towards the research into sports.

- The **'Sport Ecosystem Logic'** theory offers a framework for analyzing the dynamics of sports ecosystems and the interactions among their stakeholders. It is used to understand complex connections within the sports ecosystem based on value co-creation, engagement platforms, and sport network approaches to stimulate new research (Buser et al., 2022).
- The **'Mixed Embeddedness Theory'** is crucial for understanding digital sports–based entrepreneurial ecosystems, and it examines the intersection of digital technologies and entrepreneurship in the sports sector

TABLE 4.1

Psychology Domain Related Leading Theories in Sports Ecosystem

Leading Theory / Framework / Model	Prominent Citation	Key Relevance Points
Achievement Goal Theory (AGT)	(Angelo et al., 2022)	The AGT is a modern motivational theory utilized in sporting settings, emphasizing goal orientation and its influence on behavior. This theory is crucial for comprehending the psychological aspects of players and how the climate generated by their coach impacts their performance and pleasure.
Andersen and Williams' Model of Stress and Athletic Injury	(Junge, 2000)	This model elucidates the correlation between psychological elements and sports injuries, understanding stress theory and its effects on players' welfare. It provides a framework for comprehending how psychological factors can impact the occurrence and recovery of sports-related injuries.
Psychological Continuum Model (PCM)	(Funk & James, 2001)	It defines people's psychological connection to sports and teams. It describes four stages from awareness to allegiance: attraction, attachment, and allegiance. This paradigm emphasizes the complexity and strengthening of sport-related mental associations as crucial variables in psychological connection to a sport or team.
Grounded Theory of Psychological Resilience	(Fletcher & Sarkar, 2012)	Psychological resilience and optimal sport performance are examined. Positive personality, motivation, confidence, attention, and perceived social support help athletes manage stress and perform well. It postulates that these elements affect athletes' challenge appraisal and meta-cognitions, resulting in facilitative responses necessary for optimal performance.
Cognitive-Affective Processing Systems (CAPS) Approach	(Smith, 2006)	Social-cognitive personality theory underpins CAPS, which explains athletes' coherence and variability. It claims that situational elements and a dynamic network of cognitive, emotional, motivational, and behavior-generation units form individualized behavioral signatures. It helps sport psychologists include and enhance domain-specific frameworks like mental toughness, performance anxiety, and psychological skills training.

and investigates the influencing factors for creation of new opportunities and problems (Ratten & Thompson, 2020).

- The **'Stakeholder Theory'** is usually used for analyzing the involvement of supporters or fan engagement in sports. Jaeger, in his research (Jaeger, 2021), examines the European sports ecosystem using Stakeholder Theory (especially in European football) and explains how it allows academics to assess the connections and impacts of different stakeholders, such as fans, on the operations of the sports business.
- The notion of **'Olympism for Humanity Theory and Praxis'** is utilized to advance inclusivity, democracy, and peace through sports efforts (Lyras, 2021). This theory stems from more of an ideology that advocates using sports to promote peace and democracy in unstable areas and thereby emphasizes the transformative power of sporting environments.
- The **'Pressure-State-Response (PSR) model'** is used when assessing and scrutinizing the effective utilization and progress of national sports resources, and thereby offers valuable perspectives on the expansion and vitality of sports ecosystems (Liu & Wang, 2016). Researchers can evaluate the prevailing state and thereby deploy appropriate improvement of sports resources in specific regions by using existing evaluation models.

4.4 FITMENT OF IS THEORIES FOR 'AI-IOT-TECH IN SPORTS'

In this section, we try to understand how the adoption and propagation of AI-IoT-tech in sports sector works by analyzing through the lens of established theories, frameworks, and models in IS.

4.4.1 Technology Acceptance Theories

In this section we assess the utility of the prominent technology acceptance–related IS theories in the context of AI-IoT-tech and sports wherein we primarily refer to the work present in the existing literature on technology acceptance theories and their associated factors affecting adoption of intelligent products (Sohn & Kwon, 2019). Different theories considered are:

- Technology Acceptance Model (TAM)
- Diffusion of Innovations (DOI) theory
- Theory of Planned Behavior (TPB)
- Value-based Adoption Model (VAM)

4.4.1.1 Technology Acceptance Model (TAM)

The Technology Acceptance Model, popularly addressed as TAM, is a well-established IS theory used to understand the initial acceptance of a technology and thereafter the continued use of the same (Davis, 1989). It emphasizes that 'Perceived Utility' and 'Perceived Ease of Use' act as influencing factors in the process of adoption and further propagation of technology as depicted in Figure 4.7.

There are multiple flavors of TAM, as it has been continuously studied and expanded. The initial major upgrade was the TAM-2 (Venkatesh & Davis, 2000), and a TAM-3 (Venkatesh & Bala, 2008) has also been researched in the context of e-commerce with the inclusion of the effects of trust and perceived risk on system use. There is also a Technology Readiness Acceptance Model (TRAM). Other extensions are called the 'Unified Theory of Acceptance and Use of Technology', better known as UTAUT (Venkatesh et al., 2003), and UTAUT-2 (Venkatesh et al., 2012). Each of these extensions of TAM have their comparative strengths and limitations. However, for the purpose of brevity and the scope of this chapter, we treat these different extensions of the Technology Acceptance Model under the umbrella term 'TAM'.

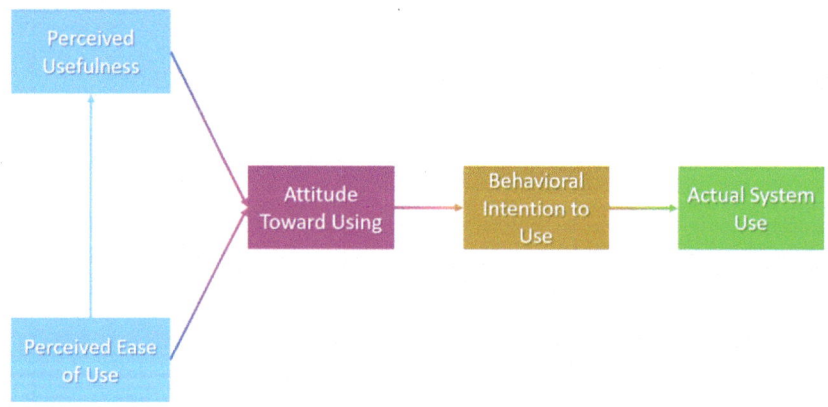

FIGURE 4.7
The Original Technology Acceptance Model. (Davis, 1989.)

A previous study in the clinical sector (Lu et al., 2021) provides valuable information on how IoT and AI are used for assessing individuals' fitness and monitoring the workload of a clinic's working staff. Such regular, continued data collection and analysis can be beneficial for improving athletic and general well-being in the sports field. There is another study in retail marketing that explores how AI plays an enabling role in ensuring end-user-centric steps into reality as it analyses how end-user adoption/ purchase intention is connected to customer engagement through emotional attachment (Bilal et al., 2024). In the context of entrepreneurial ecosystems, the impact of AI algorithmic usage on companies' decision-making has been studied (Roundy, 2022), with potential implications for sports entrepreneurs and technology providers in the sports business. IoT devices are also known to improve efficiency in manufacturing logistics and supply chain systems (Kumar et al., 2018), suggesting the possibility of leveraging these benefits in sports equipment management and athlete logistics.

As we observe from the earlier studies in other sectors, on similar lines, TAM can be used to analyze how athletes, coaches, and sports organizations perceive the presence and use of AI and IoT technologies in their sports-related activities, based on their thoughts and emotions. One wouldn't get a one-to-one mapping for fitment of AI or IoT into sports but the insights and learnings from other sectors can certainly help in fruitful adoption. The presence of AI-IoT-tech in the sports industry has enough potential to constructively affect the existing way of working for role players in the sports ecosystem and such a change can be better studied using the TAM to understand which specific features and aspects of the deployed wearables, IoT devices, and AI systems are perceived to be of better utility and simple to use. Coaches could possibly sense the enormous scope for minute-by-minute collection of the data emerging from tracking smart wearables and IoT devices that would offer historical insights and provide an advantageous foundation for enhancing future performance analysis or optimizing the existing training curriculum to prevent injury-prone routines. In other sports scenarios, the athletes would be more interested in the ease of integrating AI-IoT-tech based equipment into their extant training routines and workflows. Such scenarios would provide overall insights into the factors that influence the adoption of AI-IoT-tech in the sports arena.

Sports companies are also focusing on enhancing player performance, customizing training programs, and increasing fan engagement by utilizing AI for data analysis and decision-making. Existing systematically conducted meta-analysis-based studies indicate that IoT devices and wearables are being utilized in sports to track individual athletes' workloads (both external and internal) through monitoring of physiological status biomarker sensors and automated activity recognition (Passos et al., 2021).

Day-to-day wearables and fitness apps have brought in a sporting culture. A study conducted in Taiwanese civil sports centers used TRAM to examine how technology readiness and task–technology fit affect fitness app adoption. The integrated TRAM model focusses on consumers and sports contexts rather than the intelligence aspects of the technology, which makes the research model better suited to predict the intention of users to use these apps pertaining to fitness and thereby prefer sport-related technology (C.-J. Chang et al., 2023).

As an offshoot of studying the TAM, to promote innovation and healthy competition, the stakeholders in the sports business can strategically implement AI- and IoT-associated implementations by evaluating variables including perceived utility, simplicity of use, and their impact on performance and operations.

4.4.1.2 Diffusion of Innovations (DOI)

The Diffusion of Innovations theory, also known by the acronym DOI (Rogers, 1995a, 1995b), can be used to understand how AI and IoT are being adopted in, and their impact on, the sports ecosystem. The central idea of DOI theory states the dissemination of innovations within a social system across time, as Roger defines in his book 'Diffusion of Innovation' in the following verbatim words "the process by which an innovation is communicated through certain channels over time among the members of a social system" (refer Figure 4.8).

The implementation and usage of AI and IoT technologies can be analyzed in the context of sports using the DOI paradigm. Injury prevention of athletes plays a major role in the success of competitive sports. In a related research study (Donaldson et al., 2017), an advisory panel was constituted for the planning and implementation of an injury prevention program wherein coaches served as the main program adopters. DOI theory was used along with other frameworks to arrive at effective implementation techniques, the choice of communication channels, optimizing program resources, athlete training and the development of mentoring curriculum by coaches. There is already an extension to such research focused on 'planning injury prevention programs' using AI. AI is used in sports for injury risk assessment and

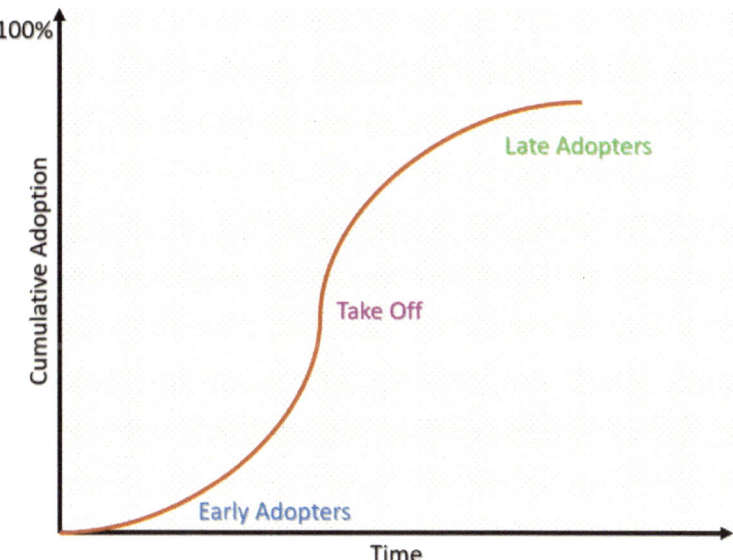

FIGURE 4.8
Diffusion of Innovations Theory. (Rogers, 1995b.)

performance prediction in team sports (Claudino et al., 2019). AI wearables and tools can assess injury risks by analyzing player performance and past records, often without any deviation or intervention to existing curriculum, leading to better decision-making.

There is also another study about using AI for preventing death of young athletes. Big match temperament and readiness for competitive sports can be stressful, especially for young athletes. As per the existing ways of working, typically a young athlete aiming for professional sports undergoes a comprehensive physical and medical exam that includes checking the family's medical history and compulsory electrocardiogram (ECG) screening. Certain quarters have strong reasons not to support the prevalent policy. They argue that sudden deaths among young athletes are rare; the ECG screening process is resource-intensive and expensive to conduct; and the rate of false positives is too high. A study (A. C. Chang, 2023) states that instead of the existing ECG screening process, a consensus-based approach – that is rooted in scientific facts and that uses easily traceable, governable tools – is needed. The study aims to reduce sudden cardiac death in young athletes by leveraging the ML and neural networking capabilities of AI and big data analytics to build an algorithm – trained on a national database of medical records, evidence-based medicine outcomes, and continued, repetitive input of real-world data like ECGs – that overcomes the limitations of the existing ECG screening process and aids in making better clinical decisions. Sports ecosystem stakeholders can use the DOI theory to propagate such solutions

Let us understand some existing research studies wherein the DOI theory is used in some sports scenario, but without any presence of an AI or IoT set-up, which will give some potential ideas on how the possible presence of AI-IoT-tech technologies can be of help in equivalent scenarios.

Adoption of AI and IoT technologies can prove challenging in sports circles as the preferences of stakeholders and ecosystem players change over time. In a related study (Xu et al., 2023), the researchers used the DOI theory to conduct a three-wave survey and found that job security worries and negative sentiments toward AI adoption among employees increased over time, and that trialability positively influenced views toward AI adoption only among employees who had a positive opinion before, and personnel already negatively predisposed were more influenced by observability and the available advantages. These findings can be put to good use whenever a sports firm adopts AI and IoT.

Observers have noticed a certain pattern since the 2004 Athens Olympics: as the demand for inexpensive labor and sexual services increases during major sports events, human trafficking peaks covertly. In an associated research study, the event organizers used the 'theory of diffusion of innovations' and the 'social event leverage framework' to initiate anti-trafficking precautions and scrutinize the anti-trafficking measures on the ground (Sant et al., 2023). In the future, AI and IoT technologies could be leveraged by making sense of the predictive patterns through big data analytics of historical data, geofencing the vulnerable population through their wearable and mobile's location data, and thus monitoring the ongoing event.

As we can see, by considering perceived advantages, compatibility with current practices, and the impact of social networks on the spread of these innovations, the DOI theory can help sports ecosystems use AI and IoT better. Applying the DOI theory can provide stakeholders in the sports sector with a better understanding of how AI and IoT are adopted and incorporated into the ecosystem and result in improved performance, decision-making, and overall user experience.

4.4.1.3 Theory of Planned Behavior (TPB)

Icek Ajzen (1985, 1991) conceptualized the Theory of Planned Behavior (TPB). It is originally a social psychology theory that tries to explain any

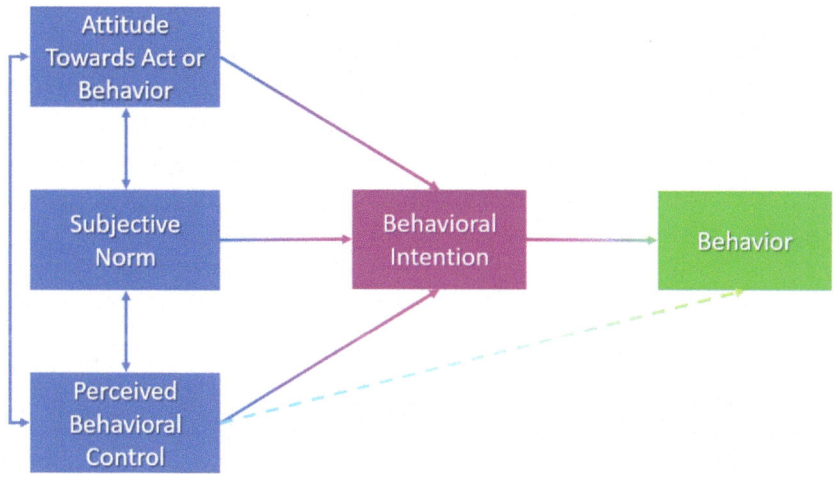

FIGURE 4.9
Theory of Planned Behavior. (Ajzen, 1991.)

human behavior by centering on the individual's intention to perform it. TPB has been studied, extended, and retrofitted to many other areas. Its key components are attitude, subjective norms, and perceived behavioral control (refer Figure 4.9).

In sports contexts, TPB can be applied to gauge the intention of coaches and athletes to use tools powered by AI or IoT.. For example, Chai et al. studied Chinese school students and their behavioral intentions to study AI were monitored (2020, 2022). The implications of their research findings could be used as a benchmark for building the curriculum of AI-associated education modules by considering the format of the content for AI training, student needs and willingness, and accompanying satisfaction in supporting the constant development of their competencies in AI. Coaches and athletes could extrapolate the observations, learnings, and conclusions from such studies to design appropriate AI-based sports training curricula. Ultimately, an AI-based mechanism is expected to help analyze athletes' performance data and/or optimize their preparation regimen.

In a Taiwan-based study (C.-J. Chang et al., 2023), IoT-based analytics was used to track the health status of the employees of more than ten financial enterprises. The researchers graded the helpful mediating effect of using a smart device (both cell phone and web-based) in influencing the staff at those firms to increase their individual physical activity. Each of these firms' occupational health nurses made sense of the analytics-based data outcome of input feed and posed evidence-based recommendations to the participating employees on how to increase their physical activity and thus promote their health. As one can sense, similar recommendations based on IoT data points are already being conducted in the context of sports. There exists well-established research (Felfernig et al., 2019) specifying an outline of sports applications based on recommendations in the IoT setting and offering new endorsement techniques on the basis of real-world IoT scenarios.

In another study, IoT-assisted improvisations have been brought into physical education training using a system based on deep reinforcement learning, wherein the system is trained to offer multiple chances to advance one's training. Students are now prompted to self-monitor their physical behavior. Based on guidance from expert recommendations, they can improve their overall physical performance and psychological benefits. The activity monitoring device assisted by IoT is projected to track students' physical training workouts and offers suggestions on how to enhance outcomes. Thus, it acts as an enabler for remote monitoring and assessment of athletes in sports training (Q. Li et al., 2022).

Another study also offers recommendations for self-training by tracking movements. It involves a low-cost, IoT-based, easy-to-use intelligent sports training and home exercise guidance solution that uses motion tracking to provide reliable correction of, and guidance on, one's form (Sun et al., 2023).

From the above discussions on TPB, we can infer that to effectively implement AI-IoT-tech in sports the stakeholders can use TPB to design interventions that tackle the key components of attitude, subjective norms, and perceived behavioral control. For example, if a given sports organization wants to encourage the use of AI in scalable livestream broadcasting and club that with wearable sensor–based live feed of athlete/player location as an input material for discussion by commentators, they could:

- Highlight the benefits of AI (positive attitude)
- Showcase contributing on-field factors for success of athletes as per live feed of their IoT wearables and related AI-assisted data analytics (social pressure)
- Provide training and support to those players whose IoT feeds suggest needing improvement in their games (perceived behavioral control)

By addressing these components, sport organizations can increase the likelihood of successful implementation of AI and IoT and adoption in sports to gain a competitive market advantage.

4.4.1.4 *Value-based Adoption Model (VAM)*

The VAM is a theoretical framework that analyzes the intention of a given user to use digital technologies. It was conceptualized in 2007 (H.-W. Kim et al., 2007). When being formulated, the prevailing technology adoption models focused on employees using organization-mandated technology; those did not consider the adoption of technology over internet or mobile. To address this gap, the study proposed a new Value-based Adoption Model (VAM) to explain the adoption of mobile internet (M-Internet) through perceived value for the individual consumer. The VAM combines the findings from technology adoption as well as value literature. It investigates how the 'perceived benefits and sacrifices' affect the 'perceived value' and how, in turn, the 'perceived value' affects the 'intention' to use (refer Figure 4.10).

In the context of IS research, the VAM is being used to understand the parameters that influence the adoption of new AI-IoT-tech based technologies in different areas. As an example, in the e-learning sector, VAM has been integrated with TAM to analyze the adoption characteristics of e-learning. The TAM's capability to assess consumers' purchase intention seems to be weak. To offset such weaknesses, the study formulated a refined model which incorporates the existing components of the TAM within the VAM theoretical framework. Quantitative measurements were ensured for the terms 'sacrifices' and 'perceived benefits' that are unique to VAM. This was done

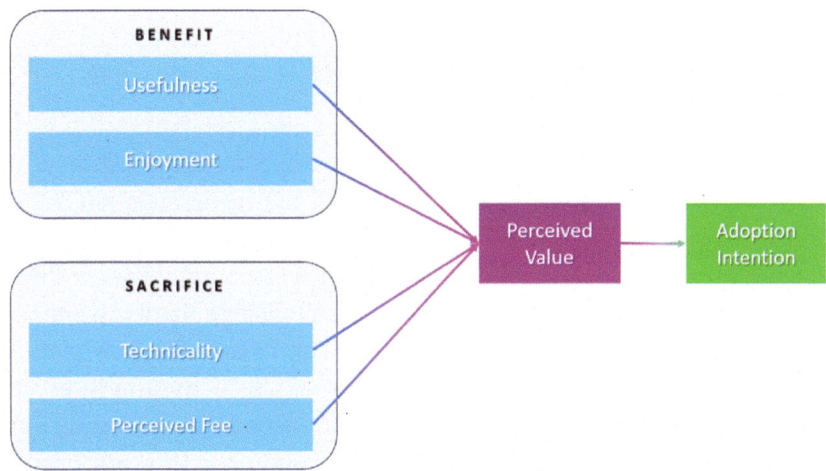

FIGURE 4.10
Value-Based Adoption Model (VAM). (H.-W. Kim et al., 2007.)

to derive practical suggestions for both e-learning service providers and researchers. The relationship between various parameters—like intention, perceived value, attitude, the intention regarding e-learning, and the facilitating role of 'e-WOM i.e., e-word of mouth'—was also scrutinized (Liao et al., 2022). On comparable lines, this can be used in the context of sports when during the onboarding of any new coach, athlete, or like role into the sports ecosystem, similar AI-&-IoT related self-help tutorials would have to be shared for adoption.

Another study, on the adoption of IoT smart home services (Y. Kim et al., 2017), was analyzed in the context of VAM. The findings suggested that it is necessary for business firms to establish and secure relevant infrastructure for inhabitants to use IoT-based smart home service, and ensuring security is also essential. In comparison, these findings can be leveraged for establishing IoT-based smart dwellings temporarily erected during mega sporting events.

As we can notice, in the sports ecosystem, VAM could carry relevance whenever end users seek perceived value of adopting AI-IoT-tech and weigh the associated 'sacrifice' before arriving at a decision to adopt them for training and performance analysis.

4.4.2 Other IS Theories

This section analyses the possibility of putting some more IS theories to good use in AI, IoT, and sports scenarios. These theories currently have relatively sparse use cases of implementation but could be significant in specific scenarios.

4.4.2.1 Attachment Theory

Sports e-commerce beckons business houses due to the sizeable profits involved. In 'a related study (Jiao et al., 2024), the researchers ran a questionnaire survey to assess how the attributes of a broadcasting platform influence the sports merchandise purchase behavior of viewers due to consumer attachment. This study applied attachment theory within the stimulus-organism-response (S-O-R) framework to examine how platform attributes of sports short video live e-commerce affect consumers' psychological states. Such research scenarios can be further extended by using a case study approach wherein researchers can have a tie-up with a given mobile sports live streaming firm that is ready to apply AI-based data analytics on the anonymized data of their viewership and analyze patterns of being influenced to click and purchase merchandise from the sports ads displayed during live streaming.

4.4.2.2 Goal-Setting Theory

AI-powered mobile fitness apps (MFA) are gaining traction. However, the extant research has not explored the basis on which users decide to continue using them. A study examines how AI features in these MFAs influences end users' perceptions of their fitness goals. The research findings suggest that by being 'more specific', AI features can bring in clarity towards the goal and make it easier to achieve; end users perceive it to be 'less difficult', which increases the likelihood of their continued usage of the app. In terms of practical implications, such findings give essential insights for fitness experts and mobile application developers on how to design AI features that keep users engaged by successfully using the perspective of goal-setting theory (Lee & Lin, 2023).

4.4.2.3 Neuro-Fuzzy Prediction Models

There is a relatively older but, nevertheless, interesting study (Boussabaine, 2001) which formulates a comparative approach for demonstrating the cost of energy in sport facilities. The study starts with explaining how energy costs are a major expense for sporting facilities and exemplifies how the constructed buildings consume a significant portion of total energy use. This study formulates methods for forecasting energy costs at sports facility leisure centers by analyzing data from multiple sports centers in Liverpool city using statistical and AI techniques. The researchers compared three modeling approaches based on linear/non-linear regression, neural networks, and neuro-fuzzy models. From a practical standpoint, models that estimate and forecast building energy cost can aid sports business investors in optimizing their decisions, especially when planning for new facilities.

4.4.2.4 Cognition-Based Models

The research by Shunjiang Ma covers human–computer interaction in augmenting college-level sports education. The author explains that with the expansion of the internet and its ubiquitous presence within different domain industries ('internet plus'), a gap emerged in the traditional approach towards higher-level sports education. This gap necessitates a conscious alteration towards mixed teaching methods, potentially combining online and offline learning, and the study proposes a problem-based 'Cognitive Reasoning Sports Teaching Model (CRSTM)' as a reasonable solution for the educational aspects of sports training (Ma, 2022). The CRSTM highlights that technology interaction skills should be incorporated, clear learning goals set, and motor skills developed through well-defined training components.

4.4.2.5 Self-Determination Theory

In 2022, two researchers commenced an interesting study on the casual, everyday sporting activities of common folks that did not carry the complexities typical of competitive professional sporting events. The authors made use of the data feed from 494 smartwatch user participants, applied 'Self-Determination' theory on the data, and investigated the moderating effect of age. This study explored how the usage of fitness trackers to track one's own sporting activity data corresponds to their sense of control and enjoyment (intrinsic motivation) and found a positive correlation between wearable data tracking and the feelings of autonomy, competence, and connection. The study had a surprising observation: only the sense of autonomy (feeling in control of one's own tracker use) directly increased enjoyment of using the device. It confirmed that age indeed played a role, with autonomy having a stronger influence on the sense of enjoyment for younger users in comparison to older users (Jung & Kang, 2022).

4.4.2.6 Theory of Reasoned Action

Another study (Perez-Aranda et al., 2021) focuses on casual everyday sporting activity of individuals using smart watches, mobile apps, and the like with focus on anticipating sport-related physical activity during tourism. It is evident that the use of mobile sports and fitness apps has become popular among the common population. However, researchers do not fully understand in what context they use these when they are traveling for tourism. Looking at both social influences and motivations, the study analyses the possible factors influencing tourists' continued determination to use sports apps. The findings suggest positive attitudes (enjoyment, ease of use, etc.) toward apps and social pressure from others using the app could potentially contribute to a tourist's intention to keep using the app during tourism. The study also observes that the previous continued usage of these fitness apps (during non-tourism periods) increases the possibility of actual use of the apps when that tourist is on trips.

4.4.3 AI-IoT-Tech Implementations in Sports

In the earlier section, we focused on theory-based analysis. Now, we move away from theories, frameworks, and models and focus on the actual implementation use cases of AI-IoT-tech in the multiple scenarios of sports to gain practical insights.

- **Range of Possibilities**: A study intends to generate a framework wherein AI-IoT-tech is integrated into the public sector enterprise by examining the potential benefits, barriers, and enabling drivers through which government agencies can aim improve public services in terms of improving device predictive capabilities, data storage, and optimizing enterprise operations, thereby resulting in better economy, efficiency, effectiveness, and overall quality of life (Ishengoma et al., 2022). Implementation of AI-based models and IoT devices ends up giving rise to extensive data from various sources, which are thereby analyzed using AI-based data analytics techniques to forecast patterns and facilitate informed decision-making (Bibri et al., 2023). This approach has been utilized in the creation of environmentally sustainable smart cities, which have default demarcated layouts for recreational activities and sports facilities. From a technical feasibility and architecture standpoint, myriads of possible implementation scenarios are possible (Zhang et al., 2022). Thus, it is incumbent on the designers and stakeholders to realize the suitability AI-IoT-tech for their business use case in sports.
- **Pandemic Scenarios**: The COVID-19 pandemic has drastically changed all aspects of sports and recreational activities—how normal populations engage in recreational fitness activities, how professional athletes train to compete, and how fans experience the sports (Glebova, Zare, et al., 2022). It is important to note that virtual reality is an applied implementation of AI-IoT-tech (Pillai et al., 2020). All recreational activities for normal populations had come to a standstill. A research group leveraged virtual reality (VR) as an inclusive platform for physical fitness activities ranging from mundane dancing to social recreational sports. The study investigated user motivations for using VR specifically for dancing (social or exercise) by analyzing responses from 292

users, wherein they identified categories including fun, fitness, social interaction, and escape from reality, thereby confirming that VR offers a unique dance experience compared to reality, with potential benefits for physical and mental well-being (Sarupuri et al., 2023).

- **Injury and Rehabilitation**: Sports-related injuries continue to be a major concern for competitive team coaches and athletes worldwide as well as normal populations, especially if the injury is associated with important functional areas like the waist, shoulder, and wrist. Poor training habits and inadequate warm-up are known to contribute to such injuries. AI-IoT-tech are being increasingly brought into the sports sector to evaluate the risk of injury and its related impact on performance analysis, proactive injury prevention and rehabilitation, and recovery efficiency (Claudino et al., 2019; Ramkumar et al., 2021). A research study focused on designing a blockchain and IoT-enabled monitoring system for sports injury rehabilitation; the system collates data of past activities from sensors to assess athletes' prevailing health and uses this data to estimate injury risk through a neural network. In comparison to traditional methods, the system could detect injury locations quickly (0.2 seconds) and offers a high tracking and recovery rate (around 94.39%), thereby offering a valuable tool for proactively identifying and preventing injuries in sports (N. Li & Zhu, 2023).

- **Training**: Research has proven that AI-IoT-tech integration can enhance sports teaching and training capabilities by analyzing the moving elements of the game-element (example: football) and the actual movement of athletes. An associated study associated with knowledge innovation confirms table tennis teaching and training improved considerably (Cui & Zhou, 2022). AI-based pattern recognition and artificial neural networks can accurately evaluate weight training results and offer athletes prompt guidance in real time (Novatchkov & Baca, 2013).

- **Scalable Fan Engagement**: The advent of digital technologies (mobile apps, big data) is fast changing how fans across the world consume sports. But research studies do not have enough qualitative perspective on 'how' or 'why'. To understand the correlation between digital technologies and sports audiences, a study interviewed sports industry professionals. The findings suggest that digital technologies are reaching broader audiences and making sports consumption more inclusive regardless of gender, age, and similar demographics (Glebova, Desbordes, et al., 2022). Further, approaches based on text analytics have been devised to quantify fan engagement in sports: a research study explores how universities leverage sentiment analysis and content categorization (using AI) to understand fan engagement from social media text data, and proposes a framework for analyzing social media content through which universities can gain insights into the positive or negative fan sentiment based on the topics they discuss, which allows for more targeted and efficient fan engagement strategies without extra costs (H. Zadeh, 2021).

- **Real-Time Analysis**: AI-IoT-tech, including neural networks, provides a foundation for intelligent decision-making and performance analysis. Expert Systems and Artificial Neural Networks (ANN) have shown limited success in sports biomechanics, whereas Evolutionary Computation has demonstrated potential in movement optimization (Bartlett, 2006). Real-time analysis of athlete performance using IoT data and AI techniques, such as game theory-based decision-making, is known to improve sports services and decision modeling. A study proposes an IoT-based framework for real-time monitoring of athlete performance and decision-making in sports, improving performance in terms of Statistical Efficacy, Classification Efficiency, Reliability, Correlation Monitoring, and Temporal Delay (Bhatia, 2021).

- **Insightful Data**: Superior data analysis methods, including data mining and ML, are transforming smart sports training across various sports domains. Smart Sport Training (SST) is coming up as a concept and is known to leverage advanced data analysis techniques to enhance performance across sports disciplines (Rajšp & Fister, 2020). AI techniques such as decision trees and neural networks are used in team sports for risk assessment and performance prediction, with soccer and basketball showing significant applications. AI and ML methods can enhance match outcome prediction and strategic decision-making in team sports, but more study is needed to overcome limitations and progress the discipline (Beal et al., 2019).

- **Expert Recommendations**: AI prediction models are effective in forecasting sports outcomes. An AI based multi-layer perceptron model can accurately predict sports results and perform well compared to human tipsters in many scenarios (McCabe & Trevathan, 2008). Pattern recognition methods and ML concepts are used in weight training to automatically assess exercise techniques and provide feedback. AIoT technology enhances data gathering, knowledge generation, and equipment usability in sports science, particularly in weight training (Chu et al., 2019). AI, including expert systems and neural networks, has potential applications in sports biomechanics for technique evaluation and movement optimization and can enhance different aspects of daily living (Poniszewska-Maranda & Kaczmarek, 2015).

4.5 THE IMPACT OF AI-IOT-TECH ON THE SPORTS ECOSYSTEM

AIoT impacts sports by improving everyday sports operations, making immediate decisions, using predictive maintenance strategies, enhancing spectator and athlete experiences, and reaching strategic goals. However, achieving these advantages involves facing difficulties and ethical considerations unique to sports. This section addresses common risks and ethical concerns and suggests strategies to reduce the obstacles to applying AI and IoT technologies to the dynamic sports industry.

4.5.1 Societal Norms and Regulatory Frameworks

The growing integration of AI-IoT-tech in sports is bringing forth societal changes that transcend the game itself, as the examples of research studies below show.

Due to the assimilation of AI and IoT in sports and, in turn, the availability and consolidation of a large number of data points, the analytical industry is in overdrive, and it has given rise to online trend-based spot betting with shorter life cycles. In earlier days, the betting industry was confined predominantly to lifestyle-oriented people with deep pockets and, most of the time, such classes indulged in betting on horse racing and the like (Estévez et al., 2017). However, with the advent of mobile apps in every stratum of society, betting has become ubiquitous (James et al., 2017), especially among the non-working segment like young adolescents and teenagers, whose inherently curious minds, and easy access, lead them to explore betting. Betting can be extremely addictive, even more than the lottery, and as the human mind is prone to lose self-control (Blanchard et al., 2000), e-sports can turn into a vicious cycle of gambling and betting beyond one's financial capabilities and into debt (Parke & Parke, 2019). Therefore, there is a need for changes to the governance of mobile application platforms and for therapy (Riley et al., 2021).

We came across a study from China exploring the economic potential of sports lottery from a knowledge-based economy perspective enhanced by AI. China continues its focus on supporting those sectors, like the sports lottery industry, which ensure a sustainable flow of money with minimal impact on environment and resources. The research (Guo & Manly, 2023) employed a panel econometric model analyzing provincial data from 2011 to 2019 and studied the role of sports lottery sales, assisted by AI, in driving China's economic growth. The findings confirm that a positive correlation exists between sports lottery sales and economic growth, wherein the presence of AI and urbanization acted as significant amplifiers. It was further noticed that the positive effect of urbanization plateaued at a certain point. Another interesting observation was that an aging population didn't necessarily hinder the growth of the sports lottery, with regional variations guided by considerations like pension plans and senior citizen leisure activities.

A human's cognitive capabilities and sensory load carry inherent limitations, apart from the possibilities of bias. These limitations and biases are known to affect even seasoned sports judges, thus making them prone to mistakes. AI-IoT-tech-assisted sport integration could be of help wherein judges have a fallback option to access a 'second opinion' from an AI assistant before declaring the outcome of their assessment. As an example, in artistic gymnastics, it is hard for judges to keep their alignment with their scoring in tandem with the gymnasts as the performing athletes tend to be faster. In such scenarios, systems driven by AI could potentially help with the judging process to maintain the accuracy and consistency of results. An in-depth case study was conducted to compare the human scoring (from multiple participating ecosystem roles such as judges, gymnasts, coaches, and fans) with the scores generated by an AI-aided system in gymnastics. This exploratory study found a few oddities with the use of AI for scoring, or what it terms 'paradoxical tensions in AI-powered evaluation systems in competitive sports'. The research emphasizes the need to understand the current judging process, how to integrate AI, and the complexities around how AI would work alongside human judges to maintain the reliability of outcomes.

The research studies discussed above may be summarized into the following points in the context of sports being integrated with AI-IoT-tech:

- China's AI assisted lottery system emphasizes the importance of extended economic influences and the need for corresponding tailored strategies and policies.

- Betting-related discussions bring out the perils of negatively impacting the younger generation in terms of maintaining financial discipline.
- AI-IoT-tech offers countries a competitive advantage to build their representative national team in elite sports and, thus, indirectly influences their ongoing investments into it.
- AI-assisted judgment of sport play carries certain advantages along with complexities.

In summary, it is worth noting that the advent of AI-IoT-tech in sports does indeed transcend the game itself and influences societal norms, economy and national policymaking regarding sports betting.

4.5.2 Changing National Avenues

Each country seeks to represent its national presence in unique ways. The following studies focus on such initiatives.

Elite sports involving competitive nationality-based teams and private professional leagues are no longer untouched by the advent of AI-IoT-tech, and it is known to yield both positive and negative societal outcomes. While investments in elite sports are anticipated to result in broader societal benefits, empirical studies demonstrate that positive impacts are not guaranteed. Many countries are hiking the percentage allocation of public money investments towards their national sports representation in various sports, often driven by the supporting point that investments in elite sports will eventually lead to more medals and give impetus to myriads of social benefits as a ripple effect of those investments (De Bosscher et al., 2021). Going by the traditional viewpoint, many governments argue that investments in elite sports benefit society, due to the 'trickle down' effect, whereas researchers seem to be skeptical in the absence of corroborating empirical evidence. In this context, a study was commenced which proposed a new framework to categorize the potential positive and negative impacts of elite sports on society and applied that framework to arrive at the understanding that the perception of the societal impact of elite sports varies (De Rycke & De Bosscher, 2019).

Another study tackles the public perception aspects of elite sports. Countries that invest heavily in national elite sports teams are hopeful about public benefits but they do not assess how people view this impact. A research study designed a survey to measure public perception of both positive and negative societal effects arising from elite sports. This was conducted in Belgium and the survey results depicted an overall favorable public perception of elite sports' impact on society (De Rycke et al., 2019).

Nations blessed with sea beaches tend to carry certain latent commercial advantages. They are now exploring a new growth-oriented trajectory involving the marriage of beach sports and the tourism business. This can be a breakthrough in terms of novel ways of seeking an economic impetus through sports tourism. Almost every country's tourism department has enough information on travel volumes, footfall spread in different regions, which aspects of sightseeing are comparatively more sought after, and in which season or like governing factor. In other words, tourism departments are seated on a hotbed of big data. If combined with tourism patterns and beach sports, a country can aim for major tourism growth. The related research study explores this novel avenue through these proposed steps. The first step is to create a national body looking into the integration of beach sports and the related tourism business. The second step is to apply the risk assessment model to evaluate the economic profit trend brought about by beach sports in the development of tourism. The third and final step is to validate the model through pilot outcomes (Zeng et al., 2023).

Challenges beckon the human spirit to survive and thrive. Adventure tourism—usually involving hiking, running, climbing, or surfing—is turning out to be a popular, growth-oriented segment in the tourism industry. Such high-adrenaline activities end up attracting investment from foreign travelers interested in practicing sports when exploring the host country. As a result, several software companies are coming up with AI-based solutions – like recommendation systems that provide tourists intelligent, personalized recommendations based on their preferences – to augment their outdoor adventure experience. Research into running and hiking has been ongoing, but other adventure sports seem to be relatively neglected. To understand the methods and techniques in adventure tourism deployed by current recommendation systems, Ivanova & Wald (2023) review over 1,000 papers and propose a unified framework for more effective, and personalized, AI-assisted recommendation systems for outdoor adventure tourism sports.

Thus, the new avenues being chartered by countries in context of sports are:

- AI-IoT-tech offers countries a competitive advantage to build representative national teams in elite sports and thus indirectly influences ongoing investment

- Assisted by big data, beach sports and tourism offer a potentially beneficial association.
- AI-assisted recommendation systems for adventure tourism sports

4.5.3 Addressing Ethical Concerns

The introduction of AI and IoT into sports brings forth numerous ethical considerations ranging from data security and privacy to the impact on athletes and the game itself. It is crucial to address ethical challenges, ensure transparency, and comprehend the broader societal implications to navigate the evolving landscape of AI-IoT-tech in sports. AI, known for its transformative force, has sparked debates on the principles guiding its development and use (Jobin et al., 2019). The advent of IoT in sports has brought significant societal transformations, particularly by empowering individuals, including women, in developing countries (Baiyere et al., 2020).

Sports technology has improved equipment, training, and biomechanics, but some argue it threatens fairness (e.g., advanced prosthetics) and as such the adoption of AI in sports comes with an inherent expectation of fair play. The study examines the use of AI in cricket umpiring and explores the ethical issues it raises for various stakeholders. Their findings can be applied to consider the broader ethics of technology use in global sports. Such observations thereby raise ethical challenges whose effects go beyond the periphery of the game potentially impacting players, administrators, and even broadcasters (DC, 2022).

A study deals with existing ineffective procedures for detecting doping in sports. It argues that if the current anti-doping system is already flawed, then introducing AI into the game to make it more effective isn't a morally right step. It posits that a more effective AI system on an existing dysfunctional doping procedure is likely to create worse ethical issues than the current system due to potential mistakes in identifying dopers, leading to wrongful accusations in terms of both false positives and false negatives, that could be devastating to the careers involved (Petersen et al., 2024).

Furthermore, the ethical concerns surrounding AI-IoT-tech in sports extend to the design and deployment of these technologies. Ethical design principles are essential to ensure that IoT devices are developed with security and privacy in mind (Baldini et al., 2016) and the lack of clarity on use of personal IoT data raises ethical questions that need to be addressed (Bourgeois & Kortuem, 2019). To summarize, the role of ethics seems to increase the complexity with advent of AI-IoT-tech in sports rather than decreasing it.

4.6 CONCLUSION

This section summarizes the overall chapter. We started with the essential understanding of the different technology terms from a layperson's standpoint. Thereafter, we deal with the definitions or perceptions as per the extant literature and make sense of the prevailing use of information systems theories in sports.

We briefly touched upon the various non-IS theories to ensure a smooth flow of reading and continuity for the reader although the focus of our chapter is on IS theories. The application of IS theories to AI-IoT-tech in sports is discussed in the context of technology acceptance theories that would aid in adoption and in the context of other IS theories that would aid in propagation. We have purposely avoided comparison between the given set of theories, frameworks, and models because the suitability of each increases or decreases based on the business conditions wherein adoption is happening and that itself can be an insightful research topic to work upon. The ending subsections deal with the impact of AI-IoT-tech on sports ecosystems and touch on the ethical concerns arising from the use of intelligent technology in sports.

Suitable diagrams have been explained at the appropriate junctures so that the discussion makes sense even to a reader who is not well versed with the subject. Our main intent was to share knowledge and so we kept the entire work plenary in nature and the mode of discussion free flowing.

ACKNOWLEDGMENTS

We thank Gartner for permission to use their images and contextual explanation on Hype Cycle and Priority Matrix for Emerging Technologies. The terms 'GARTNER' and 'HYPE CYCLE' are trademarks of Gartner Inc. and/or its affiliates.

NOTE

1 The terms 'GARTNER' and 'HYPE CYCLE' are trademarks of Gartner Inc. and/or its affiliates.

REFERENCES

Ajzen, I. (1985). From Intentions to Actions: A Theory of Planned Behavior. *Action Control*, 11–39. https://doi.org/10.1007/978-3-642-69746-3_2

Ajzen, I. (1991). The Theory of Planned Behavior. *Organizational Behavior and Human Decision Processes, 50*(2), 179–211. https://doi.org/10.1016/0749-5978(91)90020-T

Angelo, D. L., Boas, M. V, Correa, M. d. F., Souza, V. H., Moura, L. d. P., Oliveira, R. d., Bossio, M. R., & Brandão, M. R. F. (2022). Basic Psychological-Need Satisfaction and Thwarting: A Study with Brazilian Professional Players of League of Legends. *Sustainability*. https://doi.org/10.3390/su14031701

Baiyere, A., Topi, H., Venkatesh, V., Watt, J., & Donnellan, B. (2020). The Internet of Things (IoT): A Research Agenda for Information Systems. *Communications of the Association for Information Systems, 47*.

Baldini, G., Botterman, M., Neisse, R., & Tallacchini, M. (2016). Ethical Design in the Internet of Things. *Science and Engineering Ethics.* https://doi.org/10.1007/s11948-016-9754-5

Bartlett, R. (2006). Artificial Intelligence in Sports Biomechanics: New Dawn or False Hope? ©*Journal of Sports Science and Medicine, 5*, 474–479. www.jssm.org

Beal, R., Norman, T. J., & Ramchurn, S. D. (2019). Artificial Intelligence for Team Sports: A Survey. *The Knowledge Engineering Review, 34*, e28. https://doi.org/10.1017/S02698 88919000225

Bhatia, M. (2021). Intelligent System of Game-Theory-Based Decision Making in Smart Sports Industry. *ACM Transactions on Intelligent Systems and Technology, 12*(3), 1–23. https://doi.org/10.1145/3447986

Bibri, S. E., Alexandre, A., Sharifi, A., & Krogstie, J. (2023). Environmentally Sustainable Smart Cities and Their Converging AI, IoT, and Big Data Technologies and Solutions: An Integrated Approach To An Extensive Literature Review. *Energy Informatics, 6*(1), 9. https://doi.org/10.1186/s42162-023-00259-2

Bilal, M., Zhang, Y., Cai, S., Akram, U., & Halibas, A. (2024). Artificial Intelligence Is the Magic Wand Making Customer-Centric a Reality! an Investigation into the Relationship Between Consumer Purchase Intention and Consumer Engagement Through Affective Attachment. *Journal of Retailing and Consumer Services, 77*, 103674. https://doi.org/10.1016/J.JRETCONSER.2023.103674

Blanchard, E. B., Wulfert, E., Freidenberg, B. M., & Malta, L. S. (2000). Psychophysiological Assessment of Compulsive Gamblers' Arousal to Gambling Cues: A Pilot Study. *Applied Psychophysiology Biofeedback, 25*(3), 155–165. https://doi.org/10.1023/A:100955 0724836

Bourgeois, J., & Kortuem, G. (2019). Towards Responsible Design with Internet of Things Data. *Proceedings of the Design Society International Conference on Engineering Design.* https://doi.org/10.1017/dsi.2019.349

Boussabaine, A. H. (2001). A Comparative Approach for Modelling the Cost of Energy in Sport Facilities. *Facilities, 19*(5/6), 194–203. https://doi.org/10.1108/02632770110387788

Brooks, R. (1986). A Robust Layered Control System for a Mobile Robot. *IEEE Journal on Robotics and Automation, 2*(1), 14–23. https://doi.org/10.1109/JRA.1986.1087032

Buser, M., Woratschek, H., Dickson, G., & Schönberner, J. (2022). Toward a Sport Ecosystem Logic. *Journal of Sport Management.* https://doi.org/10.1123/jsm.2021-0056

Chai, C. S., Chiu, T. K. F., Wang, X., Jiang, F., & Lin, X. F. (2022). Modeling Chinese Secondary School Students' Behavioral Intentions to Learn Artificial Intelligence with the Theory of Planned Behavior and Self-Determination Theory. *Sustainability, 15*(1), 605. https://doi.org/10.3390/SU15010605

Chai, C. S., Wang, X., & Xu, C. (2020). An Extended Theory of Planned Behavior for the Modelling of Chinese Secondary School Students' Intention to Learn Artificial Intelligence. *Mathematics, 8*(11), 2089. https://doi.org/10.3390/MATH8112089

Chandrasekaran, A., & Davis, M. (2023, August 2). *Hype Cycle for Emerging Technologies, 2023.* GARTNER. www.gartner.com/document/4597499?ref=shareSummary&toggle=1&viewType=Full

Chang, A. C. (2023). Primary Prevention of Sudden Cardiac Death of the Young Athlete: The Controversy About the Screening Electrocardiogram and Its Innovative Artificial Intelligence Solution. *Pediatric Cardiology, 33*, 428–433. https://doi.org/10.1007/s00246-012-0244-5

Chang, C.-J., Yang, S.-C., & Wolzok, E. (2023). Examining the Use of Fitness Apps in Sports Centers in Taiwan: Incorporating Task-Technology Fit into a Technology Readiness Acceptance Model. *Managing Sport and Leisure, 28*(3), 283–301. https://doi.org/10.1080/23750472.2023.2165532

Chen, Z., Chan, I. C. C., Mehraliyev, F., Law, R., & Choi, Y. (2024). Typology of People–Process–Technology Framework in Refining Smart Tourism from the Perspective of Tourism Academic Experts. *Tourism Recreation Research, 49*(1), 105–117. https://doi.org/10.1080/02508281.2021.1969114

Chu, W. C.-C., Shih, C., Chou, W.-Y., Ahamed, S. I., & Hsiung, P.-A. (2019). Artificial Intelligence of Things in Sports Science: Weight Training as an Example. *Computer, 52*(11), 52–61. https://doi.org/10.1109/MC.2019.2933772

Claudino, J. G., Capanema, D. de O., de Souza, T. V., Serrão, J. C., Machado Pereira, A. C., & Nassis, G. P. (2019). Current Approaches to the Use of Artificial Intelligence for Injury Risk Assessment and Performance Prediction in Team Sports: a Systematic Review. *Sports Medicine – Open, 5*(1), 28. https://doi.org/10.1186/s40798-019-0202-3

Cui, Y., & Zhou, C. (2022). Application of Internet of Things Artificial Intelligence and Knowledge Innovation System in Table Tennis Teaching and Training. *Applied Bionics and Biomechanics, 2022*, 1–13. https://doi.org/10.1155/2022/7625626

Davis, F. D. (1989). Perceived Usefulness, Perceived Ease of Use, and User Acceptance of Information Technology. *MIS Quarterly, 13*(3), 319. https://doi.org/10.2307/249008

DC, S. (2022). Artificial Intelligence in Sport: An Ethical Issue. *Unity Journal.* https://doi.org/10.3126/unityj.v3i01.43313

De Bosscher, V., Shibli, S., & De Rycke, J. (2021). The Societal Impact of Elite Sport: Positives and Negatives: Introduction To ESMQ Special Issue. *European Sport Management Quarterly, 21*(5), 625–635. https://doi.org/10.1080/16184742.2021.1955944

De Rycke, J., & De Bosscher, V. (2019). Mapping the Potential Societal Impacts Triggered by Elite Sport: A Conceptual Framework. *International Journal of Sport Policy and Politics, 11*(3), 485–502. https://doi.org/10.1080/19406940.2019.1581649

De Rycke, J., De Bosscher, V., Funahashi, H., & Sotiriadou, P. (2019). Public Perceptions of the Societal Impact of Elite Sport: Scale Development and Testing. *Journal of Sport Management, 33*(6), 560–571. https://doi.org/10.1123/jsm.2018-0295

Donaldson, A., Lloyd, D. G., Gabbe, B. J., Cook, J., & Finch, C. F. (2017). We have the Programme, What Next? Planning The Implementation of an Injury Prevention Programme. *Injury Prevention, 23*(4), 273–280. https://doi.org/10.1136/INJURYPREV-2015-041737

Estévez, A., Rodríguez, R., Díaz, N., Granero, R., Mestre-Bach, G., Steward, T., Fernández-Aranda, F., Aymamí, N., Gómez-peña, M., Del Pino-Gutiérrez, A., Baño, M., Moragas, L., Mallorquí-Bagué, N., López-González, H., Jauregui, P., Onaindia, J., Martín-Romera, V., Menchón, J. M., & Jiménez-Murcia, S. (2017). How Do Online Sports Gambling

Disorder Patients Compare with Land-Based Patients? *Journal of Behavioral Addictions,* *6*(4), 639–647. https://doi.org/10.1556/2006.6.2017.067

Felfernig, A., Polat-Erdeniz, S., Uran, C., Reiterẹr, S., Atas, M., Tran, T. N. T., Azzoni, P., Kiraly, C., & Dolui, K. (2019). An Overview of Recommender Systems in the Internet of Things. *Journal of Intelligent Information Systems, 52*(2), 285–309. https://doi.org/10.1007/s10844-018-0530-7

Fletcher, D., & Sarkar, M. (2012). A Grounded Theory of Psychological Resilience in Olympic Champions. *Psychology of Sport and Exercise, 13*(5), 669–678. https://doi.org/10.1016/j.psychsport.2012.04.007

Funk, D. C., & James, J. (2001). The Psychological Continuum Model: A Conceptual Framework for Understanding an Individual's Psychological Connection to Sport. *Sport Management Review, 4*(2), 119–150. https://doi.org/10.1016/S1441-3523(01)70072-1

Glebova, E., Desbordes, M., & Géczi, G. (2022). Mass Diffusion of Modern Digital Technologies as the Main Driver of Change in Sports-Spectating Audiences. *Frontiers in Psychology.* https://doi.org/10.3389/fpsyg.2022.805043

Glebova, E., Zare, F., Desbordes, M., & Géczi, G. (2022). COVID-19 Sport Transformation: New Challenges and New Opportunities. *Physical Culture and Sport Studies and Research.* https://doi.org/10.2478/pcssr-2022-0011

Guo, Z., & Manly, N. E. (2023). Unlocking the Economic Potential of Sports Lottery in China: A Knowledge-Based Economy Perspective Enhanced by Artificial Intelligence. *Journal of the Knowledge Economy,* 1–27. https://doi.org/10.1007/s13132-023-01640-y

H. Zadeh, A. (2021). Quantifying Fan Engagement in Sports Using Text Analytics. *Journal of Data, Information and Management, 3*(3), 197–208. https://doi.org/10.1007/s42488-021-00052-4

Ishengoma, F., Shao, D., Alexopoulos, C., Saxena, S., & Nikiforova, A. (2022). Integration of Artificial Intelligence of Things (AIoT) in the Public Sector: Drivers, Barriers and Future Research Agenda. *Digital Policy Regulation and Governance.* https://doi.org/10.1108/dprg-06-2022-0067

Ivanova, I., & Wald, M. (2023). Recommender Systems for Outdoor Adventure Tourism Sports: Hiking, Running and Climbing. *Human-Centric Intelligent Systems, 3*(3), 344–365. https://doi.org/10.1007/s44230-023-00033-3

Jaeger, J. (2021). Football Fans and Stakeholder Theory – A Qualitative Approach to Classifying Fans in Germany. *Sport Business and Management an International Journal.* https://doi.org/10.1108/sbm-11-2020-0127

James, R. J. E., O'Malley, C., & Tunney, R. J. (2017). Understanding the Psychology of Mobile Gambling: A Behavioural Synthesis. *British Journal of Psychology, 108*(3), 608–625. https://doi.org/10.1111/BJOP.12226

Jang, M., Jung, Y., & Kim, S. (2021). Investigating Managers' Understanding of Chatbots in the Korean Financial Industry. *Computers in Human Behavior, 120,* 106747. https://doi.org/10.1016/j.chb.2021.106747

Jiao, S., Wang, X., Ma, C., & Deng, Y. (2024). How Does Sports e-Commerce Influence Consumer Behavior Through Short Video Live Broadcast Platforms? Attachment Theory Perspective. *Asia Pacific Journal of Marketing and Logistics, 36*(7), 1557–1575. https://doi.org/10.1108/APJML-08-2023-0777

Jobin, A., Ienca, M., & Vayena, E. (2019). The Global Landscape of AI Ethics Guidelines. *Nature Machine Intelligence, 1*(9), 389–399. https://doi.org/10.1038/s42256-019-0088-2

Jung, E. H., & Kang, H. (2022). Self-Determination in Wearable Fitness Technology: The Moderating Effect of Age. *International Journal of Human–Computer Interaction, 38*(15), 1399–1409. https://doi.org/10.1080/10447318.2021.2002048

Junge, A. (2000). The Influence of Psychological Factors on Sports Injuries. *American Journal of Sports Medicine*. https://doi.org/10.1177/28.suppl_5.s-10

Kim, H.-W., Chan, H. C., & Gupta, S. (2007). Value-based Adoption of Mobile Internet: An empirical investigation. *Decision Support Systems*, *43*(1), 111–126. https://doi.org/10.1016/j.dss.2005.05.009

Kim, Y., Park, Y., & Choi, J. (2017). A Study on the Adoption of IoT Smart Home Service: Using Value-based Adoption Model. *Total Quality Management & Business Excellence*, *28*(9–10), 1149–1165. https://doi.org/10.1080/14783363.2017.1310708

Kumar, S., Mookerjee, V., & Shubham, A. (2018). Research in Operations Management and Information Systems Interface. *Production and Operations Management*. https://doi.org/10.1111/poms.12961

Lee, J. C., & Lin, R. (2023). The Continuous Usage of Artificial Intelligence (AI)-Powered Mobile Fitness Applications: The Goal-Setting Theory Perspective. *Industrial Management and Data Systems*, *123*(6), 1840–1860. https://doi.org/10.1108/IMDS-10-2022-0602

Li, N., & Zhu, X. (2023). Design and Application of Blockchain and IoT-Enabled Sports Injury Rehabilitation Monitoring System Using Neural Network. *Soft Computing*, *27*(16), 11815–11832. https://doi.org/10.1007/s00500-023-08677-w

Li, Q., Kumar, P. M., & Alazab, M. (2022). IoT-Assisted Physical Education Training Network Virtualization and Resource Management Using a Deep Reinforcement Learning System. *Complex and Intelligent Systems*, *8*(2), 1229–1242. https://doi.org/10.1007/s40747-021-00584-7

Liao, Y.-K., Wu, W.-Y., Le, T. Q., & Phung, T. T. T. (2022). The Integration of the Technology Acceptance Model and Value-Based Adoption Model to Study the Adoption of E-Learning: The Moderating Role of e-WOM. *Sustainability*, *14*(2), 815. https://doi.org/10.3390/su14020815

Liu, J., & Wang, C. (2016). A Developmental Research on National Sports Resources in West China Based on PSR Model. *Advances in Physical Education*. https://doi.org/10.4236/ape.2016.64030

Lu, Z., Qian, P., Bi, D., Ye, Z., He, X., Zhao, Y., Su, L., Li, S., & Zhu, Z. (2021). Application of AI and IoT in Clinical Medicine: Summary and Challenges. *Current Medical Science*. https://doi.org/10.1007/s11596-021-2486-z

Lyras, A. (2021). Olympism for Humanity Theory and Praxis: A Call for Peace and Democracy Champions of Change. *Peace and Conflict Journal of Peace Psychology*. https://doi.org/10.1037/pac0000498

Ma, S. (2022). College Sports Intelligence Using Human–Computer Interaction System for Education. *International Journal of Human–Computer Interaction*, 1–9. https://doi.org/10.1080/10447318.2022.2104005

McCabe, A., & Trevathan, J. (2008). Artificial Intelligence in Sports Prediction. *Fifth International Conference on Information Technology: New Generations (Itng 2008)*, 1194–1197. https://doi.org/10.1109/ITNG.2008.203

Mogaji, E., Soetan, T. O., & Kieu, T. A. (2020). The Implications of Artificial Intelligence on the Digital Marketing of Financial Services to Vulnerable Customers. *Australasian Marketing Journal*, *29*(3), 235–242. https://doi.org/10.1016/J.AUSMJ.2020.05.003

Novatchkov, H., & Baca, A. (2013). Artificial Intelligence in Sports on the Example of Weight Training. ©*Journal of Sports Science and Medicine, 12*, 27–37. www.jssm.org

Parihar, V., Malik, A., Bhawna, Bhushan, B., & Chaganti, R. (2023). From Smart Devices to Smarter Systems: Evolution of AIoT with Characteristics, Architecture, Use Cases and Challenges. In B. Bhushan, A. K. Sangaiah, & T. N. Nguyen (Eds.), *AI Models for Blockchain-Based Intelligent Networks in IoT Systems. Engineering Cyber-Physical*

Systems and Critical Infrastructures (1st ed., Vol. 6, pp. 1–28). Springer. https://doi.org/10.1007/978-3-031-31952-5_1

Parke, A., & Parke, J. (2019). Transformation of Sports Betting into a Rapid and Continuous Gambling Activity: A Grounded Theoretical Investigation of Problem Sports Betting in Online Settings. *International Journal of Mental Health and Addiction*, 17(6), 1340–1359. https://doi.org/10.1007/S11469-018-0049-8

Passos, J. M., Lopes, S. I., Clemente, F. M., Moreira, P. M., Rico-González, M., Bezerra, P., & Rodrigues, L. P. (2021). Wearables and Internet of Things (IoT) Technologies for Fitness Assessment: A Systematic Review. *Sensors*. https://doi.org/10.3390/s21165418

Perez-Aranda, J., González Robles, E. M., & Urbistondo, P. A. (2021). Sport-Related Physical Activity in Tourism: An Analysis of Antecedents of Sport Based Applications Use. *Information Technology and Tourism*, 23(1), 97–120. https://doi.org/10.1007/s40558-019-00161-2

Petersen, T. S., Holmen, S. J., & Ryberg, J. (2024). AI, Doping and Ethics: On Why Increasing the Effectiveness of Detecting Doping Fraud in Sport May Be Morally Wrong. *Journal of Medical Ethics*, jme-2023-109721. https://doi.org/10.1136/jme-2023-109721

Pillai, M., Yang, Y., Ditmars, C., & Subhash, H. M. (2020). Artificial Intelligence-Based Interactive Virtual Reality-Assisted Gaming System for Hand Rehabilitation. In T. M. Deserno & P.-H. Chen (Eds.), *Medical Imaging 2020: Imaging Informatics for Healthcare, Research, and Applications* (p. 18). SPIE. https://doi.org/10.1117/12.2549372

Poniszewska-Maranda, A., & Kaczmarek, D. (2015). Selected Methods of Artificial Intelligence for Internet of Things Conception. *Selected Methods of Artificial Intelligence for Internet of Things Conception. In 2015 Federated Conference on Computer Science and Information Systems (FedCSIS)*, 1343–1348. https://doi.org/10.15439/2015F161

Rajšp, A., & Fister, I. (2020). A Systematic Literature Review of Intelligent Data Analysis Methods for Smart Sport Training. *Applied Sciences*, 10(9), 3013. https://doi.org/10.3390/app10093013

Ramkumar, P. N., Luu, B. C., Haeberle, H. S., Karnuta, J. M., Nwachukwu, B. U., & Williams, R. J. (2021). Sports Medicine and Artificial Intelligence: A Primer. *The American Journal of Sports Medicine*. https://doi.org/10.1177/03635465211008648

Ratten, V., & Thompson, A.-J. (2020). Digital Sport Entrepreneurial Ecosystems. *Thunderbird International Business Review*. https://doi.org/10.1002/tie.22160

Riley, B. J., Harris, S., Nye, T., Javidi-Hosseinabad, Z., & Baigent, M. (2021). Graded Exposure Therapy for Online Mobile Smartphone Sports Betting Addiction: A Case Series Report. *Journal of Gambling Studies*, 37(4), 1263–1275. https://doi.org/10.1007/s10899-021-10006-5

Rogers, E. M. (1995a). *Diffusion of Innovations* (E. M. Rogers, Ed.). Free Press.

Rogers, E. M. (1995b). Diffusion of Innovations: Modifications of a Model for Telecommunications. In *Die Diffusion von Innovationen in der Telekommunikation* (pp. 25–38). Springer Berlin Heidelberg. https://doi.org/10.1007/978-3-642-79868-9_2

Roundy, P. T. (2022). Artificial Intelligence and Entrepreneurial Ecosystems: Understanding the Implications of Algorithmic Decision-Making for Startup Communities. *Journal of Ethics in Entrepreneurship and Technology*, 2, 23–28. https://doi.org/10.1108/jeet-07-2022-0011

Salzman, M., Matathia, I., & O'Reilly, A. (2003). *BUZZ: Harness the Power of Influence and Create Demand* (M. Salzman & I. O. A. Matathia, Eds.). Wiley.

Sant, S.-L., Maleske, C., Wang, W., & King, E. J. (2023). Leveraging Sport Events for the Promotion of Human Rights in Host Communities: Diffusion of Anti-Trafficking

Campaigns at Super Bowl LIV. *Sport Management Review, 26*(2), 203–223. https://doi.org/10.1080/14413523.2022.2120010

Sarupuri, B., Kulpa, R., Aristidou, A., & Multon, F. (2023). Dancing in Virtual Reality as an Inclusive Platform for Social and Physical Fitness Activities: A Survey. *Visual Computer,* 1–16. https://doi.org/10.1007/s00371-023-03068-6

Smith, R. E. (2006). Understanding Sport Behavior: A Cognitive-Affective Processing Systems Approach. *Journal of Applied Sport Psychology, 18*(1), 1–27. https://doi.org/10.1080/10413200500471293

Sohn, K., & Kwon, O. (2019). Technology Acceptance Theories and Factors Influencing Artificial Intelligence-Based Intelligent Products. *Telematics and Informatics.* https://doi.org/10.1016/j.tele.2019.101324

Suciu, G. (2016). Big Data and Internet of Things—Challenges and Opportunities for Accelerated Business Development Beyond 2050. In R. Prasad & S. Dixit (Eds.), *Wireless World in 2050 and Beyond: A Window into the Future!* (pp. 111–128). Springer Series in Wireless Technology. Springer, Cham. https://doi.org/10.1007/978-3-319-42141-4_10

Sun, S., Peng, T., Huang, H., Wang, Y., Zhang, X., & Zhou, Y. (2023). IoT Motion Tracking System for Workout Performance Evaluation: A Case Study on Dumbbell. *IEEE Transactions on Consumer Electronics, 69*(4), 798–808. https://doi.org/10.1109/TCE.2023.3320183

Thomas, M. A., Li, Y., Sistenich, V., Diango, K. N., & Kabongo, D. (2023). A Multi-Stakeholder Engagement Framework for Knowledge Management in ICT4D. *Journal of the Association for Information Science and Technology, 74*(12), 1384–1400. https://doi.org/10.1002/asi.24703

Venkatesh, V., & Bala, H. (2008). Technology Acceptance Model 3 and a Research Agenda on Interventions. *Decision Sciences, 39*(2), 273–315. https://doi.org/10.1111/j.1540-5915.2008.00192.x

Venkatesh, V., & Davis, F. D. (2000). A Theoretical Extension of the Technology Acceptance Model: Four Longitudinal Field Studies. *Management Science, 46*(2), 186–204. https://doi.org/10.1287/mnsc.46.2.186.11926

Venkatesh, V., Morris, M. G., Davis, G. B., & Davis, F. D. (2003). User Acceptance of Information Technology: Toward a Unified View. *MIS Quarterly, 27*(3), 425. https://doi.org/10.2307/30036540

Venkatesh, V., Thong, J. Y. L., & Xu, X. (2012). Consumer Acceptance and Use of Information Technology: Extending the Unified Theory of Acceptance and Use of Technology. *MIS Quarterly, 36*(1), 157. https://doi.org/10.2307/41410412

Xu, S., Kee, K. F., Li, W., Yamamoto, M., & Riggs, R. E. (2023). Examining the Diffusion of Innovations from a Dynamic, Differential-Effects Perspective: A Longitudinal Study on AI Adoption Among Employees. *Communication Research.* https://doi.org/10.1177/00936502231191832

Yang, L., Henthorne, T. L., & George, B. (2019). Artificial Intelligence and Robotics Technology in the Hospitality Industry: Current Applications and Future Trends. In B. George & Y. Paul (Eds.), *Digital Transformation in Business and Society: Theory and Cases* (pp. 211–228). Springer. https://doi.org/10.1007/978-3-030-08277-2_13

Zeng, G., Ren, Z., Zhou, H., Wang, H., Tang, J., & Tang, H. (2023). Exploration of Profit Model of Beach Sports Based on Data Drive. In Y. Zhong (Ed.), *Fifth International Conference on Computer Information Science and Artificial Intelligence (CISAI 2022)* (p. 74). SPIE. https://doi.org/10.1117/12.2667560

Zhang, Y., Yu, H. Z., Zhou, W., & Man, M. (2022). Application and Research of IoT Architecture for End-Net-Cloud Edge Computing. *Electronics.* https://doi.org/10.3390/electronics12010001

SUGGESTED ADDITIONAL READING

This is given in the order of significance and not alphabetically ordered.

- Pretorius, A., & Parry, D. A. (2016, September). Human Decision Making and Artificial Intelligence: A Comparison in the Domain of Sports Prediction. In *Proceedings of the Annual Conference of the South African Institute of Computer Scientists and Information Technologists* (pp. 1–10).
- Schmidt, S. L. (2020). *21st Century Sports*. Springer International.
- Araújo, D., Couceiro, M., Seifert, L., Sarmento, H., & Davids, K. (2021). *Artificial Intelligence in Sport Performance Analysis*. Routledge.
- Chase, C. (2020). The Data Revolution: Cloud Computing, Artificial Intelligence, and Machine Learning in the Future of Sports. *21st Century Sports: How Technologies Will Change Sports in the Digital Age*, 175–189.

5

Artificial Intelligence (AI): A New Window to Smart Stadiums

Sardar Mohammadi, Seyyed Iman Ghaffarisadr, and Manuel Alonso Dos Santos

5.1 INTRODUCTION

Today's stadiums face increasing competition from home-viewing options – powered by better camera angles and multiplatform, multimedia experiences – while at the same time the monetary costs to operate and maintain a stadium remain the same (Molnár, 2023). Another development, according to Bernhold et al. (2014), is that in Europe and further afield most stadiums were built more than 35 years ago, and these outdated stadiums are unable to fulfill the expectations of today's fans (Bernhold et al., 2014). These trends are harming the financial viability of the key stakeholders of the stadiums, and many stadiums do not realize their business case opportunities.

Concurrent with these trends is the increase in computing power and the near-ubiquity of the smartphone, which gives even the most remote user access to the benefits of this technology. Today's smartphone owner carries a device with processing power that would have required a computer the size of a stadium 50 years ago (van Heck et al., 2021). These technological developments have the potential to measure in real time the use of a stadium. The information that is generated is affecting the decision-making of managing a stadium, thus the real estate management of a stadium. In real estate management, in general, the focus is on the match between demand and supply which can result in a 'competitive advantage', leading to different 'added values' for an organization in the end (Beckers et al., 2015). To keep attracting fans to stadiums, it is important that demand and supply are in line with each other. Using technological developments to measure the real-time use of stadiums has the potential to match demand and supply more efficiently. This can be done by the technology of so-called 'smart tools', a "service or product which collects real-time information on space use to improve the space use on the current campus on the one hand, whilst supporting decision making on the future space use on the other hand" (Valks et al., 2016, p. 23). The implementation of smart tools in the built environment has the potential to align real estate portfolios to the needs of users more frequently in time, due to the provision of real-time information, and to a higher level of detail in space. According to Buckman, Mayfield and Beck (2014) "the reason for providing this information will lead to improving certain aspects, which can be grouped in the following categories: energy and efficiency, longevity, and comfort and satisfaction" (Buckman, Mayfield & Beck, 2014, p. 104).

Within the context of stadiums, a lot of data can be made available due to the implementation of smart stadiums. Since stadiums gather a lot of people for a specific, short period of time, it creates challenges. As shown in different studies (D'Orazio & Guaragnella, 2015; Dong, 2015; Panchanathan et al., 2017; O'Brolcháin, Colle & Gordijn, 2019), integrating smart tools can improve specific touchpoints of stadiums, such as safety, fan experience, sustainability, and energy reduction. These touchpoints are affecting the competitive advantage of a stadium (Sartori & Nienhoff, 2013). This means that a stadium can differentiate itself from other stadiums and reduce operational costs (van Heck et al., 2021).

However, the integration of smart tools in stadiums is a new development that is in its infancy. One of the main elements in smart stadiums is AI, which casts a shadow like an umbrella over other activities carried out in these structures. In this chapter, the authors try to highlight the role of AI in this process. It will help stadium stakeholders to gain knowledge in this field and make informed decisions.

5.2 AI IN STADIUM DOMAIN

AI is a term that refers to technology that mimics human functions and, in many cases, uses machine learning (ML) to learn from data how to outperform these jobs (Shabbir & Anwer, 2018). In sports domains, it is used to analyze a plethora of data to improve the performance of players and teams and enhance the experiences and engagement of fans (Araújo et al., 2021). The global AI in sports market was valued at $1.4 billion in 2020, and it is projected to reach $19.2 billion by 2030, growing at the rate of 30.3% from 2021 to 2030 (Nadikattu, 2020). This technology also plays an essential role in reducing human errors and in supporting referees and umpires in making the right decision. AI in Stadium refers to the implementation of AI technologies and solutions in sports venues to enhance the overall fan experience, optimize stadium operations, and improve player performance. AI in Stadium encompasses various applications, such as facial recognition, predictive analytics, virtual reality (VR), chatbots, and smart stadium infrastructure (Ding et al., 2021). The increase in the number of participants in sporting events is expected to propel the growth of the AI in Stadium market going forward. Sports events refer to organized competitions or gatherings where athletes or teams compete in various sports disciplines. The application of AI in stadiums implements AI technologies and systems to enhance performance analysis, improve the fan experience, assist referees, enable predictive analytics, and optimize stadium operations (Ding et al., 2021). For instance, in 2020, according to Tourism Economics, a Philadelphia-based information services organization, there were 96 million travelers attending sporting events in the US. That number increased to 175 million travelers in 2021 (Kim et al., 2021). Further, in February 2023, according to the Sports & Fitness Industry Association (SFIA), a US-based promoter of sports and fitness participation, around 77.6% of all Americans, or 236.9 million people, participated in at least one activity (SFIA, 2023). Therefore, the increase in the number of participants in sporting events is driving the growth of the AI in Stadium market.

Advancements in technology are a key trend gaining popularity in AI in the stadium market. Major companies operating in the AI in Stadium market are adopting new technological advancements to sustain their position in the market (Ogle & Lamb, 2019). For instance, in November 2022, SoFi Stadium, a US-based sports and entertainment venue, and YouTube Theater, a US-based indoor entertainment venue, launched AI-based security screening by Evolv Technology (Cappellini, 2023). Evolv Technology is a US-based company that provides advanced security screening solutions using AI and ML technologies. This new AI-based security screening is launched to make the entrances to the events safer and more effective in detecting threats. Evolv's Express technology is used in SoFi Stadium and YouTube Theater to enable danger detection at an unprecedented volume and speed. It combines sophisticated sensor technology with AI. Fans can bypass long queues, go straight through each venue's entrances, and pass the sensors without always stopping (Cappellini, 2023).

North America was the largest region in covered in the AI in Stadium market in 2022. The regions covered in the AI in Stadium Report are the Asia-Pacific, Western Europe, Eastern Europe, North America, South America, the Middle East, and Africa (Lazzeretti et al., 2023). The countries covered in the AI in Stadium Market Report are Australia, Brazil, China, France, Germany, India, Indonesia, Japan, Russia, South Korea, UK, the US, Italy, Spain, and Canada (Ozkaya & Demirhan, 2023). The global AI in Stadium market is set to experience robust growth, ascending from $1.37 billion in 2022 to $11.85 billion by 2027, with a remarkable compound annual growth rate (CAGR) of 53.4% (Ameco Research, 2023). The repercussions of the Russia-Ukraine war have instigated a series of global economic upheavals, prompting the adoption of AI technologies in stadiums to optimize operations and enhance security measures amid uncertain geopolitical landscapes (Vyas et al., 2023).

The outlook of the AI in Stadium market is highly positive. The increasing demand for enriching fan experience, increasing revenue streams, and improving safety and security measures in sports venues are driving the adoption of AI technologies. AI-powered technologies offer personalized fan experiences, real-time analytics, and efficient stadium operations, which are expected to attract more investments in this market (Li & Huang, 2023).

A key trend in the AI in Stadium market includes AI-based technologies (Rathi et al., 2020). Major companies operating in the AI in Stadium market are concentrating on creating innovative technologies, such as AI-driven imaging platforms for disease management, to sustain their position in the market. For instance, in April 2023, Twinn.health, a US-based company engaged in fitness, AI, and ML, launched an AI-driven imaging platform for the early detection of age-related diseases. The new platform is the first to incorporate magnetic resonance imaging (MRI) data for the risk evaluation of frailty. It is a potent tool for early intervention and prevention since it detects chronic age-related disorders earlier than conventional molecular signals and helps manage these conditions at an early stage (Twinn.health, 2023).

According to Jan Kees Mons, Consultant and Sports Commentator at Eurosport, stadiums will be instrumental as they will become major content and data providers in order to deliver the ultimate customer journey inside a stadium, and hence satisfy the demands of the fans. In fact, stadiums and fan platforms will become 'data temples'. Equipped with this data, tailor-made marketing campaigns, games and sales recommendations, can be made, which should add to the fan experience. The entire future customer journey of a fan will be hugely affected by AI. Imagine yourself wanting to go to a football match. Ordering your tickets will be determined by chatbot-assisted

AI, your AI-assisted car will drive itself to the stadium, drop you off at the entrance and find itself a parking spot. You won't have to queue as AI-powered crowd management systems will take care of congestion assisted by facial recognition etc. Once in the stadium, AI will recognize who you are and what fan profile you have, so it can provide you with a tailor-made experience instead of a one-for-all experience. AI-powered chatbots will give you a personal treatment like never before, making you feel like a VIP. Whether it is related to food, merchandise or social media, AI will come up with the right suggestions. An AI-assisted control centre with security personnel will oversee and monitor your safety so that you do not have to worry about terrorist threats or hooligans. Once at home, AI will take care of all your personal highlights during the game, so you have something great to remember (Tuck, 2022, p. 1).

Therefore, the need for smart stadiums based on AI will be unavoidable now and in the future.

5.3 SMART STADIUMS

Over the past years, stadiums have faced increasing competition from home-viewing options (van Heck et al., 2021), with which they have to compete in order to avoid remaining empty. In recent years, the so-called "At-Home Experience" has been improved, because of developments such as the availability of high-quality streaming services, high-definition video and audio, access to live statistics via laptops, the availability of replays from different angles, and other technological improvements (van Heck et al., 2021). Furthermore, it is expected that through VR, fans will be able to watch a football match from the side of the pitch or from the goalkeeper's perspective, or experience what it is like to walk on the pitch (Baker, 2018). Stadium technology is also changing the way spectators experience live events. By increasing the attractiveness of their facilities and services, stadiums can remain competitive (van Heck et al., 2021).

As a response to this development, the concept of 'smart stadium' is gaining ground. Stadiums are typically characterized by the gathering of a lot of people in a short period of time in a limited space, which creates challenges relating to logistics and safety. Recent advancements in technology have enabled the real-time measurement of how the stadium is being used: today's smartphone owner carries a device with processing power that would have required a computer the size of a stadium 50 years ago (van Heck et al., 2021). Providing (real-time) information to the users of a stadium can lead to improvements along many different objectives of stadiums, such as safety and security, the satisfaction and experience of the fan, sustainability, energy reduction, efficiency, and longevity (van Heck, 2019). In addition to this, the information acquired from smart tools can be used to develop long-term plans and real estate strategies, thereby supporting decision-making processes (Valks et al., 2018). The principle of integrating these tools into stadiums to improve certain processes can be defined as the concept of a smart stadium. O'Brolcháin, Colle and Gordijn (2019) give a definition for smart stadiums: "the way sports stadiums are designed and managed by using smart technologies in order to enhance the experience of attending a live match through innovative and improved services for the audience, as well as for the players, vendors and other stadium stakeholders".

In this regard, there is an increasing usage of AI to efficiently build and expand stadiums; create a safer, healthier, and secure live sports environment; analyze data streamed from closed circuit television (CCTV) cameras and other cameras to report incidents in real-time; and enhance the efficiency of stadium entryways. The exponential surge in the participation rate in sporting events is a key driving force behind the growth of the AI in Stadium market. The integration of AI technologies in stadiums serves to streamline performance analysis, enrich fan experiences, and facilitate predictive analytics, ushering in a new era of transformative sports engagement and management (Mahajan et al., 2023). In this chapter, the authors try to examine the impact of AI on stadiums.

5.3.1 Opportunities for AI in Smart Stadiums

It is an interesting proposition that a smart stadium is not so much a definition or an achievement but rather a process, where a platform is a foundation for new technologies and innovations that will improve and enhance the experience of different stakeholders. In their research, O'Brolcháin, Colle, and Gordijn (2019) focus on the potential advantages of AI for smart stadiums by distinguishing five opportunities: enhanced entertainment; commercial opportunities and improved customer service; enhanced safety and security; sustainability, reduced environmental impacts, and energy costs; and athletic performance (Figure 5.1).

FIGURE 5.1
Opportunities of the AI for Smart Stadiums. (Author.)

5.3.1.1 Enhanced Entertainment

This opportunity is based on the value of entertainment, or the experience of attending a live event in a stadium. AI can enhance the entertainment possibilities available to many of the relevant stakeholders (O'Brolcháin, Colle & Gordijn, 2019). There are various examples that support this opportunity. The audience can be stimulated by AI to encourage greater crowd participation during games, which can enhance the entertainment value.

5.3.1.2 Commercial Opportunities and Improved Customer Service

Smart stadiums have the opportunity to promote commerce. Stadiums are becoming 'tradiums', where leisure is linked with spending (Bale, 2000, p. 93). There are a lot of good reasons to promote commercial opportunities and customer services. Stadiums are economically significant entities, which can bring commercial activity to an area, create employment, and earn revenues. Also, audiences will benefit, as smart stadium innovations will make it easier for them to purchase goods and services easily (O'Brolcháin, Colle & Gordijn, 2019).

5.3.1.3 Enhanced Safety and Security

With such large gatherings of people, as seen in stadiums, there are significant risks to public safety. In terms of stadium and public security, AI solutions employ facial recognition and video analytics to ensure safety. By improving the understanding of the behavior of large crowds of people within a stadium, it can help maintain safety and security (Panchanathan et al., 2017, p. 4). Crowd disasters have taken many lives and are a serious threat in stadium environments. The Love Parade disaster in Duisburg, 2010; the Ellis Park Stadium disaster in Johannesburg, 2001; and the PhilSports Stadium stampede in Manila, 2006, are just a few examples. One of the major factors contributing to crowd disasters is critically dense spots (Georgievska et al., 2019). Sensor technologies can determine if crowds are behaving and how this impacts the safety of visitors. As a result, emergency situations can be detected earlier, and the response time will be more rapid.

In addition to crowd control, AI technology can also enable security or health services to respond quickly to emergencies and facilitate security for criminal and terroristic threats (O'Brolcháin, Colle & Gordijn, 2019). AI technology could also be used in the aftermath of an event to detect antisocial abuse and violence in the stadium.

Also, to ensure fan safety, a comprehensive real-time view of stadium activities is essential. AI video analytics comes to the rescue by providing real-time monitoring of video footage, simplifying the detection of and response to potential security threats (Ganesh Babu et al., 2021). This technology seamlessly integrates with existing CCTV and video monitoring solutions (VMS) infrastructure, along with other Internet of Things (IoT) devices, offering dynamic insights and reducing response times (Simić et al., 2020).

Furthermore, advanced AI video analytics extends its monitoring capabilities to multiple access points, including entrances, exits, parking lots, dressing rooms, and queues. Inside the stadium, AI video analytics monitors for loitering and potential security risks, enabling prompt intervention. This dynamic response not only guarantees fan safety but also fosters an atmosphere of trust (Rai et al., 2019).

5.3.1.3.1 How AI Is Shaping Stadium Security

Stadiums must always stay up to date with the latest security technologies to ensure they offer their customers and staff the maximum level of safety. This is especially true for large venues that host tens of thousands of people.

Among the various risks spectators and stadium workers face, we find violent hooliganism, theft, vandalism, drug dealing, and even terrorism.

FIGURE 5.2
The Elements of AI-Powered Security in Stadiums. (Author.)

Traditional stadium security measures to counter these threats include metal detectors, security cameras, and bag inspections. However, by themselves, they can't always provide the desired level of security (Jarczewski & Bogdalski, 2019).

Fortunately, the introduction of AI provides stadiums with new ways to minimize or entirely neutralize the risks that exist. Let's focus on how AI-powered security works and how stadiums can benefit from it (Figure 5.2).

5.3.1.3.1.1 Analyzing Large Quantities of Data from Multiple Sources   AI uses ML and advanced algorithms to analyze large volumes of information from multiple sources. First, data is collected from the stadium's VMS, elevator security system, fire detectors, and other security devices. Then, this information is analyzed to determine patterns and spot anomalies which, in turn, trigger alerts to security personnel or even automatic actions, such as blocking access to certain areas of the stadium (Sarker, 2021).

What previously would have taken days or weeks can now be done in seconds or minutes, thus drastically shortening the response time. For instance, by analyzing a network of security cameras, an AI system can detect unusual patterns, such as large groups gathering in a certain area or people loitering for extended periods of time. The system can also monitor existing lines to detect long wait times and can be used to respond rapidly to problems before they escalate into something more serious (Şengönül et al., 2023).

5.3.1.3.1.2 Detecting Threats Faster and More Effectively than Traditional Metal Detectors   People trying to access stadiums while carrying weapons have always been a major security concern for stadium managers.

Traditional metal detectors are still reliable tools to detect concealed weapons. However, they are often slow and inaccurate, as they need human operators to assess the scans. An AI-powered system can make searches quicker and more efficient by automatically scanning people as they walk in. Spectators can enter the stadium at a regular walking pace, and AI will alert security only when an issue is detected (Castro & New, 2016). AI weapons detectors tend also to be more accurate than traditional metal detectors, which often detect metal objects that are not a weapon and may fail to detect weapons that are not made of metal (Castro & New, 2016).

5.3.1.3.1.3 Monitoring Spectators' Behavior and Detecting Threats   AI can also be used to detect suspicious behavior among spectators. An AI system can analyze a camera feed in real-time and look for patterns indicating aggressive or dangerous behavior. For example, an AI system may recognize when people start shouting or running, which could indicate a fight or other incidents. In this way, security personnel can act before it is too late and stop potential threats before they escalate further (Yang et al., 2019).

5.3.1.3.1.4 Recognizing   Security   Shortcomings   and   Suggesting Improvements   In addition to detecting and responding to security threats, AI can also help stadiums improve their current security measures (Talbot & Jakeman, 2011). These systems can detect weak areas in the security infra-structure and inform managers of potential vulnerabilities (Talbot & Jakeman, 2011). For example, an AI system may recognize that certain areas are not monitored by CCTV cameras and suggest improvements such as installing additional cameras (Khan et al., 2020). The AI system can also recommend how to strengthen access control procedures or even offer tips on where staff members should be stationed for maximum effectiveness (Khan et al., 2020).

5.3.1.3.1.5 Freeing Security Staff for Other Activities   Finally, AI can also be used to free up security personnel from tedious tasks and allow them to focus on more important activities. For instance, by automating the process of searching through video security footage for suspicious behavior, AI systems can greatly reduce the amount of time that security personnel need to spend examining the mentioned footage. This allows them to devote their time and energy to other activities, such as patrolling or responding to emergencies (Davenport & Ronanki, 2018).

5.3.1.3.1.6 Enhancing Cybersecurity   In addition to physical threats, stadiums are also exposed to the risk of cyberattack, which may result in personal data theft and the disruption of operations. This can result in significant financial loss and reputational damage.

By leveraging AI, stadiums can respond to cyber threats quickly and effectively. For example, AI systems can also be used to monitor access logs and detect abnormal behavior that may indicate a cyberattack. AI-powered solutions can also be used to detect malicious software and prevent it from entering the stadium's networks (Kinyua & Awuah, 2021).

5.3.1.3.1.7 Cutting Security Costs   The features we described in this article can also help stadiums achieve significant savings in terms of security costs. AI-powered systems can reduce the need for a large physical security staff, which in turn reduces payroll costs. Moreover, AI systems can save time, which in turn translates into cost savings (Mathew et al., 2023).

Both the improvements in security and the cutting of costs achieved by AI make it an invaluable tool for stadiums looking to ensure the safety of their people and assets (Mathew et al., 2023).

5.3.1.4 Sustainability, Reduced Environmental Impacts, and Energy Costs

In a time when sustainable development is important, the environmental impacts of sporting events are commanding increasing attention, and quantifying these is becoming increasingly important. Sustainable development commitments are becoming more mainstream (Collins, Jones & Munday, 2009, p. 837). To better understand the working of a stadium, sensor technologies can inform the stadium management about waste products, air quality, carbon footprint, and energy consumption. This information can be made available in real time and over the course of the life of the stadium (O'Brolcháin, Colle & Gordijn, 2019). Sensors can also be used to detect the property's status, which can be linked to property and maintenance services. For example, sensors could detect something broken in the stadium which must be repaired.

Also, energy efficiency renovations in large sports venues are challenging and time-consuming because of the enormous energy consumption and the wide variety of energy loads that must be met. Power monitoring methods using SE-AI (Stadium Electricity-Artificial Intelligence) are used to manage this in the stadium. With AI, it is possible to monitor power capacity and output and control the error rate of loading and unloading in a defect detection system (Tam et al., 2021).

In the end, the insights are valuable for optimizing stadium resources use, utilizing energy more efficiently, and managing and reducing noise and emissions. Also, costs can be made more explicit, which will make them better understood and considered, and can lead to reduced environmental impacts and lower energy expenses..

5.3.1.5 Athletic Performance

As stated by O'Brolcháin, Colle and Gordijn (2019), another opportunity for AI is to improve athletic performance. Data gathered from athletes can be used to analyze their performance and by these insights improve their performance. Due to AI, motion sensing is made more accessible and prevalent than ever before. Multimodal feedback is more and more ubiquitous through the introduction of haptic, visual, and audio feedback mechanisms in different devices. In addition to this, we see also that there is a rise of low-cost motion-sensing hardware (Panchanathan et al., 2017, p. 4).

5.3.2 Leveraging AI to Elevate Fan Experience

Projects to enrich a fan's experience were identified by considering the entire 'journey' of an event attendee; that is, not only his or her interactions, behaviors, and actions within the stadium but all the activities involved in attending an event. For example, a fan's journey may include extensive preparation, perhaps months prior, to attend an upcoming event; planning and coordination to travel to and from the stadium; their involvement on social media leading up to an event as well as during and after an event itself; and activities carrying over to relevant events and gatherings happening before, during, and after the stadium event itself (Panchanathan et al., 2017). This work presents three fan-focused projects targeting efficiency/convenience, safety, and engagement. These projects include: (i) Crowd Understanding: Improved safety via vision-based and non-vision-based crowd behavior understanding and analytics; (ii) Athletic Demonstrator Platform: Interactive serious gaming stations to support fan engagement while promoting motor learning and athletic training; and (iii) Wait Time and Queue Estimation: Real-time, accurate access via a mobile app to wait time estimates of lines across a stadium's concession stands, souvenir stands, and restrooms (Panchanathan et al., 2017). AI's potential to enhance fan experience knows no bounds. Here are some intriguing applications (Mons, 2020):

- Immersive VR Experiences: AI-powered VR lets fans feel like they're in the thick of the action, heightening their engagement.
- Stadium Navigation: AI-assisted face recognition matches fans with their ticket information, helping them find their seats in the stadium.
- Personalized Content: AI curates game highlights tailored to individual fan preferences, enhancing their viewing experience.
- Player Interaction: AI chatbots facilitate interaction with fans' favorite players, answering queries and providing player-related information.
- Social Media Monitoring: AI can gauge fan sentiment on social media, enabling teams to address any negative buzz promptly.
- Stadium Traffic Flow Optimization: AI tracks fans' movements in the stadium to improve layout and traffic flow.
- Biometric-based Experiences: AI uses biometric data like heart rate to gauge when fans are most excited during a game (Nalepa et al., 2019). Take the Chicago Cubs, for instance, who use AI to monitor player fatigue levels. In a similar vein, the Cleveland Indians employ AI to keep track of players' sleep patterns. These intelligent systems identify players potentially at risk of injuries, thereby aiding in their prevention. The Seattle Seahawks have upped the ante by creating software leveraging ML to spot players at potential risk of injuries. Such valuable insights can guide decisions about player rotations and game strategies, prioritizing player safety. On a broader scale, the NFL is investing in AI to develop a system that can detect concussions promptly. Such technological advancements play a crucial role in enhancing player safety measures, underscoring the tremendous potential of AI in sports injury prevention and overall athlete well-being (Peranzo, 2023).
- Streamlined Food and Ticket Purchasing: AI chatbots ask fans about their preferences and suggest relevant games for ticket purchases.

- Customized Discounts: AI chatbots identify fans' interest in certain products or services and offer tailored discounts.
- Parking Assistance: AI uses face recognition and license plate matching to assist fans in finding parking spaces.
- AI's revolutionary impact is indeed turning sports stadiums into smart arenas, crafting a more personalized, immersive, and hassle-free experience for fans.
- Automated Journalism: Media outlets are leveraging AI-driven automation to expand their sports coverage capabilities and increase revenue. AI-driven platforms are currently being used to translate hard data from baseball into narratives, using natural language, providing content to fans including coverage of the minor leagues. AI also enables coverage to be fairer, with matches shown based on how exciting they are rather than who is playing, drawing more fans to watch games that initially may not necessarily have attracted attention (Chan-Olmsted, 2019).

5.4 COVID-19'S IMPACT ON THE USE OF AI IN STADIUMS

The COVID-19 outbreak had a negative impact on the growth of the AI in sports market owing to the shutdown of the majority of stadiums and the decrease in overall investment in AI by the sports industry. However, the number of applications being used in the sports industry increased exponentially during the lockdown to keep the fan base growing (Wang & Zeng, 2020)

The Business Research Company's Artificial Intelligence in Stadium Global Market Report 2023 identifies chronic diseases as the major driver for the AI in Stadium market's growth in the forecast period. Chronic disease refers to a health condition or disease that is persistent or long-lasting in its effects, usually lasting for three months or longer, and may get worse over time (Openpr, 2023).

As many college stadiums and athletics programs are evolving their COVID policies by the week or the day, being able to provide a venue's visitors with accurate, real-time answers is important. To accomplish this, collegiate athletics is relying on conversational AI solutions that allow health and safety information not only to be accessed by fans easily but also to be updated quickly by team management. AI-powered solutions streamline communication, and provide flexibility to adjust rapidly changing answers and learn about the most frequently asked questions over time, which provides a scalable solution. This gives fans the confidence that the information they're receiving is the most up to date, making a school's website the go-to source of information (White, 2021).

Moreover, COVID-19 brings a series of challenges for sports event managers. Stadium security has never been easy, but post-COVID requirements are going to make it even more complex. Along with ensuring people have secured access to the right areas and monitoring the perimeter, stadiums also must comply with COVID-19 regulations (White, 2021).

These tasks can only be carried out using smart video surveillance. AI-based solutions can turn existing CCTV and stationary cameras into surveillance machines that analyze data streamed from CCTV and other cameras and report incidents in real-time (White, 2021).

Below we introduce some measures taken by AI to solve the problems caused by COVID-19 and bring back spectators and fans to the stadiums (Irex, 2020).

- **Providing Behavioral Analytics:** Almost all stadiums these days have many CCTV cameras, but these are seldom effective. Discrepancies occur largely due to manual monitoring by a small security team, who are expected to watch and inspect live streams from hundreds of cameras simultaneously. Such a tedious routine often ends up with human errors and, as a result, fails in preventing physical threats. Event organizers can prevent such mishaps by deploying a powerful AI-based video surveillance system at the stadium. Analyzing the data collected through existing camera infrastructure, real-time behavior recognition, and anomaly detection solutions can identify dangerous behavioral patterns, detect suspects, and report threats to authorities before they escalate (Irex, 2020).
- **Crowd Metrics:** Arming stadiums with AI-powered surveillance tools can detect crowd metrics such as "people counting" and "group statistics". This ensures stadium personnel can monitor social distancing with precision, accuracy, and immediacy. Alerts can be set up throughout parts of the stadium to alert senior staff members when overcrowding can appear with real-time videos, analytics, and photos to their handheld devices such as smartphones (Irex, 2020).
- **Fever Detection:** Thermal cameras have been implemented throughout facilities including stadiums and help spot people with elevated temperatures. What IREX.ai implements is an alert system, coupled

with facial recognition of any individual(s), that read an elevated body temperature. This alert system then provides security and health officials with a photo of the individual with the elevated body temperature, meaning staff can react quicker to prevent this individual from entry.

- **Pandemic Monitoring by Facial Recognition:** Thermal cameras have been implemented throughout facilities including stadiums and are helping spot people with elevated temperatures. Through facial recognition, staff members can locate individuals by uploading a photo. It has never been easier to find a person of interest. With masks becoming an everyday part of society, facial recognition has come under scrutiny regarding the accuracy when a mask is worn. Irex.ai still maintains a 96% accuracy with individuals wearing masks and can set up alerts for any individuals not wearing a mask. Another important aspect of facial recognition is finding people of interest quickly through technology like IREX.ai's "searchveillance". The future is here. Designated staff can track a person from when they enter the stadium by simply uploading their photograph. An example of how this can assist stadium personnel is to help relocate lost children inside the stadium with their guardians/parents when they are separated. Another attribute would be any individuals banned from entering the stadium would trigger alerts once they appear under surveillance, a fantastic collaborative tool to use with law enforcement (Irex, 2020).
- **Return on Investment:** With security solutions, one of the biggest issues with any security investment is a lack of return on investment (RoI). This is where AI security is breaking the mold. The ability to provide business analytics, consumer/fan behaviors, traffic patterns, etc., allows other departments within the organization to gain vital information that can assist with their strategies and practices (Irex, 2020).

5.5 MAJOR MARKET PLAYERS

One of the key players in the competitive AI in Stadium market is Cisco Systems. Founded in 1984, Cisco Systems is a multinational technology conglomerate known for its networking hardware, software, and telecommunications equipment. With a strong focus on innovation and research, Cisco has been at the forefront of driving technological advancements in various industries, including sports (ASPIRE RESEARCH, 2023).

Over the years, Cisco Systems has witnessed significant growth and has established itself as a leading provider of AI solutions for stadiums. Their state-of-the-art technologies cater to the unique requirements of large sporting venues, providing enhanced fan experiences, operational efficiency, and improved safety and security. Cisco's portfolio includes solutions such as stadium analytics, connected stadiums, and immersive experiences (ASPIRE RESEARCH, 2023).

Another notable player in the market is IBM Corporation. Founded in 1911, IBM is a renowned technology company with a rich history of innovation. IBM has been actively involved in the sports industry and has developed AI solutions specifically designed for stadiums. Through its AI-powered technologies, IBM enables stadiums to collect and analyze large amounts of data, providing valuable insights to enhance fan experiences and boost operational efficiency (ASPIRE RESEARCH, 2023).

While specific sales revenue figures for the listed companies are not provided, it is worth mentioning that some of the companies have reported substantial growth in recent years. For instance, Cisco Systems reported total revenue of $49.3 billion in the fiscal year 2020, showcasing its strong market presence and success in the industry (ASPIRE RESEARCH, 2023).

Overall, the competitive landscape of the AI in Stadium market consists of prominent players such as Cisco Systems and IBM Corporation. With their innovative solutions and strong market presence, these companies are driving the growth of AI technologies in stadiums and helping shape the future of the sports industry (ASPIRE RESEARCH, 2023).

5.6 AI IN STADIUM MARKET REGIONAL ANALYSIS

AI is increasingly being utilized in the stadium market across various regions including North America (NA), the Asia-Pacific (APAC), Europe, the US, and China. These regions are witnessing significant adoption of AI-powered applications to enhance stadium operations, fan engagement, and overall sports experiences (Sigridrobel, 2023).

In North America, AI is revolutionizing stadium management by streamlining ticketing processes, optimizing facility operations, and enhancing security with intelligent surveillance systems. The region's technologically advanced infrastructure enables the seamless deployment of AI solutions, leading to operational efficiency and improved fan satisfaction (Sigridrobel, 2023).

The Asia-Pacific, particularly China, is experiencing a rapid expansion of AI in the stadium market. Chinese stadiums are leveraging AI for crowd management, personalized fan experiences, and advanced analytics for player performance evaluation. The country's immense population size and growing sports culture present substantial opportunities for AI adoption in stadiums (Sigridrobel, 2023).

Europe is witnessing increased AI integration in various components of stadium management. AI-driven solutions are optimizing energy consumption, enhancing stadium security, and enabling personalized marketing efforts. European stadiums are progressively adopting AI-powered chatbots and virtual assistants to cater to fan queries and provide real-time information (Sigridrobel, 2023).

In the US, where the sports industry holds immense significance, AI is revolutionizing fan engagement. Innovations such as AI-powered VR experiences, real-time video analytics, and AI-driven content recommendations are reshaping the stadium experience. The US market showcases a strong appetite for AI-driven innovations, leading to early adoption and continuous market growth (Sigridrobel, 2023).

Growing countries such as India, Brazil, and Russia are increasingly investing in sports infrastructure, presenting significant opportunities for AI in the stadium market. These countries are leveraging AI to improve stadium operations, enhance fan experiences, and drive revenue generation. With a rising spectator base and growing interest in sports, AI adoption in these countries is poised for substantial growth (Sigridrobel, 2023).

Overall, the global stadium market has witnessed a rapid integration of AI solutions across regions, including NA, APAC, Europe, the US, and China. With the increasing demand for enhanced fan experiences and the implementation of smart stadium technologies, AI is expected to play a vital role in the future, transforming stadiums into intelligent, connected, and immersive environments (Sigridrobel, 2023).

5.7 DRIVERS, CONSTRAINTS, AND OPPORTUNITIES

Rise in demand for monitoring and tracking data of players, demand for chatbots and virtual assistants to interact with followers, and requirement of real-time data analytics to improve performance drive the growth of the global AI in sports market. However, the lack of trained and skilled professionals and the high cost of implementation and maintenance constrain the market growth (Najjar, 2023). On the other hand, the rise in demand for AI to make future predictions will create new opportunities in the coming years. Other constraints are the negative factors which hinder the market growth and development in the near future. Some of the constraining factors – including strict government regulations, supply chain disruptions, and changing consumer preferences – may affect market growth in the near future (Dwivedi et al., 2021). For example, the outbreak of COVID-19 affected most of the industries. However, concerns related to data privacy and security pose challenges to the widespread adoption of AI in stadiums. Constraining factors are important to analyze, and companies should develop strategies to overcome their negative impact on the growth of the market.

5.8 CONCLUSION

With the potential to revolutionize the stadium experience and improve operational efficiency, AI technology will continue to play a significant role in the future of stadiums. The deployment of AI in stadiums works toward enhancing numerous aspects such as fan engagement, operational efficiency, security, and more, introducing a data-driven decision-making system for personalized experiences for attendees. With the primary algorithms focused on digital content management and crowd management among other areas, AI application in stadiums brings forth a novel approach to organizing, storing, and distributing digital content in an effective manner.

Generative AI, powered by real-time data streaming, holds the key to revitalizing the stadium experience. Whether you're a business professional, technologist, or an enthusiastic fan, the integration of these technologies offers an exciting realm to explore. By embracing personalization, interactive engagement, and streamlined entry processes, the stadium of the future promises to be a place where technology-driven enhancements create unforgettable memories for all. So, the next time you consider staying home for the big game, remember the incredible technology-driven experiences awaiting you at the stadium.

REFERENCES

Ameco Research. (October 27, 2023). Artificial Intelligence in Sports Market is Forecasted to Reach USD 8,592 Million by 2030, Growing at a CAGR of Around 32.8%. Market Research. www.linkedin.com/pulse/artificial-intelligence-sports-market-forecasted-reach-62lzf/

Araújo, D., Couceiro, M., Seifert, L., Sarmento, H., & Davids, K. (2021). *Artificial intelligence in sport performance analysis*. Routledge.

Aspire Research. (October 2, 2023). Artificial Intelligence in Stadium Market Research Report Provides thorough Industry Overview, which offers an In-Depth Analysis of Product Trends. LinkedIn. www.linkedin.com/pulse/artificial-intelligence-stadium-market-research-report/

Baker, T. A. (2018). *Coming home through football: A geographic exploration of long-distance fandom* (Doctoral dissertation, The University of Waikato).

Bale, J. (2000). The changing face of football: Stadiums and communities. *Soccer & Society, 1*(1), 91–101.

Beckers, R., van der Voordt, T., & Dewulf, G. (2015). Aligning corporate real estate with the corporate strategies of higher education institutions. *Facilities, 33*(13/14), 775–793.

Bernhold, T., Lattuch, F., & Riemenschneider, F. (2014). Success dimensions for major real estate projects: The case of stadium development. *Baltic Journal of Real Estate Economics and Construction Management, 2*, 23–29.

Buckman, A. H., Mayfield, M., & BM Beck, S. (2014). What is a smart building?. *Smart and Sustainable Built Environment, 3*(2), 92–109.

Cappellini, V. (2023). Electronic imaging & the visual arts. EVA 2023 Florence.

Castro, D., & New, J. (2016). The promise of artificial intelligence. *Center for Data Innovation, 115*(10), 32–35.

Chan-Olmsted, S. M. (2019). A review of artificial intelligence adoptions in the media industry. *International Journal on Media Management, 21*(3–4), 193–215.

Collins, A., Jones, C., & Munday, M. (2009). Assessing the environmental impacts of mega sporting events: two options? *Tourism Management, 30*(6), 828–837.

Davenport, T. H., & Ronanki, R. (2018). Artificial intelligence for the real world. *Harvard Business Review, 96*(1), 108–116.

Ding, J., Chen, C., & Yu, K. (2021). Application Status and Prospect of Artificial Intelligence Big Data in Stadium Management. In *2020 International Conference on Data Processing Techniques and Applications for Cyber-Physical Systems: DPTA 2020* (pp. 791–797). Springer Singapore.

Dong, J., Wang, G., Yan, H., Xu, J., & Zhang, X. (2015). A survey of smart water quality monitoring system. *Environmental Science and Pollution Research, 22*(7), 4893–4906.

D'Orazio, T., & Guaragnella, C. (2015). A survey of automatic event detection in multi-camera third generation surveillance systems. *International Journal of Pattern Recognition and Artificial Intelligence, 29*(01), 1555001.

Dwivedi, Y. K., Hughes, L., Ismagilova, E., Aarts, G., Coombs, C., Crick, T.,... & Williams, M. D. (2021). Artificial Intelligence (AI): Multidisciplinary perspectives on emerging challenges, opportunities, and agenda for research, practice and policy. *International Journal of Information Management, 57*, 101994.

Ganesh Babu, R., Elangovan, K., Maurya, S., & Karthika, P. (2021). Multimedia security and privacy on real-time behavioral monitoring in machine learning IoT application using big data analytics. *Multimedia technologies in the Internet of Things Environment*, 137–156.

Georgievska, S., Rutten, P., Amoraal, J., Ranguelova, E., Bakhshi, R., de Vries, B. L.,... & Klous, S. (2019). Detecting high indoor crowd density with Wi-Fi localization: A statistical mechanics approach. *Journal of Big Data*, 6(1), 31.

Irex. (August 20, 2020). The new marriage between AI and Stadiums. https://irex.ai/blog/tpost/la9a7at2e1-the-new-marriage-between-ai-and-stadiums

Jarczewski, W., & Bogdalski, P. (2019). Social determinants of crime and hatred incidents at mass sports events in Poland. *Przegląd Strategiczny, 12*, 215–231.

Khan, P. W., Byun, Y. C., & Park, N. (2020). A data verification system for CCTV surveillance cameras using blockchain technology in smart cities. *Electronics, 9*(3), 484.

Kim, M., Choi, K. H., & Leopkey, B. (2021). The influence of tourist risk perceptions on travel intention to mega sporting event destinations with different levels of risk. *Tourism Economics, 27*(3), 419–435.

Kinyua, J., & Awuah, L. (2021). AI/ML in security orchestration, automation and response: Future research directions. *Intelligent Automation & Soft Computing, 28*(2).

Lazzeretti, L., Innocenti, N., Nannelli, M., & Oliva, S. (2023). The emergence of artificial intelligence in the regional sciences: A literature review. *European Planning Studies, 31*(7), 1304–1324.

Li, A., & Huang, W. (2023). A comprehensive survey of artificial intelligence and cloud computing applications in the sports industry. *Wireless Networks*, 1–12.

Mahajan, K., Pal, A., & Desai, A. (2023). Revolutionizing fan engagement: Adopting trends and technologies in the vibrant Indian sports landscape. *International Journal of Management Thinking, 1*(2), 116–135.

Mathew, D., Brintha, N. C., & Jappes, J. W. (2023). Artificial Intelligence Powered Automation for Industry 4.0. In *New Horizons for Industry 4.0 in Modern Business* (pp. 1–28). Springer International Publishing.

Molnár, A. (2023). Okos stadionok–Hogyan reformálja a digitális ökoszisztéma a sportinfrastruktúra üzemeltetését és a sportszolgáltatások modelljét. *Jelenkori Társadalmi és Gazdasági Folyamatok, 18*(1–2), 141–163.

Mons, J. (July 21, 2020). 8 great ways how AI will impact fan engagement. Sport Tomorrow. https://sporttomorrow.com/8-ways-how-ai-will-greatly-impact-fan-engagement/

Nadikattu, R. R. (2020). Implementation of new ways of artificial intelligence in sports. *Journal of Xidian University, 14*(5), 5983–5997.

Najjar, M. C. (2023). Legal and ethical issues arising from the application of data analytics and artificial intelligence to traditional sports. *Albany Law Journal Science & Technology, 33*, 51.

Nalepa, G. J., Kutt, K., Giżycka, B., Jemioło, P., & Bobek, S. (2019). Analysis and use of the emotional context with wearable devices for games and intelligent assistants. *Sensors, 19*(11), 2509.

O'Brolcháin, F., de Colle, S., & Gordijn, B. (2019). The ethics of smart stadia: a stakeholder analysis of the Croke Park project. *Science and Engineering Ethics*, 25(2), 737–769.

Ogle, A., & Lamb, D. (2019). The role of robots, artificial intelligence, and service automation in events. In S. Ivanov & C. Webster (Eds.), *Robots, Artificial Intelligence, and Service Automation in Travel, Tourism and Hospitality* (pp. 255–269). Emerald Publishing.

Openpr. (November 30, 2023). Artificial Intelligence in stadium market overview – forecast market size, top segments and largest region. www.openpr.com/news/3311160/artificial-intelligence-in-stadium-market-overview-forecast

Ozkaya, G., & Demirhan, A. (2023). Analysis of countries in terms of Artificial Intelligence technologies: PROMETHEE and GAIA method approach. *Sustainability, 15*(5), 4604.

Panchanathan, S., Chakraborty, S., McDaniel, T., Tadayon, R., Fakhri, B., O'Connor, N. E.,... & Monaghan, D. (2017). Enriching the fan experience in a smart stadium using internet of things technologies. *International Journal of Semantic Computing*, *11*(02), 137–170.

Rai, M., Husain, A. A., Maity, T., Yadav, R. K., & Neves, A. J. R. (2019). Advance intelligent video surveillance system (AIVSS): A future aspect. *Intelligent Video Surveillance*, *37*.

Rathi, K., Somani, P., Koul, A. V., & Manu, K. S. (2020). Applications of artificial intelligence in the game of football: The global perspective. *Researchers World*, *11*(2), 18–29.

Sarker, I. H. (2021). Machine learning: Algorithms, real-world applications and research directions. *SN Computer Science*, *2*(3), 160.

Sartori, A., & Nienhoff, H. (2013). A blueprint for successful stadium development. Retrieved from https://assets.kpmg/content/dam/kpmg/pdf/2013/11/blueprint-successful-stadium-development.pdf

Şengönül, E., Samet, R., Abu Al-Haija, Q., Alqahtani, A., Alturki, B., & Alsulami, A. A. (2023). An analysis of Artificial Intelligence techniques in surveillance video anomaly detection: A comprehensive survey. *Applied Sciences*, *13*(8), 4956.

SFIA. (February 22, 2023). *SFIA's topline report shows physical activity rates increased for a fifth consecutive year*. Sport and Fitness Industry Association (SFIA). https://sfia.org/resources/sfias-topline-report-shows-physical-activity-rates-increased-for-a-fifth-consecutive-year/

Shabbir, J., & Anwer, T. (2018). Artificial intelligence and its role in near future. *arXiv preprint arXiv:1804.01396*.

Sigridrobel. (December 8, 2023). Artificial intelligence in stadium market: Trends, forecast, and competitive analysis to 2030. Medium. https://medium.com/@sigridrobel/artificial-intelligence-in-stadium-market-trends-forecast-and-competitive-analysis-to-2030-c4a13db550bb.

Simić, M., Perić, M., Popadić, I., Perić, D., Pavlović, M., Vučetić, M., & Stanković, M. S. (2020). Big Data and development of Smart City: System architecture and practical public safety example. *SJEE*, *17*(3), 337–355.

Talbot, J., & Jakeman, M. (2011). *Security risk management body of knowledge* (Vol. 69). Wiley.

Tam, K., Hopcraft, R., Crichton, T., & Jones, K. (2021). The potential mental health effects of remote control in an autonomous maritime world. *Journal of International Maritime Safety, Environmental Affairs, and Shipping*, *5*(2), 40–55.

Tuck, A. (March 17, 2022). How AI platforms are transforming sports fan engagements. AI & Machine Learning. https://technologymagazine.com/ai-and-machine-learning/how-ai-is-transforming-sports-fan-engagement

Twinn.health. (April 26, 2023). Twinn.health launches revolutionary AI-Driven imaging platform for early detection of age-related diseases. Businesswire. www.businesswire.com/news/home/20230425005990/en/Twinn.health-Launches-Revolutionary-AI-Driven-Imaging-Platform-for-Early-Detection-of-Age-related-Diseases

Valks, B., Arkesteijn, M. H, & Den Heijer, A. (2018). Smart campus tools 2.0: An international comparison. Delft University of Technology.

Valks, B., Arkesteijn, M. H., Den Heijer, A. C., & Vande Putte, H. J. (2016). Smart campus tools: Adding value to the university campus by measuring space use real-time. *Journal of Corporate Real Estate*, *20*(2), 103–116.

van Heck, S. (2019). Smart Stadium Tools: An explorative case study of the Johan Cruijff ArenA: identification and optimization of smart tools in stadiums. Delft University of Technology. http://resolver.tudelft.nl/uuid:4e3536e0-f6c3-458c-8ac0-ba81b85a5ba3 (open in a new window).

van Heck, S., Valks, B., & Den Heijer, A. (2021). The added value of smart stadiums: A case study at Johan Cruijff Arena. *Journal of Corporate Real Estate, 23*(2), 130–148.

Vyas, P., Vyas, G., & Dhiman, G. (2023). Ruemo: The classification framework for Russia-Ukraine war-related societal emotions on twitter through machine learning. *Algorithms, 16*(2), 69.

Wang, Y., & Zeng, D. (2020). Development of sports industry under the influence of COVID-19 epidemic situation based on big data. *Journal of Intelligent & Fuzzy Systems, 39*(6), 8867–8875.

White, D. (January 26, 2021). How Artificial Intelligence has helped College Stadiums? *Sportstravelmagazine*. www.sportstravelmagazine.com/how-artificial-intelligence-has-helped-college-stadiums/

Yang, K. C., Varol, O., Davis, C. A., Ferrara, E., Flammini, A., & Menczer, F. (2019). Arming the public with artificial intelligence to counter social bots. *Human Behavior and Emerging Technologies, 1*(1), 48–61.

6

Game Theory in the Digital Age

Yvan J. Kelly

6.1 THE ORIGIN OF GAME THEORY

While heavily developed in the second half of the 20th century, game theory owes its origins to a French mathematician, Antoine Augustin Cournot, whose initial work in the field took place over a century earlier. Cournot's famous work *Recherches sur le principes mathématiques de la théorie des richesses*, published in 1838, explores mathematical economics (Ekelund & Hebert, 2014). In the work, Cournot proposes a theory of how a duopoly, a market which contains only two firms, would find a solution to the problem of how much quantity each firm would produce of the product being sold (Landreth & Colander, 1989). The two firms are in competition with each other, but each firm is dependent upon the action that the other firm takes and upon the strategy decisions it makes. Graphically described as reaction curves, Cournot finds that the optimal solution is not determined solely by what one firm chooses to do; instead, it is determined by each firm's reaction to what the other firm is doing. With both firms acting in this manner, their interaction eventually leads to a stabilizing solution.

Other scholars did not readily pick up on Cournot's work, and the topic remained dormant until the 1940s. Mathematician John von Neumann teamed up with economist Oskar Morgenstern to explore the topic, which resulted in their seminal work *The Theory of Games and Economic Behavior* (McCain, 2004). Intending to produce a short work, their theory of games begins by exploring two-person games, then expands to three-person games, then four-person games. Games were included that have two strategy choices, then three strategies, then four strategies – all this resulting in a monumentally large work (von Neumann & Morgenstern, 1990). In all their games, the

DOI: 10.1201/9781032665191-6

strategy choices of one player depended on what the strategy choices were for their opponent.

von Neumann and Morgenstern's solutions to games were lacking a generalized theory that could help to predict the behaviors of the players in games. Their models predicted well for games that were constant sum games (that is, those in which the payoffs for the players always total to the same amount) but not for other cases.

The theoretical solution for non-cooperative games was created by a Princeton graduate student named John F. Nash (Kuhn & Nasar, 2002). His solution has come to be known as the Nash equilibrium and is used extensively in the field of game theory. His theory finds the best response to the best strategy played by an opponent, and results in a stable solution. Nash's theory led to him being awarded the Nobel Prize in 1994 (Kuhn & Nasar, 2002). It also eventually led to a bestselling book and a movie made about his life, both titled *A Beautiful Mind*. With stable solutions to games able to be found, the field of game theory exploded with scholars researching the topic and finding further enhancements and theories as well as a variety of applications.

6.2 WHAT IS A GAME?

To understand how game theory can be useful, we first need to look at just what constitutes a game. All games have three elements: players, strategies, and payoffs. There can be 2, 3, or n number of players. The game presents the players with 2 or more strategies from which the players must choose. The payoffs are what the players in the game receive at the end of the game. This can be signified as a win or a loss, a dollar amount, a certain amount of pollution, the amount of troops killed, or any other type of consequence of the game.

Ariel Rubenstein has said that whoever came up with the name "game theory" was a marketing genius. If the field had been named "models of rationality and decision making in interactive situations" no one would have been interested (Rubenstein, 2007). Through the years, I have had some students become disappointed when they discover their introductory game theory class was not about the design of video games (although that could be a use for game theory) or that the class was about gambling (though von Neumann and Morgenstern's first work in the field did include an examination of bluffing when playing poker). Game theory is nothing more than an analysis of strategy. Using it, we can predict what strategy choices the players in the game will make.

6.3 NASH EQUILIBRIUM

To begin to understand how a Nash equilibrium comes into play, let us examine a game that has two players and two strategies. This game is commonly referred to as the Prisoner's Dilemma. It was created by Albert Tucker and first presented in a lecture at Stanford in 1950 (McCain, 2004).

Here is the story for this game. Two people have been arrested, Allie and Henry. The police separate the prisoners and begin to interrogate them. The police make an offer to Allie, telling her that if she confesses to the crime she will get a reduced sentence and Henry will get a lengthy sentence. The police also make the same offer to Henry. The two players have to make their decision not knowing what their opponent (their former partner in crime) is choosing. For payoffs, let's say that if Allie confesses and Henry does not, she will go free but Henry will get 20 years in prison. If Allie confesses and Henry confesses, then they each get 10 years in prison. If Henry confesses and Allie does not, he will go free and Allie will go to prison for 20 years. However, if neither confesses, the district attorney can only gain a conviction on a lesser charge resulting in one year in prison for both players. The goal for Allie is to minimize her prison time. The same is true for Henry. Because they have individual goals that would conflict with each other, this is referred to as a non-cooperative game.

Game theory puts the players, strategies, and payoffs into a table (Table 6.1) referred to as the normal form presentation of the game.

Allie is the row player, Henry is the column player. The payoffs in each cell are listed for the row player first, and then for the column player. With the game set up in this manner, we can find the Nash equilibrium.

Let us examine Allie's best response if Henry chooses the strategy to 'confess'. Allie would have a choice of a payoff in that column of either 10 years if she confesses or 20 years if she does not. Ten years is preferable, so to get that payoff she would choose the strategy to 'confess'. If Henry were to choose 'don't confess', Allie would have a choice of payoffs of either 0 time in jail for a confession or 1 year if she does not. Zero would be preferred to 1 year, and

TABLE 6.1

The Prisoner's Dilemma

		Henry	
		Confess	Don't
Allie	Confess	10 years, 10 years	0, 20 years
	Don't	20 years, 0	1 year, 1 year

to reach this she would need to choose the strategy of 'confess'. So, regardless of which strategy Henry chooses, Allie's best response is to choose 'confess'. 'Confess' is referred to as a dominant strategy.

Henry faces the same type of decision. If Allie were to select 'confess', the payoffs for Henry in that row are 10 years or 20 years. To get the lighter sentence he would choose 'confess'. If Allie were to select 'don't confess', the payoffs to Henry in that row are 0 or 1 year. Again, he would choose 'confess' in order to get zero time in prison. His dominant strategy, like Allie's, is to choose 'confess'. Therefore, without knowing what the other player is choosing, they both decide to play the 'confess' strategy. This solution is stable because neither player can improve their payoffs by switching strategy choices; it is the Nash equilibrium for the game (Nash, 1996). Ironically, had they both chosen not to talk they would have had lower jail times (this is referred to as a 'social dilemma'). This, no doubt, is why police separate prisoners when they are interrogated. Even if both chose not to confess, that solution is not stable. Each player would have an incentive to change their strategy in order to gain a lesser sentence. Since both face the same incentives, we would see them return to the 'confess, confess' solution.

6.4 MIXED STRATEGY SOLUTIONS

Suppose we have a tennis player named Bill. Bill is better at hitting the ball down the line than he is hitting the ball crosscourt. Does this mean that hitting down the line is a dominant strategy for Bill? It may be what he does best, but it is not a dominant strategy. We know this because of the result were he to choose to play that strategy all the time. No doubt his opponent would position themselves on that side of the court and return his shots, and Bill would lose the match. What Bill needs to do is to occasionally hit the ball crosscourt. In sports this is oftentimes referred to as 'keeping the opponent honest'. What it actually means is that Bill wants to keep his opponent off guard by altering his strategy. What it also means is that for Bill to be successful, that is, for him to win the match, he must sometimes choose a strategy that is not what he does best. But in doing what he does not do best, he can win the match, which is his goal. In choosing some combination of the strategies he will play, he is using a mixed strategy equilibrium. Let's explore how these come about.

Let us begin with a situation we all face fairly frequently. Two people approach a doorway, coming from opposite sides of the door, and arrive at the door at the same time. Who goes through the door first? Our two players in this game are named Fred and Maribeth. If Fred goes through the door first, he gets to where he is going more quickly, which has a value of 3 (the payoff values are the amount of utility derived from the outcome of the game). Maribeth would be momentarily delayed if Fred goes first and her payoff is 2. It is not as good a payoff as Fred's because she has had a slight delay. If Maribeth goes first, she will receive the 3 and Fred will have a payoff of 2. If neither of them moves, and they both stand at the doorway staring at each other, there is a long delay as they try to sort out who goes first, and the payoff for both would be 0. Should they both try to move first they will collide in the doorway and get stuck. This is not only a longer delay but also a great embarrassment and so has a payoff for both players of −1. The goal of the players is to maximize their payoffs. Placing these players, strategies, and payoffs into a normal form table, we can see the game in Table 6.2.

We begin the analysis of this game looking for a Nash equilibrium. If Fred chooses 'wait', Maribeth's best response is 'go', because the payoff of 3 is greater than 0. If Fred chooses 'go', Maribeth's best response is 'wait', because she would rather have a payoff of 2 than −1. We can see that there is no dominant strategy for Maribeth – there is no strategy that she should play every time.

Examining this game from Fred's perspective, if the row player, Maribeth, chooses 'wait', Fred's best response is to choose 'go', as that will give him a payoff of 3 versus 0. If Maribeth chooses 'go', Fred would respond with 'wait', as that would give him a payoff of 2 and not −1. Since we have defined a Nash equilibrium as a solution in which neither player can improve their payoffs by changing strategies, we can see that this game has two Nash equilibria. The combination of 'wait' and 'go' is a Nash equilibrium. But so is the combination of 'go' and 'wait'. In games that have more than one Nash equilibrium, the solution is found using a combination of the two available strategies. Players will choose between the two strategies with some probability. This leads to the questions: How many times should Maribeth play the 'wait' strategy? And how many times she should play the 'go' strategy? Game theory allows us a way to determine these probabilities.

Looking at this from Maribeth's point of view, let p be the probability that Fred chooses 'wait' as his strategy. For the alternative 'go' strategy, the

TABLE 6.2

Doorway Game

		Fred	
		Wait	Go
Maribeth	Wait	0, 0	2, 3
	Go	3, 2	-1, -1

probability would be 1 − p. Looking at her payoffs, if she plays the 'wait' strategy she will receive:

$$0p + 2(1 − p)$$

This can be reduced to:

$$2 − 2p$$

If Maribeth plays the 'go' strategy, her payoff would be:

$$3p − (1 − p)$$

Which reduces to:

$$4p − 1$$

Setting the payoffs for the two strategy choices equal to each other we find:

$$2 − 2p = 4p − 1$$

Solving for p:

$$p = ½$$

For Maribeth, the mixed strategy equilibrium is to play the 'wait' strategy half the time and the 'go' strategy the other half of the time. This is the mixed strategy equilibrium. I must admit that in experimenting with this solution, I decided that one day on campus the first door I encountered I would go through and the next I would wait, and that I would repeat this pattern all day. My results were fairly successful, only colliding once with a student as we both chose to go. What we do in real life also involves signaling. Were Fred to be a gentleman he may look at Maribeth and signal for her to go first. Other methods would be a head nod, some type of eye contact, or body movement indicating what that person's strategy choice is. A detailed look into signaling is beyond the scope of this chapter; however, you can look for these in real life and see just how many times we actually do this.

Having laid the foundation for the Nash equilibrium and the mixed strategy solution, we can now turn to three examples of game theory in the world of sports.

6.5 SPORTS EXAMPLES OF GAME THEORY

Baseball. In baseball, a pitcher will most likely have a preferred pitch. A pitch they throw the best. Suppose it is a fastball. Does this mean that the pitcher would always choose to throw a fastball? No, for the same reason that the tennis player would never try to hit every shot down the line. The pitcher must use a mixed strategy equilibrium between the fastball and the other pitches at his disposal. The goal for the pitcher is to not throw his best pitch every time, it is to get the batter out.

For the purpose of this game, let's limit the pitcher to having two pitches, that is, two strategy choices, fastball and change-up. From the batter's perspective, they also have two strategy choices. If the pitch is a fastball, the batter is more successful if they swing early and try to make contact with the ball. Should the batter delay, the pitch will go past him and he won't be able to get a hit, which is his goal. If the pitch is a change-up, if the batter swings early, the ball will not yet be at the plate and the chances of getting a hit are small. The player would be better off swinging later, giving him better timing on the slower pitch, and a greater chance of getting a hit.

To heighten the excitement of this game, we will assume that there is a full count, three balls and two strikes. What this means is, for those who are not well versed in the rules of baseball, the next pitch is the last chance for the batter to get a hit or for the pitcher to get an out. As we simplify the game for the sake of this example, we also simplify the payoffs. If the batter hits the fast ball, it would be a home run and give the batter a 10 and the pitcher a −10. These payoffs don't represent the runs scored in the game, but instead represent the utility gained (the happiness to the players) from that result. If the batter hits the change-up, it would result in a single that has a value of 3 for the batter and a −3 for the pitcher. Should the pitcher fool the batter by throwing a change-up when the batter was expecting a fastball, the batter would strike out and be a −5 for the batter and a 5 for the pitcher. The same payoffs apply if the batter swings for a change-up but the pitcher threw a fastball, −5 for the batter and 5 for the pitcher. Table 6.3 contains the players, strategies, and payoffs for this baseball game.

For the batter, what portion of the time should he swing for a fastball and what portion of the time should he swing for a change up? These can be calculated using the mixed strategy approach. Let p be the probability that the pitcher will throw a fastball. The payoff for the swing early strategy would

TABLE 6.3

The Baseball Game

		Pitcher	
		Fastball	Change-up
Batter	Swing early	10, -10	-5, 5
	Swing late	-5, 5	3, -3

be total of the payoffs for the fastball and the change-up. He would receive a 10 with p probability and would receive the payoff of −5 with the remaining probability of 1 − p. The payoffs then for the swing early strategy are:

$$10p - 5 (1 - p)$$

Which is reduced to:

$$15p - 5$$

The payoff for the swing late strategy would be:

$$- 5p + 3(1 - p)$$

Which is simplified to:

$$3 - 8p$$

The batter does not want the pitcher to exploit any predictability on his part, he will adjust his strategy choices so that they are unpredictable to the pitcher. Since the batter wishes to have the same payoffs for playing each strategy, the payoff for swing early strategy is set equal to the payoff for the swing late strategy:

$$15p - 5 = 3 - 8p$$

Solving for p, we find

$$p = 8/23,$$

which means that the batter should swing early 8/23 of the time and swing late 15/23 of the time. These types of swings need to be kept in that proportion, but they must be chosen randomly so as not to have a pattern be detectable and give the pitcher an advantage. Notice that in this game there has been no mention of what the pitcher's best pitch may be. It would not matter. Say the pitcher prefers to throw a fastball. If it is detected that the pitcher is more likely to throw that pitch, the batter will react to that discovery and swing early. It is only by keeping their opponent guessing that the players would be successful.

Football. The game of American football is a ground acquisition game. The team with the ball tries to move the ball down the field in order to score. The opponents in the game are on defense and trying to prevent the other team from advancing the ball. The offense will call a play in a huddle, thus keeping their strategy choice a secret from their opponent. The opponent will set their defense according to their expectation of what the offense will choose. Each play has a payoff as the teams either gain or lose yardage.

For simplicity's sake, we will limit the offense to two choices of plays. The first is a pass, where the quarterback will drop back and throw the ball to a receiver. The other play is a draw play. With a draw play the team fakes a pass and instead runs the ball.

The defense can choose to set their defense to defend either type of play but not both simultaneously. If they choose to guard against the pass, they will rush their lineman in order to put pressure on the throw of the quarterback, while other defenders drop back to cover the possible receivers downfield. If the defense sets itself to defend the run, then they will keep defenders closer to the line of scrimmage in order to make the tackle at the earliest moment. Should they guess wrong and set themselves to defend the run while a pass play has been called, the quarterback will have more time to throw and fewer defenders will be downfield in protection. Should they choose to defend the pass when a run play was called, their players would drop back making the line of scrimmage more vulnerable to a run and resulting in a longer yardage run. Table 6.4 contains the players, strategies, and payoffs of this game. The payoffs are the yards gained or lost on the play.

To solve this game and see what proportion of the two strategies the defense should utilize, we can use the mixed strategy solution. Assume the p represents the probability that the offense will choose the pass strategy. The payoffs for the pass defense would then be:

$$-1p - 3(1-p)$$

This reduces to:

$$2p - 3$$

The payoffs for the run defense strategy are:

$$-4p + 1(1-p)$$

Which is simplified to:

$$1 - 5p$$

TABLE 6.4

American Football Game

		Offense	
		Pass	Draw Play
Defense	Pass defense	-1, 1	-3, 3
	Run defense	-4, 4	1, -1

Setting these two payoffs equal to each other results in:

$$2p - 3 = 1 - 5p$$

Solving, we find: p = 4/7

In order to get the greatest payoffs from these two strategies, the defense should set itself to protect against the pass 4/7 of the time and defend against the run 3/7 of the time. Substituting this probability value back into the payoff equations for each strategy, we find that the expected value payoff for each strategy for the defense is − 1.85 yards. The pass defense yields:

$$2 (4/7) - 3 = - 1.85 \text{ yards}$$

And the run defense results in 1 − 5 (4/7) = − 1.85 yards

Tennis. Let's return to the example of Bill the tennis player. At the time I am writing this, Novak Djokovic is the world's top-rated men's player. Let's say that Bill has a match against him. When serving the ball, Bill can choose to either hit toward Djokovic's forehand side or to his backhand side. Just as with the choice of going down the line or going crosscourt, Bill needs to use a mixed strategy approach to have any chance for success. (Success in this case may simply be winning one point against the world's #1 player!)

Djokovic, who is going to be receiving Bill's serve, can either guess forehand or guess backhand. In doing so, he would prepare himself both mentally and physically to return that type of serve. Should he guess correctly, the chances of him winning the point are greater than if he chose incorrectly.

Let's assume the following outcomes. If Bill serves towards the forehand and Djokovic guesses forehand, Bill will win the point 40% of the time and lose the point 60% of the time. But, if he serves to the forehand and Djokovic guesses backhand, Bill will win the point 60% of the time and Djokovic will win 40% of the time. If Bill serves to the backhand and Djokovic guesses forehand, Bill will win 60% of the time and Djokovic will win 40% of the time. Should Bill serve to the backhand and Djokovic guesses backhand, Bill will win 50% of the time and Djokovic will win 50% of the time. Table 6.5 contains the players, strategies, and payoffs of this game.

TABLE 6.5

The Tennis Game

		Djokovic	
		Guesses forehand	Guesses backhand
Bill	Serves to forehand	40%, 60%	60%, 40%
	Serves to backhand	60%, 40%	50%, 50%

The percentage of serves Bill should make towards his opponent's forehand and backhand can be determined using a mixed strategy approach. Let p equal the percentage of serves that Djokovic guesses forehand. Then, the payoff for the service to the forehand will be

$$.4 p + .6 (1 - p)$$

Which reduces to:

$$.6 - .2p$$

The payoff for the service to the backhand would be:

$$.6p + .5(1 - p)$$

Which simplifies to:

$$.1p + .5$$

The mixed strategy equilibrium is found by setting the payoffs from the two strategies equal to each other:

$$.6 - .2p = .1p + .5$$

The solution is found to be:

$$1/3 = p$$

This means that Bill should serve to Djokovic's forehand 1/3 of the time and serve to his backhand 2/3 of the time. When the p value of 1/3 is inserted into the payoff equations for both strategies, we find that both strategies result in a success rate of 53.3% of the points played. Maybe Bill has a chance to win the match! Should he deviate from this mixed strategy equilibrium, and should his opponent detect it, we would expect his 53.3% winning percentage to fall quickly. If he stays with the strategy mix found, no matter what Djokovic guesses, Bill should win 53.3% of the points.

6.6 UTILIZING ANALYTICS AND GAME THEORY

One limitation of utilizing game theory has been the precise calculation of the payoffs. Others have been simplifying the number of strategies utilized in a game and also determining the probabilities of achieving the payoffs. Each of these limitations have been used for purposes of simplicity or because the data did not allow for a more thorough and accurate assessment of the elements of the game. With improvements in technology and the ability to use larger datasets, researchers would be able to provide more robust findings, produce more accurate predictions, and improve the decision-making as a result. Here are a few examples of areas where analytics would help game theory in its analysis of strategies within the sports world.

By analyzing large sets of data of previous outcomes given certain strategy choices, improved determination of game payoffs could be provided. For example, as we determine what the defense's strategy mix should be in a football game, having more accurate determinations of the number of yards yielded on a play will determine a more precise choice of strategies. This will result in improved decision-making about strategy choices. It will not necessarily improve the outcomes for the players of the games, but it will provide them with more accurate payoffs, from which they can determine their strategy.

Along similar lines, the probability assignment in games could be improved if large datasets allowed for a more precise determination of what the true probabilities are. As was explored in the strategy choices made by Bill in the tennis game, his mix of strategy choices was made according to what he believed to be the probability of success he would have in each situation. If that probability could be more accurately determined, he would be able to more accurately predict the result and thus be able to improve his mix of strategy choices.

Oftentimes, for the sake of simplicity, the number of strategy choices is limited by those constructing the game. This is done for the purpose of teaching or to make decisions easier. The real world, though, is not limited to dichotomous strategy choices. There are oftentimes three, four, or more strategies available to choose from. The more complete the strategy choices are, the better the decisions that can be made. In the baseball example, if the pitcher has a variety of pitches, those could be tracked, and their career data could be analyzed to examine what the probability is for each type of pitch to be thrown, and thus improve the batter's performance by being able to form a more comprehensive game plan. Certainly, football coaches have multiple plays they can select from as well. The more complete the presentation of the game, the better the chance of making the correct defensive decision.

Beyond the examples used in this chapter, analytics opens the door for improved scouting of team tendencies and the outcomes of those choices. If two cities were vying for an expansion franchise in a league, that league could evaluate the situation as a game with two or more cities (players) and include all the relevant variables in arriving at their final decision about the location. College athletic departments and leagues could use a game theoretic approach using large datasets to analyze conference realignments. Should a particular university be invited to join? Should a university accept that invitation?

The NCAA basketball tournament could benefit from a game theoretic approach using a multiple-player game technique to analyze not only which schools should be included in the tournament but also the seedings and pairings of the early games. Public finance decisions about new stadium construction could be analyzed using game theory as well. Should a city fund a stadium? If so, to what degree? The price of tickets to a sporting event can also be considered to be a multiplayer game and the relevant variables could be utilized using large datasets. The optimal ticket prices, number of ticket pricing tiers, and optimal number of seats in each tier can be examined. A major sports league negotiating a new broadcast contract can use the game theoretic approach of bargaining theory, with the hope that it is not a prisoner's dilemma game!

There clearly are many, many more situations within the world of sports that can be analyzed using game theory principles. The use of analytics and big data will allow for better strategy choices to be made. Improved decision making with better opportunities for finding optimal solutions would be the result.

REFERENCES

Ekelund, R. B. & Hebert, R. F. (2014). *A history of economic theory and method*, 6th ed. Long Grove, IL: Waveland Press.

Kuhn, H. W. & Nasar, S. (2002). *The essential John Nash*. Princeton, NJ: Princeton University Press.

Landreth, H. & Colander, D. C. (1989). *History of economic theory*, 2nd ed. Boston, MA: Houghton Mifflin.

Leeds, M. & von Allmen, P. (2014). *The economics of sports*, 5th ed. Upper Saddle River, NJ: Pearson.

McCain, R. (2004). *Game theory*. Mason, OH: Thompson South-Western.

Nash, J. F. (1996). *Essays on game theory*. Cheltenham: Edward Elgar.

Rubinstein, A. (2007, October 10). *John Nash: A beautiful mind and game theory*. Lecture at Georgetown University.

von Neumann, J. & Morganstern, O. (1990). *Theory of games and economic behavior*. Princeton, NJ: Princeton University Press.

7

Computational Approaches to Sport Outcome Prediction

Sadegh Sulaimany and Sardar Mohammadi

7.1 INTRODUCTION

The concept of using data to predict sports outcomes gained prominence with the success story of the Major League Baseball team "Oakland Athletics" as depicted in the book *Moneyball*. The team used in-game play statistics to assemble an exceptional team, despite their relatively small budget. This data-driven approach led to the playoffs in 2002 (Chmait & Westerbeek, 2021). This showed that the ability to predict outcomes accurately not only benefits athletes and coaches but also guides the development of sports (Zhou, 2022).

In the last two decades, artificial intelligence (AI) and machine learning (ML) have transformed the way we consume and analyze sports. AI and ML have been applied to various areas in the sports industry, including match outcome modeling, in-game tactical decision-making, player performance in fantasy sport games, and managing professional players' sport injuries. AI can track player movements, identify key events in a game, and even predict future outcomes using computer vision algorithms. This information is invaluable for coaches and players, allowing them to make informed decisions during a game and adjust their strategies accordingly (Bonidia et al., 2018).

Sport outcome prediction is a growing field of research that aims to predict the results of sporting events using ML and statistical analysis. Recent studies have focused on using ML algorithms to predict the outcomes of different fields (Lu et al., 2021; Zhao et al., 2023). Sports performance prediction can help schools, sports teams, and sports training institutions develop scientific training methods. Athletes and coaches can use these predictions as a basis for reforming physical education and training. Accurate prediction of sports achievement can guide the development of sports. It is of great significance in promoting scientific training and improving sports performance. However, the development of sports as a special cultural phenomenon has a profound and extensive influence on the development of sports culture, which in turn affects the development of other related cultures in society (Zhou, 2022). Therefore, sport outcome prediction plays a pivotal role in sports decision-making. It not only enhances performance and training but also guides the development of sports and influences sports culture.

This chapter delves into the world of predictive analytics in sports, taking a comprehensive journey. We begin by exploring the field with a broad perspective, offering an overarching categorization and understanding of the potential applications of this powerful tool. Next, we shift our focus to a critical initial step in sport outcome prediction: data preparation. We delve into the importance of meticulously preparing data for accurate calculations, ensuring its suitability for ML algorithms. Following this, we propose a general workflow for preprocessing and data transformation specifically designed for forecasting purposes.

As we progress through the chapter, we introduce feature selection and engineering techniques, empowering the reader to refine and extract valuable insights from the sports data. We then provide an overview of the diverse ML methods that have attracted significant research interest in the realm of sport outcome prediction. This section will be further enriched by referencing existing review papers in the field. To broaden the understanding of potential research avenues, "Exploring a Spectrum of Sports through Computational Prediction" is presented as a separate subsection, highlighting promising areas for future investigation. Finally, the chapter concludes by summarizing the key takeaways and outlining potential future directions for research. We also acknowledge some limitations associated with the presented work, fostering transparency and providing a foundation for further exploration.

7.2 OVERVIEW OF PREDICTIVE ANALYTICS AND ITS APPLICATION IN SPORTS

The realm of sports has undergone profound transformation due to the integration of data science and advanced analytical methods, particularly predictive analytics. By leveraging historical performance data, ML models, and

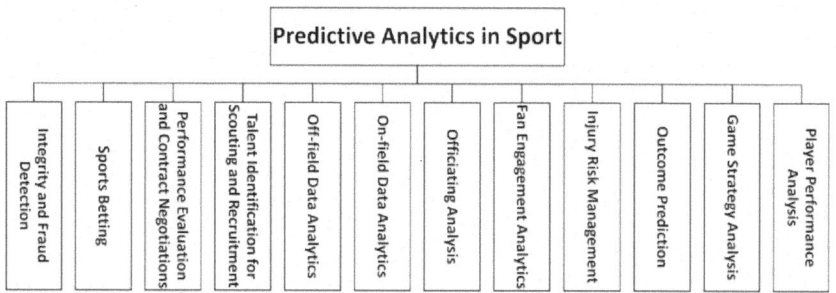

FIGURE 7.1
An Overview of Predictive Analytics Applications in Sport.

computational power, teams and athletes now possess an unprecedented ability to forecast trends, anticipate challenges, and optimize strategy.

Predictive analytics refers to the practice of extracting patterns and relationships within large datasets to generate predictions or probabilities regarding future occurrences. In sports, it encompasses various applications (Kaur et al., 2021) that we have tried to provide a comprehensive list as bellow, and in Figure 7.1.

1. **Player Performance Analysis**: Leverages tracking data and ML models to analyze movement patterns, skills, and abilities. This aids in talent identification, training optimization, and injury prevention.
2. **Game Strategy Analysis**: Involves the analysis of team/player statistics, tendencies, and scenarios to gain strategic insights for planning tactics and lineups.
3. **Outcome Prediction**: Utilizes ML models to predict match outcomes, player injuries, career longevity, transfers, etc., based on historical data.
4. **Injury Risk Management**: Monitors player workload, fatigue, and movement mechanics and correlates it with injury data to develop injury risk profiles.
5. **Fan Engagement Analytics**: Analyzes fan demographic, media consumption, and purchasing behavior data to create targeted marketing campaigns.
6. **Officiating Analysis**: Reviews game footage and referee positioning in relation to players to evaluate decision quality for training and recruitment.
7. **On-field Data Analytics**: Tracks key on-field data metrics to influence methodologies that may be used to improve in-game strategies,

nutrition plans, and other vital areas that could ethically boost athletes' performance levels.

8. **Off-field Data Analytics**: Focuses on the business side of sports. It involves monitoring important off-field data metrics such as ticket sales, merchandise sales, fan engagement, etc.

9. **Talent Identification for Scouting and Recruitment**: Teams use analytics to identify promising athletes and make informed recruitment decisions.

10. **Performance Evaluation and Contract Negotiations**: Teams value players based on their analytical performance alongside traditional metrics.

11. **Sports Betting**: Sportsbooks use analytics to set accurate odds.

12. **Integrity and Fraud Detection**: Sports organizations use analytics to identify and prevent fraudulent activities.

7.3 DATA COLLECTION AND PREPROCESSING TECHNIQUES

The world of sports is awash with data, from player statistics to weather conditions and fan sentiment. Analyzing this data effectively holds the key to unlocking valuable insights, including predicting game outcomes. A wealth of data sources – including sporting events, individuals involved in those events, and even the devices used – can generate valuable information for predicting outcomes. However, each source produces different types of data, so careful consideration is necessary to effectively utilize them for prediction purposes. Here is a clear and concise list of different types of data commonly used for sports outcome prediction (Figure 7.2):

1. **Player Performance Data**: Statistics that quantify the past performance of players and teams like goals scored, assists completed, rebounds made etc. Help predict scoring potential and offensive strengths.

2. **Injury Data**: Details on player injuries, surgeries, recovery time, missed games etc. Informs availability and fitness modeling which impacts expected performance.

3. **Tracking Data**: Granular data from video analysis and wearables on factors like speed, distance covered, acceleration, heart rate variability. Used to model physical capacities.

FIGURE 7.2
Data Types Used for Prediction in Sport.

4. **Scouting Data**: Subjective ratings and comparisons of attributes – like dribbling ability, vertical jump – from talent scouts. Helps uncover less quantifiable skills. In comparison with player performance data, scouting data predicts future potential, while player performance data evaluates past and present impact.

5. **Match Results Data**: Outcomes, scores, margins from historical contests to derive offensive and defensive strengths between teams and for different venues, weather conditions etc.

6. **Biomechanics Data:** Measurable characteristics of movements and technique like release angle of shots, quality of tackles etc. Help quantify skill execution.

7. **Context Data**: Travel schedules, rivalries between opponents, lineup changes provide additional situational explanations.

Note that the data used for prediction is not limited to these categories, and researchers are constantly exploring new sources and developing novel analysis techniques to improve the accuracy of outcome prediction. The effectiveness of this data depends on the specific sport, prediction model, and the quality of data collection and preprocessing (Jain et al., 2021).

FIGURE 7.3
General Workflow for Data Preparation for Sport Outcome Prediction.

While the data type may vary, effective sports result prediction hinges on meticulous preprocessing. This includes careful collection and transformation before feeding it into prediction algorithms. Let us delve deeper into this critical stage, in Figure 7.3.

1. **Identifying the Right Data:** The first step is to determine the data relevant to your prediction goals. For example, predicting a football match outcome might require player performance data, team formation, historical records, and even weather conditions. This data can be sourced from official league websites, sports media platforms, or even specialized data providers.

2. **Gathering the Data:** Data collection methods vary depending on the source. Web scraping tools can automate data extraction from websites, while APIs offer programmatic access to structured data. Manual data entry might be necessary for less readily available information.

3. **Cleaning and Standardizing:** Raw data often contains inconsistencies, missing values, and formatting errors. The preprocessing stage tackles these issues. Data cleaning involves identifying and correcting errors, while standardization ensures consistency across different data sources. This might involve converting units, scaling values, or imputing missing data using appropriate techniques.

4. **Feature Engineering:** Not all raw data directly contributes to the prediction. Feature engineering involves transforming raw data into meaningful features that can be used by prediction models. This might involve creating new features based on existing ones, such as calculating player efficiency metrics or team win streaks. This will be explained in more detail in the next section.

5. **Dealing with Imbalance:** In some sports, certain outcomes (e.g., upsets) might be less frequent than others. This imbalance can skew prediction models. Techniques like oversampling or under sampling can be used to address this issue and ensure the model considers all outcomes fairly.

6. **Preparing for the Algorithm:** Finally, the preprocessed data needs to be formatted for the chosen prediction algorithm. This might involve splitting the data into training and testing sets, encoding categorical variables, and scaling numerical features to appropriate ranges.

By carefully collecting and preprocessing your data, you lay the foundation for accurate and reliable sports outcome predictions. Remember, the quality of your predictions hinges on the quality of your data, so invest time and effort in this crucial stage of the game!

7.4 FEATURE SELECTION AND ENGINEERING TECHNIQUES

The field of sports outcome prediction has experienced significant progress due to the integration of ML and data science techniques. Central to achieving accurate predictions is the meticulous selection and crafting of features that encapsulate the most pertinent information regarding the game. For example, imagine predicting NBA game winners. You start with a mountain of data: player points, rebounds, team turnovers, even home court advantage. But not all are equally important. Feature selection helps you sift through it. First, you leverage basketball knowledge, choosing relevant statistics like free throw percentage. Then, you analyze the data, removing redundant features and identifying key trends. Next, you employ techniques like chi-square tests to find statistically significant indicators of wins. Finally, you evaluate different feature combinations by training models and comparing their accuracy. Through this process, you emerge with a streamlined set of features most likely to predict victory, like free throws, points, and defensive rating, giving you a sharper edge in predicting the outcome of the game.

Feature selection is the process of identifying the most relevant variables or features from a larger set. In the context of sports outcome prediction, these features could include player statistics, team rankings, historical performance, and even factors like weather and location. The goal is to select a subset of features that contribute the most to the predictive model, thereby improving its accuracy and efficiency. Feature engineering, on the other hand, involves creating new features from the existing ones. This could involve combining two or more features, transforming a feature into a different scale or format, or even creating entirely new features based on domain knowledge. For instance, a feature like 'team momentum', which is not directly available in the data, could be engineered from the team's recent performance statistics (Lu et al., 2021).

The choice of features, both in selection and engineering, can significantly impact the performance of the predictive model. For example, a study by Bunker and Susnjak (Bunker & Susnjak, 2022) found that selecting and engineering an appropriate feature set appears to be more important than having many instances. They also highlighted the potential for greater interdisciplinary collaboration between sport performance analysis, a subdiscipline of sport science, and ML.

Different sports may require different features for accurate prediction. For instance, in basketball, features like player shooting percentage, team rebounding stats, and home-court advantage may be critical. On the other hand, in football, features like possession stats, team form, and player injuries may be more relevant. Therefore, domain knowledge of the specific sport is crucial in feature selection and engineering.

Despite the advancements in feature selection, engineering, and ML techniques, sports outcome prediction remains a challenging task due to the unpredictable nature of sports. However, with the increasing availability of sports-related data and the continuous development of new analysis techniques, the accuracy of sports outcome prediction is expected to improve (Lu et al., 2021).

In conclusion, feature selection and engineering are critical components of sports outcome prediction. By choosing the most relevant features and engineering new ones, we can improve the accuracy of our predictive models. As we continue to gather more data and develop more sophisticated analysis techniques, the field of sports outcome prediction will continue to evolve and improve.

7.5 MACHINE LEARNING ALGORITHMS AND COMPUTATIONAL METHODS

Machine learning (ML) is a subset of AI that uses statistical techniques that enable machines to learn and improve from data analysis without explicit programming (Sarker, 2021). Here is a compact review of the most popular ML methods, in Figure 7.4. Each of these methods has its strengths and

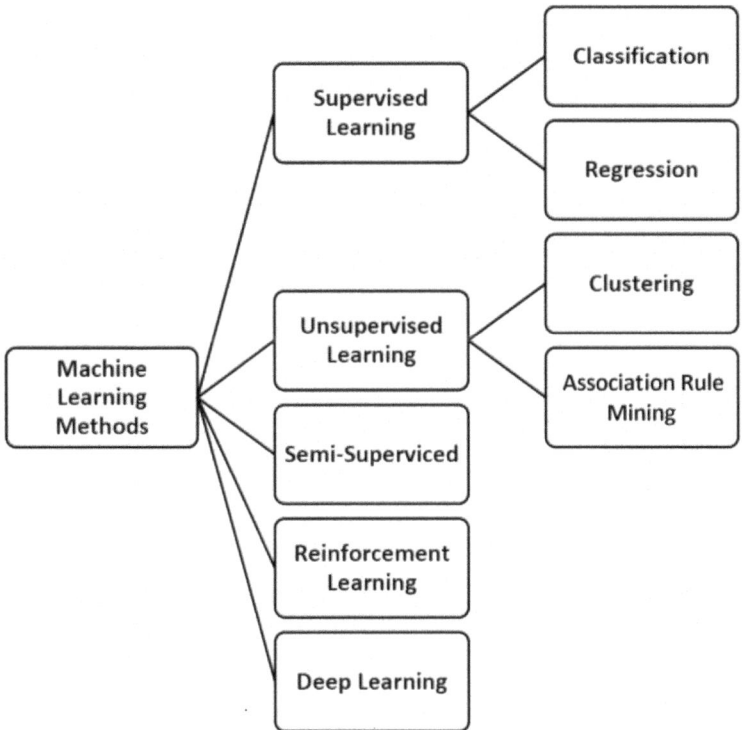

FIGURE 7.4
A General Categorization of Machine Learning Methods.

weaknesses, and the choice of method often depends on the specific task and the nature of the data.

1. **Supervised Learning Algorithms:** These algorithms are trained using labeled data, i.e., input data paired with correct output. The algorithm learns a mapping from inputs to outputs and uses this to predict outcomes for unseen data. Examples include Linear Regression, Decision Trees, k-Nearest Neighbors, and Support Vector Machines (SVM).

2. **Unsupervised Learning Algorithms:** Unsupervised learning involves training an algorithm with no labels, leaving it to find structure in its input on its own. This can mean clustering the data into different groups or reducing the dimensionality of the data. Examples include k-Means, Hierarchical Clustering, and Principal Component Analysis. Another useful and popular subfield of unsupervised learning is Association rule mining, that helps researchers discover interesting relations between variables in large databases.

3. **Semi-Supervised Learning Algorithms:** These algorithms fall somewhere between supervised and unsupervised learning as they use both labeled and unlabeled data for training. The systems that use this method can considerably improve learning accuracy.

4. **Reinforcement Learning Algorithms:** Reinforcement learning is about interaction with an environment. An agent takes actions in an environment to achieve a goal. The agent receives rewards or penalties for the actions it performs and aims to maximize the total reward.

5. **Deep Learning Algorithms:** Deep learning is a subset of ML that's based on artificial neural networks with representation learning. It can process a wide range of data resources, requires less data preprocessing by humans, and can often produce more accurate results than traditional ML models (Pichler & Hartig, 2023).

There are several review papers about using ML in sport result prediction. This shows the importance of the research in this area. Table 7.1 presents a brief review of the important survey papers, demonstrating their differences and distinguishing properties. The table shows research interest in this field

TABLE 7.1

Review Papers about the Sport Outcome Prediction

No	Title	Year	Journal	Authors Country	IF	Reference
1	Machine learning application in soccer: a systematic review	2023	Biology of Sport	Spain, Portugal, Austria	5.6	(Rico-González et al., 2023)
2	The Application of Machine Learning Techniques for Predicting Match Results in Team Sport: A Review	2022	Journal of Artificial Intelligence Research	Japan New Zealand	5	(Bunker & Susnjak, 2022)
3	The use of machine learning in sport outcome prediction: A review	2020	Wiley Interdisciplinary Reviews-data Mining and Knowledge Discovery	Croatia	7.8	(Horvat & Job, 2020)
4	Forecasting the outcomes of sports events: A review	2020	European Journal of Sport Science	Germany	3.2	(Wunderlich & Memmert, 2020)
5	Artificial intelligence for team sports: A survey	2019	The Knowledge Engineering Review	UK	2.1	(Beal et al., 2019)

is growing, with studies published from 2019 to 2023. Besides, the studies are published in various journals, reflecting the diverse academic landscape relevant to sport science and data analysis. Moreover, the research teams come from different countries, showcasing the international collaboration in this field. It is noteworthy that most authors of sport prediction review papers come from European countries. Finally, higher impact factor (IF) – which indicates the average number of citations received by articles published in a particular journal in the past two years – often suggests greater influence within the field, though it is not a definitive measure of research quality. Here, "The Use of Machine Learning in Sport Outcome Prediction: A Review" has the highest IF (7.8). Finally, some of the papers are about a special type of sport, such as soccer. Surprisingly, a comprehensive review of the literature reveals no dedicated review paper on deep learning methods for sport outcome prediction. This suggests a potential gap in the research landscape that could be further explored.

Numerous statistical and ML approaches are employed in sports predictive analytics, and the majority of them fall into the ML categories, and so ML techniques play a vital role in sports outcome prediction. Common methodologies include regression modeling, time series analysis, classification algorithms, clustering, and deep neural networks. Based on the above reviews, major ML algorithms used for sport result forecasting are Artificial Neural Networks, Decision Tree, Support Vector Machine, Naïve Bayes, Boosting, Bayesian Network, k Nearest Neighbor, Linear Regression, Random Forest, Logistic Regression, Rule Set, Ensemble Methods, Linear Discriminant Analysis, ... (Bunker & Susnjak, 2022). Recent advancements in these fields enable more accurate and nuanced predictions, leading to improved team performance and competitive advantage.

7.6 EXPLORING A SPECTRUM OF SPORTS THROUGH COMPUTATIONAL PREDICTION

The application of computational methods for predicting outcomes in various sports has been a subject of growing interest within the academic community. Identifying the most frequently studied sports in this field can be highly beneficial for researchers, fostering the exploration of potential gaps and uncharted territories within the domain. This can pave the way for the expansion of the field's boundaries and the generation of novel insights.

TABLE 7.2

Some Example Sports Investigated for Outcome Prediction with a Recent Instance Reference for Each One

American Football (Gifford & Bayrak, 2023)	Soccer (Mattera, 2023)	Basketball (Lampis et al., 2023)	Baseball (Li et al., 2022)
Hockey (Ice) (Chin et al., 2023)	Tennis (Yue et al., 2022)	Horse Racing (Chavan et al., 2024)	Golf (Chae et al., 2021)
Rugby (Bennett et al., 2021)	Volleyball (Gabrio, 2021)	Chess (Drezewski & Wator, 2021)	Cricket (Goel et al., 2021)
Swimming (Wu et al., 2021)	Gymnastics (Pion et al., 2017)	Wrestling (L. Zhao et al., 2020)	Cycling (Kholkine et al., 2020)

Table 7.2 exemplifies this concept by providing a breakdown of 16 example sports where computational approaches have been employed for outcome prediction. Each entry in the table showcases a recent reference that demonstrates the utilization of such methods within the respective sport. As the field continues to evolve, it is crucial to not only acknowledge the existing areas of focus but also to actively seek opportunities to delve into unexplored territories, enriching the landscape of sports prediction through computational methods.

7.7 FUTURE DIRECTIONS AND CHALLENGES IN SPORT OUTCOME PREDICTION

In conclusion, this chapter has provided an overview of the emerging field of using computational methods for sports outcome prediction. We began with a high-level perspective on the diverse applications of predictive analytics in sports before diving into critical considerations around data collection and preprocessing. Meticulous data preparation is crucial for ensuring accurate predictions. We then explored techniques like feature selection and engineering that empower practitioners to extract meaningful insights from sports data.

An overview of popular ML algorithms commonly used for sports forecasting was presented, enriched by key insights from existing literature reviews on the topic. This highlighted the predominance of methods like neural networks, SVM, random forests, and regression in this domain. We also showcased the breadth of sports where computational techniques have been or could be applied, from mainstream choices like soccer and basketball to less investigated options like gymnastics and cycling.

While the discipline has made great strides, there remain unexplored avenues and challenges around dealing with the inherent complexity and randomness of sports. As data quality and quantity continue improving alongside analytical techniques, the field will unlock new levels of performance optimization, fan engagement, and, potentially, even social impacts. We hope this chapter provides a robust foundation to guide future efforts in stretching the boundaries of computational sports prediction.

Despite significant progress, several obstacles remain in implementing predictive analytics effectively in sports. Firstly, ensuring data privacy and security is crucial given the sensitive nature of athlete health records and proprietary team tactics. Secondly, integrating multiple sources of heterogeneous data requires robust data management frameworks and interoperability standards. Thirdly, overreliance on quantitative metrics might overshadow qualitative aspects of athletic performance, necessitating a balanced approach to evaluation.

As technology continues to evolve at an exponential rate, predictive analytics will undoubtedly play a pivotal role in shaping the landscape of modern sports. However, it remains essential to strike a balance between technological innovation and human expertise while maintaining ethical considerations. Ultimately, embracing predictive analytics offers exciting opportunities to improve athlete wellbeing, drive team success, and elevate fan engagement. Finally, leveraging novel computational techniques holds the potential to unlock significant value-added opportunities in the field, not only by enhancing sport outcome prediction performance but also by opening doors to new and exciting applications.

REFERENCES

Beal, R., Norman, T. J., & Ramchurn, S. D. (2019). Artificial intelligence for team sports: A survey. *Knowledge Engineering Review, 34*, e28. https://doi.org/10.1017/S026988891 9000225

Bennett, M., Bezodis, N. E., Shearer, D. A., & Kilduff, L. P. (2021). Predicting performance at the group-phase and knockout-phase of the 2015 Rugby World Cup. *European Journal of Sport Science, 21*(3), 312–320. https://doi.org/10.1080/17461391.2020.1743764

Bonidia, R. P., Brancher, J. D., & Busto, R. M. (2018). Data mining in sports: A systematic review. *IEEE Latin America Transactions, 16*(1), 232–239. https://doi.org/10.1109/TLA.2018.8291478

Bunker, R., & Susnjak, T. (2022). The Application of Machine Learning Techniques for Predicting Match Results in Team Sport: A Review. *Journal of Artificial Intelligence Research, 73*, 1285–1322. https://doi.org/10.1613/JAIR.1.13509

Chae, J. S., Park, J., & So, W. Y. (2021). Victory prediction of Ladies Professional Golf Association Players: Influential factors and comparison of prediction models. *Journal of Human Kinetics, 77*(1). https://doi.org/10.2478/hukin-2021-0023

Chavan, P., Kunekar, P., Musale, P., Shinde, M., Shinde, A., & Shinde, N. (2024). Horse Race Prediction Using Machine Learning Algorithms. In *Proceedings of the Fifth International Conference on Computer and Communication Technologies (IC3T 2023)* (pp. 329–336). Springer. https://doi.org/10.1007/978-981-99-9704-6_30

Chin, J. S., Juwono, F. H., Chew, I. M., Sivakumar, S., & Wong, W. K. (2023). Predicting Ice Hockey Results Using Machine Learning Techniques. In *2023 International Conference on Digital Applications, Transformation and Economy, ICDATE 2023*. https://doi.org/10.1109/ICDATE58146.2023.10248726

Chmait, N., & Westerbeek, H. (2021). Artificial intelligence and machine learning in sport research: An introduction for non-data scientists. *Frontiers in Sports and Active Living, 3*, 682287. https://doi.org/10.3389/fspor.2021.682287

Drezewski, R., & Wator, G. (2021). Chess as sequential data in a Chess match outcome prediction using deep learning with various chessboard representations. *Procedia Computer Science, 192*, 1760–1769. https://doi.org/10.1016/J.PROCS.2021.08.180

Gabrio, A. (2021). Bayesian hierarchical models for the prediction of volleyball results. *Journal of Applied Statistics, 48*(2), 301–321. https://doi.org/10.1080/02664763.2020.1723506

Gifford, M., & Bayrak, T. (2023). A predictive analytics model for forecasting outcomes in the National Football League games using decision tree and logistic regression. *Decision Analytics Journal, 8*. https://doi.org/10.1016/j.dajour.2023.100296

Goel, R., Davis, J., Bhatia, A., Malhotra, P., Bhardwaj, H., Hooda, V., & Goel, A. (2021). Dynamic cricket match outcome prediction. *Journal of Sports Analytics, 7*(3). https://doi.org/10.3233/jsa-200510

Horvat, T., & Job, J. (2020). The use of machine learning in sport outcome prediction: A review. *Wiley Interdisciplinary Reviews: Data Mining and Knowledge Discovery, 10*(5), e1380. https://doi.org/10.1002/WIDM.1380

Jain, P. K., Quamer, W., & Pamula, R. (2021). Sports result prediction using data mining techniques in comparison with base line model. *OPSEARCH, 58*(1), 54–70. https://doi.org/10.1007/s12597-020-00470-9

Kaur, A., Kaur, R., & Jagdev, G. (2021). Analyzing and exploring the impact of Big Data analytics in sports sector. *SN Computer Science, 2*(3), Article 184. https://doi.org/10.1007/s42979-021-00575-y

Kholkine, L., De Schepper, T., Verdonck, T., & Latré, S. (2020). A Machine Learning Approach for Road Cycling Race Performance Prediction. In M. Berlingerio, F. Bonchi, T. Gärtner, N. Hurley, & G. Ifrim (Eds.), *Machine Learning and Data Mining for Sports Analytics* (Vol. 1324, pp. 103–112). Springer. https://doi.org/10.1007/978-3-030-64912-8_9

Lampis, T., Ioannis, N., Vasilios, V., & Stavrianna, D. (2023). Predictions of European basketball match results with machine learning algorithms. *Journal of Sports Analytics, 9*(2), 171–190. https://doi.org/10.3233/jsa-220639

Li, S. F., Huang, M. L., & Li, Y. Z. (2022). Exploring and selecting features to predict the next outcomes of MLB games. *Entropy, 24*(2), 288. https://doi.org/10.3390/e24020288

Lu, C. J., Lee, T. S., Wang, C. C., & Chen, W. J. (2021). Improving sports outcome prediction process using integrating adaptive weighted features and machine learning techniques. *Processes*, *9*(9), 1563. https://doi.org/10.3390/PR9091563

Mattera, R. (2023). Forecasting binary outcomes in soccer. *Annals of Operations Research*, *325*(1), 115–134. https://doi.org/10.1007/s10479-021-04224-8

Pichler, M., & Hartig, F. (2023). Machine learning and deep learning: A review for ecologists. *Methods in Ecology and Evolution*, *14*(4), 994–1016. https://doi.org/10.1111/2041-210X.14061

Pion, J., Hohmann, A., Liu, T., Lenoir, M., & Segers, V. (2017). Predictive models reduce talent development costs in female gymnastics. *Journal of Sports Sciences*, *35*(8), 806–811. https://doi.org/10.1080/02640414.2016.1192669

Rico-González, M., Pino-Ortega, J., Méndez, A., Clemente, F. M., & Baca, A. (2023). Machine learning application in soccer: A systematic review. *Biology of Sport*, *40*(1), 249–263. https://doi.org/10.5114/biolsport.2023.112970

Sarker, I. H. (2021). Machine learning: Algorithms, Real-World applications and research directions. *SN Computer Science*, *2*(3), 160. https://doi.org/10.1007/s42979-021-00592-x

Wu, P. P. Y., Babaei, T., O'Shea, M., Mengersen, K., Drovandi, C., McGibbon, K. E., Pyne, D. B., Mitchell, L. J. G., & Osborne, M. A. (2021). Predicting performance in 4 x 200-m freestyle swimming relay events. *PLOS ONE*, *16*(7), e0254538. https://doi.org/10.1371/JOURNAL.PONE.0254538

Wunderlich, F., & Memmert, D. (2020). Forecasting the outcomes of sports events: A review. *European Journal of Sport Science*, *21*(7), 944–957. https://doi.org/10.1080/17461391.2020.1793002

Yue, J. C., Chou, E. P., Hsieh, M.-H., & Hsiao, L.-C. (2022). A study of forecasting tennis matches via the Glicko model. *Plos One*, *17*(4), e0266838.

Zhao, K., Du, C., & Tan, G. (2023). Enhancing Basketball game outcome prediction through fused graph convolutional networks and random forest algorithm. *Entropy*, *25*(5), 765. https://doi.org/10.3390/E25050765

Zhao, L., Liu, R., Wu, J., & Guo, L. (2020). Wrestling performance prediction based on improved RBF neural network. *Journal of Physics: Conference Series*, *1629*(1), 012012. https://doi.org/10.1088/1742-6596/1629/1/012012

Zhou, Q. (2022). Sports achievement prediction and influencing factors analysis combined with deep learning model. *Scientific Programming*, *2022*, Article ID 3547703. https://doi.org/10.1155/2022/3547703

8

Analytics in Sports: A Review and Exploration of Financial and On-Field Performance of Football Clubs

Ziad Zein, Ashish Kumar Jha, and K. Mohammed Jasim

8.1 INTRODUCTION

With the growth of the analytics field and the fast emergence of big data over the past few years, most if not all industries have been impacted with this transformation. Companies and organizations are leveraging the data available, in addition to other new technologies and analytical techniques, to improve and enhance their businesses. The sports industry is no exception to this transformation (Razzaq and Yang, 2023). With vast amounts of data being generated daily from a wide range of competitions and matches across multiple sports, sports organizations can derive valuable insights for their businesses. The world's biggest sports businesses, clubs, and teams are being highly impacted with the presence of data and analytical techniques and efficiently using it to improve their businesses, enhance their performances, increase their revenues, expand their fan base engagement, and more (Liu et al., 2023).

Henry Chadwick, an American sportswriter, was the first person to introduce analytics to the sport industry in 1858. Chadwick developed a metric called the "box score", which let baseball teams quantitively evaluate the performance of their players using a tabular form (Kashyap, 2021). Multiple other attempts took place in the 19th and 20th centuries where a lot of researchers tried to incorporate analytics to sports, but they all failed. In 1977, Bill James, an American baseball writer and statistician, invented the field of "Sabermetrics", which is the use of mathematical and statistical analysis of baseball records to understand the science behind the sport (Kashyap, 2021). In 2003, Billy Beane, former American professional baseball player and current executive vice president of the Oakland Athletics, published a book titled *Moneyball. Moneyball* focuses on the use of analytics in baseball to achieve outstanding results and he describes his role as a General Manager in the Oakland Athletics at that time and his use of advanced analytical techniques to clinch the American League West Title in 2002 (Kashyap, 2021). In 2011, *Moneyball* was directed as a movie and was considered a huge hit at the box office, shedding light on the importance of analytics in sports. Since then, the popularity of this field started emerging, and the global market size for sports analytics increased at an accelerated rate and is projected to reach over $4.5 billion by 2026 (Kashyap, 2021).

With its expansion to all sports, sports analytics has become an indispensable tool in sports organizations, especially in the world's greatest sports competitions like National Basketball Association (NBA), Fédération Internationale de Football Association (FIFA), Major League Baseball (MLB), and many more. Multiple clubs have implemented data analysis techniques into their organizations to efficiently leverage the data available, allowing them to improve their performances, and thus achieving better outcomes and increasing revenues. Real Madrid C.F, one of the world's greatest football clubs in history, partners with Microsoft Analytical Tools to manage the team's and players' performances, operations, and relationship with millions of global fans (Kashyap, 2021). The top premier clubs like Liverpool and Manchester City hired experienced data analysts a few years back to beef up their internal analysis (Worville, 2021). The result is their dominance in English and European football for the past 5-6 years, performing at the top level and clinching titles more than ever before. More and more teams are investing in sports analytics and understanding its wide range of applications and importance in achieving and sustaining better results. Sports analytics also allows for better operations within sports organizations and has proven its strong positive impact in multiple areas of application. In turn, this will allow sports clubs to expand and grow and accumulate more and more revenue.

After in-depth analysis of the areas of application of sports analytics, one area that is not researched and emphasized enough is the interrelation between financial performance and on-field performance for sports teams and clubs. The objective of this research is to develop an understanding for football clubs in terms of financial and on-field performance and identify the impact of field performance on financial revenues. Research will mainly follow explanatory data analysis to identify the correlation of both factors of European football clubs and a predictive analysis model to forecast revenues for three clubs for the calendar years 2022-2024. The research will conclude with prescriptive analysis using the results obtained to allow clubs to understand their stream of revenues and how to increase them using sports analytics. The following are the research questions (RQ) this study aims to answer and explore as we progress through our research:

RQ1: How can sports analytics identify the correlation between on-field and financial performance and how does performance impact revenues of sports clubs?

RQ2: How can sports analytics allow sports clubs to identify streams of revenues from different departments and help increase these numbers?

RQ3: How can sports analytics allow football clubs to use historical financial data to predict upcoming financial revenues?

RQ4: How can sports analytics develop better on-field performance?

8.1.1 Purpose of the Study

The purpose of this study is to get a deeper understanding of sports analytics, its areas of application, data and data sources available, and impact on sports organizations. Our paper will include two approaches: descriptive and analytical. The descriptive approach explores the areas of research within the field of sports analytics and digs deep to understand the data available and data analytical tools applied. The analytical approach will introduce two analytical models: exploratory data analysis and a forecasting model. Multiple data explanatory techniques are done on European football clubs using on-field performance and financial data. These analytical techniques are applied to understand the correlation between financial and on-field performances and the financial impact of performances on various football clubs. The forecasting model implemented will use the historical financial data of three European football clubs to predict the revenues for the next three calendar years using various models.

8.2 LITERATURE REVIEW

The main objective of this literature review is to get a deeper understanding of sports analytics and gain more knowledge about this field. Various scholarly articles, books, papers, and dissertations are published online that discuss and talk about sports analytics in general and some dig deeper into specific areas of sports analytics and the application of sports data with various analytical techniques and machine learning models (Romanov et al., 2023; Srivastava et al., 2023). To get a detailed understanding of sports analytics literature, our review will follow a structured approach where we will understand the areas of research, available data and data sources, methodologies, and the application of sports analytics in various areas.

8.2.1 Sports Analytics

The era of big data has caused a huge impact on the development of the sports industry. The availability of sports data such as exercise performance, health data, and training and performance statistics and their analysis has allowed sports organizations to analyze and efficiently derive insights (Sarlis and Tjortjis, 2020; Tiwari et al., 2024). In turn, this can effectively help athletes in daily training and developing game strategies that are indispensable for winning competitions (Bai and Bai, 2021). The efficient use of sports big data and its application with the relevant analytical techniques provides meaningful insights, creating a slight advantage for teams and players during competitions. However, sports analytics is not only limited to enhance performance and achieve advantages over other teams or players. Although analytics is often associated with performance, player personnel decisions, and team selection, professional sports teams are now relying on analytical techniques to optimize ticket pricing strategies, increase sponsorship return on investment, and enhance customer relationship management (Mondello and Kamke, 2014). Sports analytics can also help teams make predictions for upcoming talents and recruit the best athletes, and identify a player's market value and the possibility of injuries and prevent them (Apostolou and Tjortjis, 2019).

Sports analytics is not only restricted to sports organizations or athletes. Other corporations have leveraged extensive analysis of all sports data available to develop betting and gambling algorithms (Pantzalis and Tjortjis, 2020). Sports analytics is a vast field that incorporates multiple applications in various areas that sports organizations can leverage to enhance their performances, increase revenues, and engage in better customer relationship management, and for betting purposes (Khan et al., 2022). A majority of sports fans are interested in viewing advanced statistics for teams and players during and after matches and efficiently assessing the performance of their best teams and players. Clubs use sophisticated devices and software such as GPS Tracking System to gather and analyze data generated by players during training sessions and matches and present them using advanced visualization techniques (Deng et al., 2021). They process these data to use for short-term decision-making and long-term organization development (Pantzalis and Tjortjis, 2020).

With the growth of sports analytics and with the availability of more sports big data, sports analytics can be applied to all sports in multiple areas. Bai and Bai (2021) suggest the sports big data framework to better understand how, and which, data are used in the application of sports analytics. The framework of sports analytics consists of five different layers that represent the chronological order of data source, collection, manipulation, analysis, and the application stages. The framework also expands to demonstrate how the data is collected, processed, cleaned, and manipulated to be used in data mining and other machine learning models. The most common and most used applications of sports analytics are the following: (i) performance evaluation, (ii) performance prediction, (iii) injury prediction and prevention, (iv) scouting and athlete recruitment, (v) betting, and (vi) marketing and fan base management.

Another area where sports analytics is heavily applied is betting, which has been considered an ongoing tradition in many countries. However, over the past few years, sports gambling and betting have been increasing at an exponential rate as more and more countries have legalized sports wagering. In 1992, the U.S. issued the Professional and Amateur Sports Protection Act (PASPA), a federal law restricting almost every state but Nevada from legalizing sports gambling (STATS Predictive Data Brings Innovation to Sports Gambling Market – Stats Perform, 2022). According to *The New York Times*, the U.S. accumulates around $150 billion of illegal sports gambling (STATS Predictive Data Brings Innovation to Sports Gambling Market – Stats Perform, 2022).

As of October 2021, sports gambling has become legal in over 30 states and more states are expected to legalize it soon (American Gaming Association,

2022). With more sports big data being generated daily, sports gambling has interfered in every sport utilizing predictive analysis techniques to predict match outcomes. These predictive analysis techniques rely on historical performance data as well as other data necessary for the outcome prediction of this game such as home team, away team, available players, weather conditions, and more. All this data combined allows for estimating the probability that one of each team will win or a draw will occur. In hand, these probabilities are converted into odds presenting the chances that a specific team will win or draw.

Probabilities can be estimated on either player-specific basis, by accumulating predictive analysis probabilities of scoring or conceding goals using their historical performance data, or on team-specific basis. However, probabilities of a match outcome estimated on team-specific basis allow for better and more efficient calculation of odds for a specific match (Dixon and Coles, 1996). Multiple researchers have studied the impact of other features in a game of football and their ability to impact the predictive analysis of match outcomes. Ridder et al. (1994) investigated the effect of a player being sent off from a football match. Reep and Benjamin (1968) studied the effect of the number and types of passes in a football match on outcome. Other researchers have studied the impact of the number of goals scored in a previous match (Dixon and Coles, 1996). There are a lot of internal and external factors that play a role in the estimation of the probability of match outcomes, where researchers have developed several predictive models with various features. Multiple sports websites have established themselves as leading sports gambling, such as Betway, Bet365, Boylesports, Paddy Power and more, with their access to all sports competitions and events and their respective data to perform predictive analysis and estimate match outcome probabilities.

In the 21st century, sports teams have become more than just clubs competing in events and matches. With social media interaction and engagement, these clubs and advanced university athletic programs have become more like communities rather than sports teams. Direct interaction between sports clubs and fans allows for an increase in commercial activities such as retail, social media interaction, and more resulting in more revenues for the clubs. Sentiment and text analysis can be performed by sports clubs to understand the polarity of their fans and sentiments and level of engagement (Zadeh, 2021). Multiple insights can be derived from this analysis and sports clubs' management and analytics teams should know how to use the data available and formulate new strategies to attract a bigger fanbase and

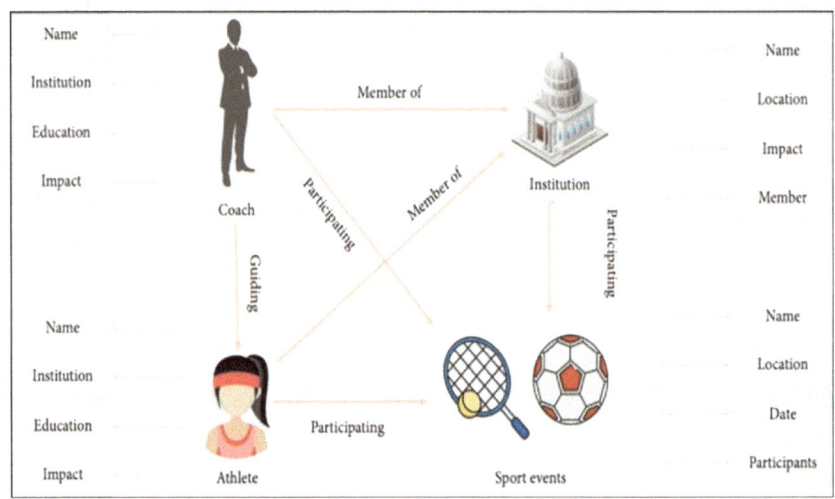

FIGURE 8.1
Example of Entities and Their Relationships in Sports Big Data.

allow more engagement with fans. Figure 8.1 illustrates the entities and their relationships in sports big data.

8.3 METHODS

The major objective of this study is to determine any patterns from financial and performance data and identify correlation between those different variables. In addition to that, we try to test the impact of the performance of clubs on their revenues for that respective season. Exploratory data analysis helps you in summarizing the data available using summary statistics and visualization techniques such as graphical representations (Patil, 2018). This will allow for better understanding of the data and deeper dissection of every football club to assess their on-field and financial performance. In addition to that, exploratory data analysis allows for comparison of football clubs for the season 2020/2021 using various metrics such as total revenue, wins, trophies, and more. Clustering of the data also allows us to group these football clubs according to similar characteristics and variables, which will allow for better comparison using financial and performance data. K-means Clustering is used to cluster the observations and derive the most useful information from these clusters (Ikotun et al., 2023).

8.3.1 Data Sources

Hundreds of millions of sports data are being generated daily from different sports events, competitions, matches and more. The main objective is to mine knowledge from sports big data to provide better sports services for athletes, coaches, competition-related decision-makers, and the public (Bai and Bai, 2021). Sports big data analysis relies on data mining, network analysis, and statistical analysis techniques to derive valuable information for sports enterprises, managers, coaches, and players (Patel et al., 2020). This valuable information is displayed through visualization to be easily presented and understood by sports professionals allowing them to evaluate athletes and formulate new strategic plans. Sports data analysis can also help coaches and athletes understand the strengths and weaknesses of their opponents and simulate game strategies and plans to counter them and achieve better results (Bai and Bai, 2021). Sports data generated can be in various forms with different functions and values. The most common and most valuable sports data are categorized into four different groups (Bai and Bai, 2021):

    i. Physical fitness data such as height, weight, muscle mass, body fat percentage, and more.
    ii. Physical exercise behavior and trajectories such as running, swimming, football, basketball, and more.
    iii. Personal Information such as gender, age, ethnicity, and more.
    iv. Various competition results and performance statistics such as final score, goals scored and conceded, shots missed, and more.

Each of these different kinds of data provide different value to sports organization and its players. Athletes' physical fitness and exercise behaviors and performances are analyzed to predict potential athletes (Bai and Bai, 2021). For example, all NBA teams' draft basketball players from college teams to join their teams and perform at the highest level. These players are drafted based on their performances and physical fitness, where recruiters analyze and study the athlete's data and pick the player with the best statistics and potential. In addition to that, some typical big data services such as exercise performance, health data, training statistics, and analysis can effectively help coaches and athletes in daily training and customizing game strategies and play an immeasurable role in winning competitions (Sestino et al., 2020; Bai and Bai, 2021). Leveraging the data available and insights derived can help professional teams to adjust their training and game strategies by relying on their strengths to enhance their performances and improve their results.

Due to the complexity of sports data and its presence in a variety of unstructured forms, the process of data acquisition and management is complex and not easy. A particularly important feature of sports big data is its diversity. Sports big data are extremely broad and complex (Bai and Bai, 2021). Figure 8.1 demonstrates the complexity of sports big data and shows an example of entities and their relationship within one sports organization. Each entity has its own specific attributes and explicit data such as name and physical fitness data of athletes, name and results of sports events, and so on. Data extracted from these entities in their natural unprocessed format do not maximize the valuable insights that can be derived. These data should be restructured, labeled, and cleaned to be used in machine learning models and acquire the most insights possible. The process of data labeling and data cleaning can be done manually or automatically, using other machine learning models, depending on the complexity of the data extracted.

8.4 RESULTS

8.4.1 Descriptive Measures

Figure 8.2 represents the total revenue for the 19 football clubs for the calendar year 2021. The data is formatted in descending order where Manchester City tops the rest of the clubs with a total revenue of €645m. Real Madrid comes in at second spot with only a total of €4m difference with Manchester City. Revenues for these clubs decrease gradually between one another where Wolves (Wolverhampton Wanderers), Everton, and AC Milan occupy the last three places with a total revenue of €219m, €218m, and €216m respectively. We identify a huge gap between first and last place with a range of €429m, and average revenue across clubs for the year 2021 comes in at €420m.

Figure 8.3 represents the commercial revenue for the clubs for the year 2021. We identify a reshuffle in the order of football clubs compared to the total revenues. Bayern Munich tops the list with a total of €345m earned from commercial activities. Paris Saint Germain (PSG) comes in at second place followed by Real Madrid and then Manchester City at fourth place. Revenues from commercial activities can result from hundreds of different actions, as previously defined, which is why there is such a large fluctuation – about

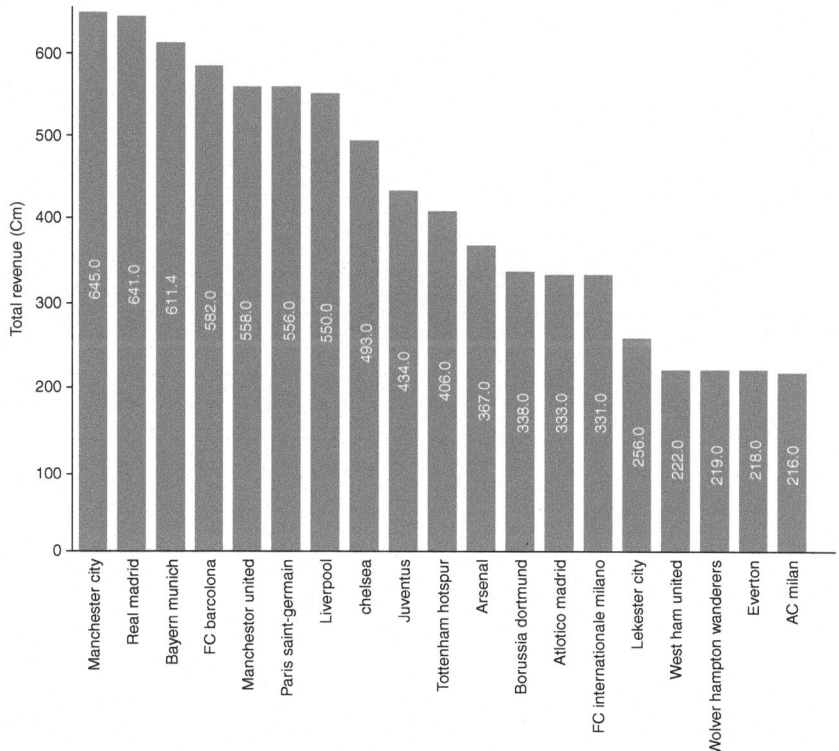

FIGURE 8.2
Total Revenue – Year 2021.

€317.8 m – between the highest- and lowest-earning clubs. For example, Real Madrid have started a project in 2020, expected to be done by 2023, to renovate their stadium, Santiago Bernabue, which requires a lot of investment and money (Caulfield and Jha, 2022). Despite this project, Real Madrid was still able to clinch third spot and rely on other commercial activities to bring them in more revenue. In turn, this new stadium is expected to be a technological and innovative change in sports stadiums and most likely to bring in thousands of euros in return. Also, Real Madrid have agreed big money deals with Sixth Street and Legends, asset management and consulting firms helping them in reconstruction and optimizing management, worth around €340m to be earned right after project completion in 2023 (Kemble, 2022). In turn, this is considered a gigantic financial boost for Real Madrid starting early next year.

Figure 8.4 represents the total number of social media followers for each club across 5 different platforms: Facebook, Instagram, Twitter, YouTube, and

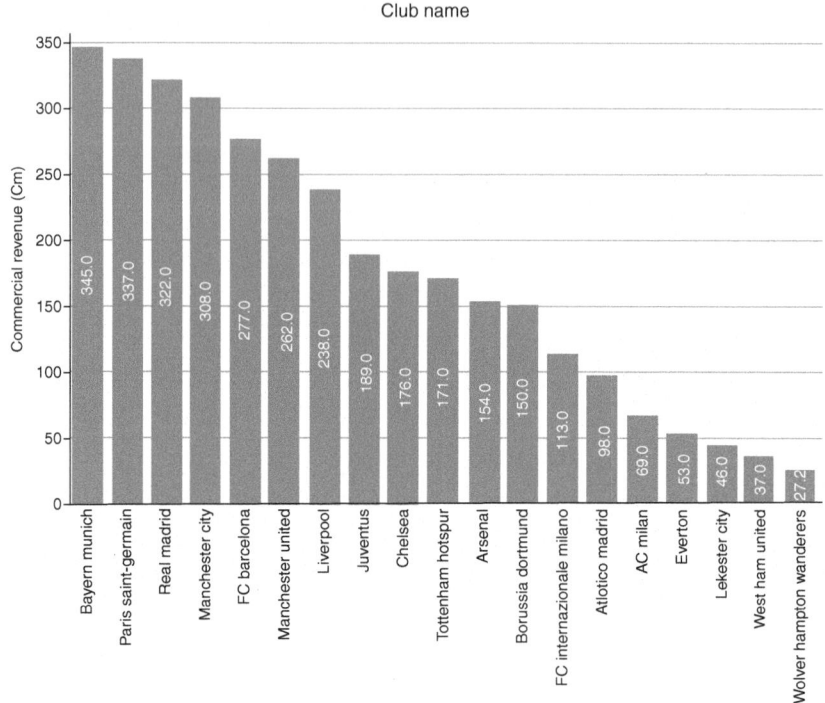

FIGURE 8.3
Commercial Revenue – Year 2021.

TikTok. Real Madrid and FC Barcelona easily secure the top two spots with a total of 277.4 million followers and 263.9 million followers respectively. With these two clubs considered the biggest and most successful clubs in Europe, we can identify a huge fan base for these two clubs. This also explains why Real Madrid ranks third in commercial revenue, as the club benefits from a large fan base both locally and globally, which drives its commercial activities and generates significant revenue. The average number of followers across all clubs is calculated to be 91.94 million people which shows the high fan base for these clubs.

8.4.2 Correlation

A correlation matrix was run on the numerical variables in the dataset, which are all variables excluding club name and country, and presented in Figure 8.5. The following scale was set to identify the strength and sign of correlation: Strong negative correlation: [−1,−0.7], Moderate negative

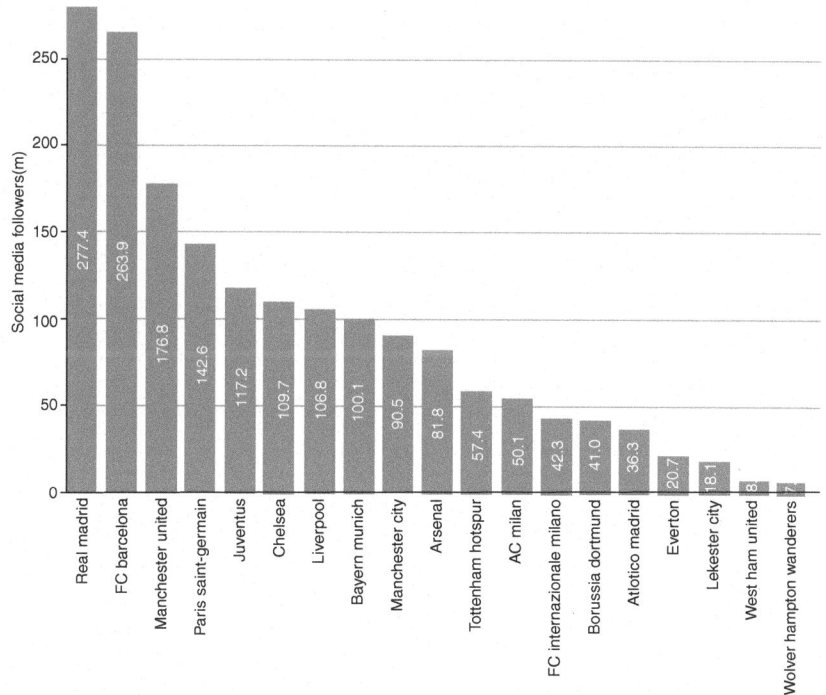

FIGURE 8.4
Social Media Followers – Year 2021.

correlation: [−0.7,−0.3], Weak negative correlation: [−0.3,0], No correlation: 0, Weak positive correlation: [0,0.3], Moderate positive correlation: [0.3,0.7], and Strong positive correlation: [0.7,1]. We obtain the correlation matrix and heatmap for the variables presented in Figure 8.5, which allows us to better visualize the correlations between the variables and their strength.

A strong positive correlation exists between the number of social media followers and total revenue of the club, matchday revenue, commercial revenue, and a moderate positive correlation with broadcast revenue. The number of social media followers may give us insights into how big a club is in terms of supporters and fan engagement. More followers indicate that a lot of fans are staying up to date with the latest games and fixtures of a team either by attending stadiums and watching in person or by watching live broadcasts on TV. The higher the number of people watching, the more revenue these football clubs will accumulate. More fans also mean more retail sales and more commercial activities, resulting in higher revenues for the club.

A moderate positive correlation exists between the total revenue of a club and total trophies won that year and number of wins in the league. A strong

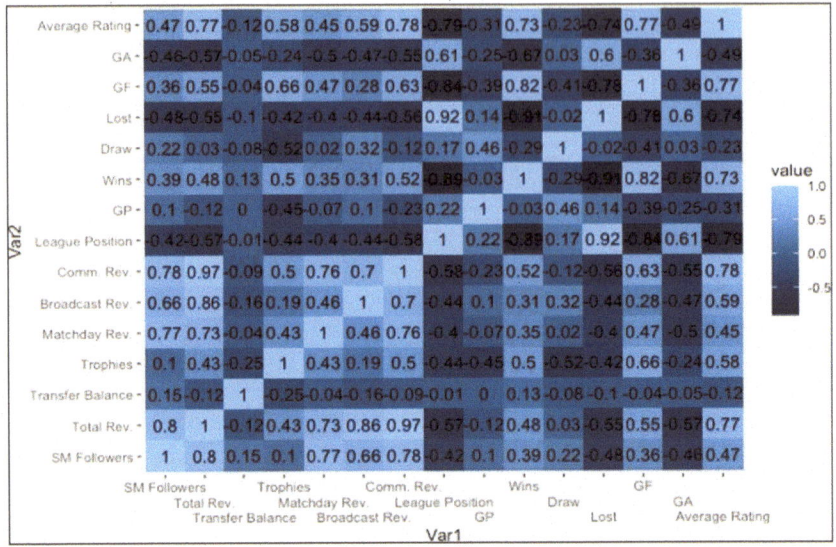

FIGURE 8.5
Correlation Heatmap.

positive correlation exists between total revenue and average rating. A football club's main priority is that the players perform well and the team achieves good outcomes while winning matches and trophies. Achieving higher ratings in-game reflects on the team's performance, which means the higher the average rating, the better the performance was – most likely achieving a win. Winning matches leads to winning trophies which results in rewards for teams and more revenue for the clubs. This also explains the moderate negative correlation between total revenue and the variables league position and lost. The more games a team loses the lower their position in the league will be, thus less chances of winning a trophy at the end of the season, and more chances of not satisfying the fans and reducing total accumulated revenue.

A moderate positive correlation exists between trophies, number of wins, and number of goals scored. A moderate negative correlation exists between trophies and league position and number of draws and number of losses in a season. Clinching the league title in any country is not as easy as it seems, due to the level of competition and all the factors that affect performance. However, statistically, it all comes down to the team that accumulates the highest number of points within the total number of games played. Thus, achieving more wins (+3 pts.) and less draws (+1 pts.) and losses (0 pts.) by scoring more goals and conceding fewer ones results in more points for the team, allowing them to top their league and clinch a title.

A strong positive correlation exists between total revenue and the 3 other financial variables related to revenue: Matchday Rev., Broadcast Rev., and Comm. Rev. That is expected because total revenue is the sum of the other three. But it is important to notice that commercial and broadcast revenue are more correlated to total revenue compared to matchday revenue. That can be explained due to the lack of fans in the season of 2020/2021, due to the Covid-19 pandemic, which minimized the total revenue accumulated by clubs from matchdays and tickets sold, as explained earlier. We identify that the performance variables are relatively highly correlated to each other, whether positively or negatively. For example, league position is affected by number of wins and losses, so that is why we see a strong negative correlation and strong positive correlation respectively. Goals scored and goals conceded also are correlated with the number of wins achieved throughout the season and the final position in the league.

8.4.3 K-Means Clustering

To derive more insights, we performed clustering of the 19 different clubs according to a K-means clustering model. The model clusters the clubs into two different groups. To determine the accurate number of clusters to separate the clubs into we used two different methods: the Elbow Point Technique and the Silhouette Method. Both methods identify that the best number of clusters to use is k=2 because we observe a bend in the curve at k=2 in the Elbow Point Technique and the Silhouette Method maximizes the average silhouette length at k=2. Figures 8.6 and 8.7 represent the ideal number of clusters in our K-means clustering model.

To optimize the K-means model on our dataset using k = 2 and we obtain the following 2 clusters presented in Figure 8.8.

Figure 8.8 presents the two different clusters generated by our model, and we can determine that the K-means model was able to reduce the dimensions of the variables into two principal components while maintaining around 94% of the data without losing its value. Cluster 1 includes a total of 10 clubs whereas Cluster 2 includes the remaining 9 clubs. Table 8.1 presents the different clubs in each cluster.

After deriving the cluster means from R and presenting them in Table 8.1, we can analyze and identify the features of every cluster and compare both. Cluster 1, which includes 9 out of the 19 clubs, is considered the elite cluster or the cluster where football clubs have better on-field and financial performance. These clubs are also considered the most successful in the past

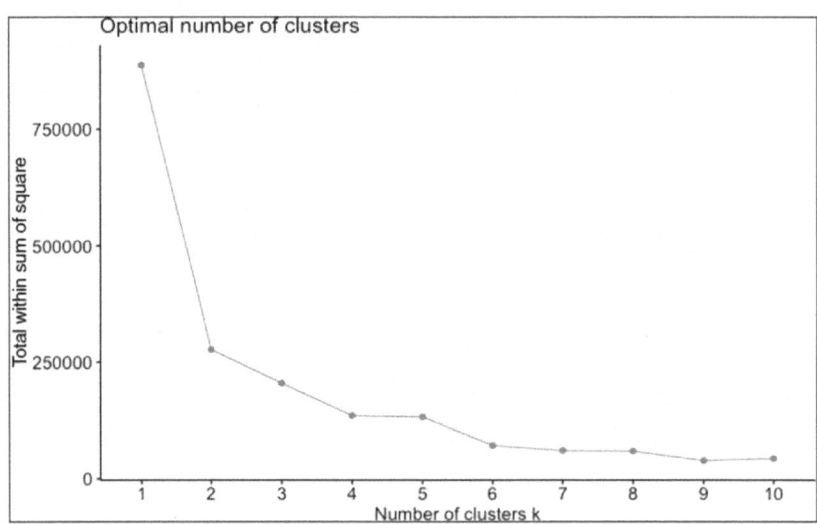

FIGURE 8.6
Optimal Number of Clusters Using Elbow Point Technique.

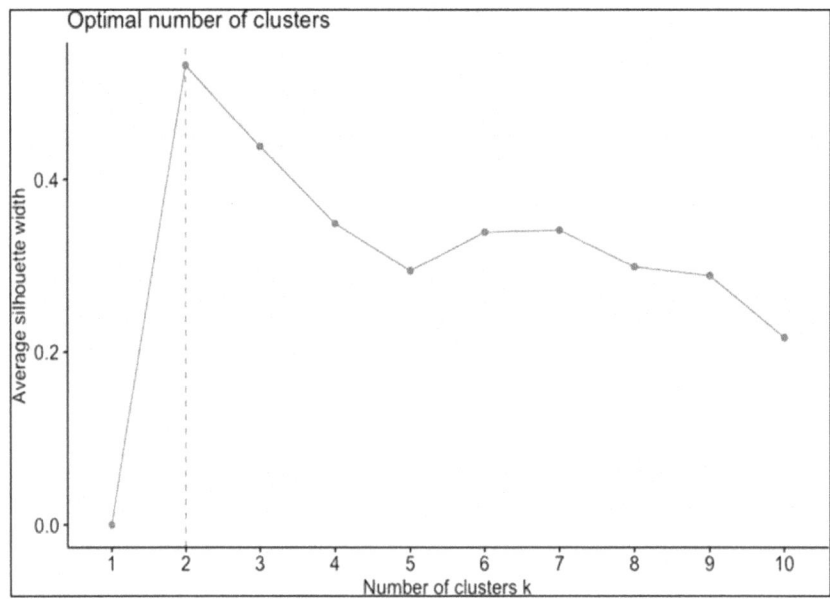

FIGURE 8.7
Optimal Number of Clusters Using Silhouette Method.

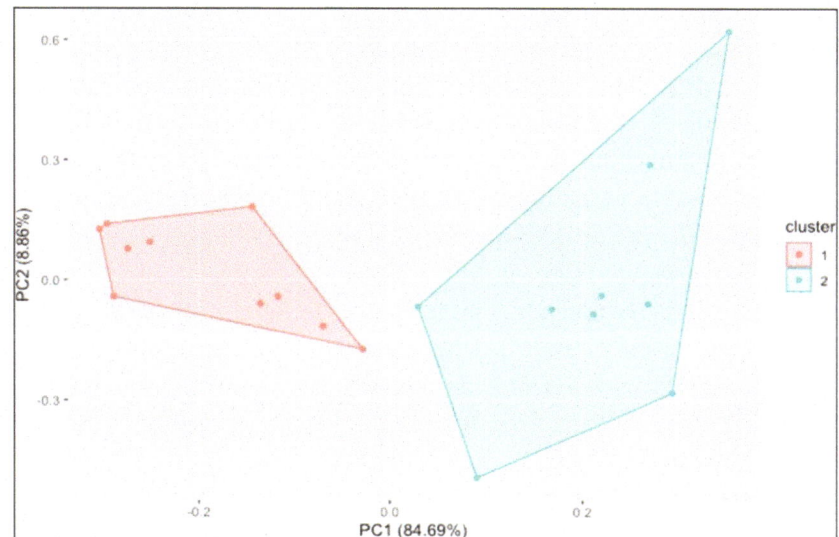

FIGURE 8.8
Clusters Obtained Using K-Means Clustering.

TABLE 8.1

Clubs K-Means Clustering Results

Variables	Cluster 1	Cluster 2
Social Media Followers (m)	153.8	36.3
Total Revenue (€m)	563.38	290.6
Transfer Balance (€m)	-74.47	-50.5
Trophies	1.22	0.5
Matchday Revenue (€m)	9.8	1.58
Broadcast Revenue (€m)	281.3	197
Commercial Revenue (€m)	272.67	91.82
League Position	2.44	5.6
GP (Games Played)	37.6	37.6
Wins	23.22	20.2
Draws	7.8	7.1
Lost	6.6	10.3
Goals For (GF)	77.3	64.1
Goals Against (GA)	34.3	42.8
Average Rating	6.88	6.77

years in terms of financial and on-field performance. The remaining 10 clubs in Cluster 2 performed worse financially and in terms of performance compared to the clubs in Cluster 1. The clubs in Cluster 1 are showed to have an average of around 154 million followers on social media compared to only 36 million followers for Cluster 2 clubs. This indicates that clubs in Cluster 1 have a much bigger fan base and more engagement on social media platforms. To consider the financial features, clubs in Cluster 1 have much higher revenues from all different sources: matchday, broadcast, and commercial. Total revenue for clubs in Cluster 1 on average is almost double compared to clubs in Cluster 2. These clubs have managed to secure much higher sources of revenue from commercial activities, which might be due to more fans and social media followers, allowing more interaction and engagement with the clubs.

As for broadcast revenue, clubs in Cluster 1 might have secured more broadcasting rights due to bigger fanbases, and that is why we see higher average broadcast revenue compared to clubs in Cluster 2. Now let's focus on the performance features and compare the performance of clubs in Cluster 1 to clubs in Cluster 2. The average league position after all games of the season concluded of clubs in Cluster 1 is 2.44, which means that these clubs were able to secure at least the top 3 spots in their leagues in different countries. In turn, this allows for UEFA Champions League qualification for the next season, which brings in more revenue and rewards for the clubs. Considering the average final league standing for clubs in Cluster 2, we can determine that these clubs have performed worse than clubs in Cluster 1 as they secured an average league position of 5.6. This indicates that these clubs fall behind 3rd and 4th place in the league standings in each country where some have failed to secure promotion to the UEFA Champions League for the next season.

The number of games played in both clusters is identical; however, clubs in Cluster 1 secured slightly more wins and lost fewer games. This performance difference contributes to their higher league standing, supporting the cluster's league position grouping. With better performances, clubs in Cluster 1 managed to score more goals and concede fewer goals, allowing them to win more games and achieve better outcomes and results. Explanatory Analysis of football clubs using accurate and relevant financial and performance data shows a strong association between performances and revenues in different metrics and variables.

8.4.4 Naïve Method

According to the naïve method, which forecasts the revenue for the upcoming 3 years using the last observation of the historical financial data, which includes total revenue in 2021, we obtain Table 8.2.

According to the results obtained from the naïve forecasting method presented in Table 8.2, we can identify that the total revenues for Manchester United forecast for the next 3 years will be €558m, with the confidence interval increasing every year, and a 95% chance that the total revenues will be within the interval for every year. Figures 8.9, 8.10, and

TABLE 8.2

Naive Method Forecasting Results

| Date | Manchester United | | Real Madrid | | Bayern Munich | |
	Point Forecast (€m)	95% Confidence Interval	Point Forecast (€m)	95% Confidence Interval	Point Forecast (€m)	95% Confidence Interval
2022	558	[437, 679]	641	[561, 720]	611.4	[531, 692]
2023	558	[387, 729]	641	[528, 753]	611.4	[497, 726]
2024	558	[348,767]	641	[503,779]	611.4	[472,751]

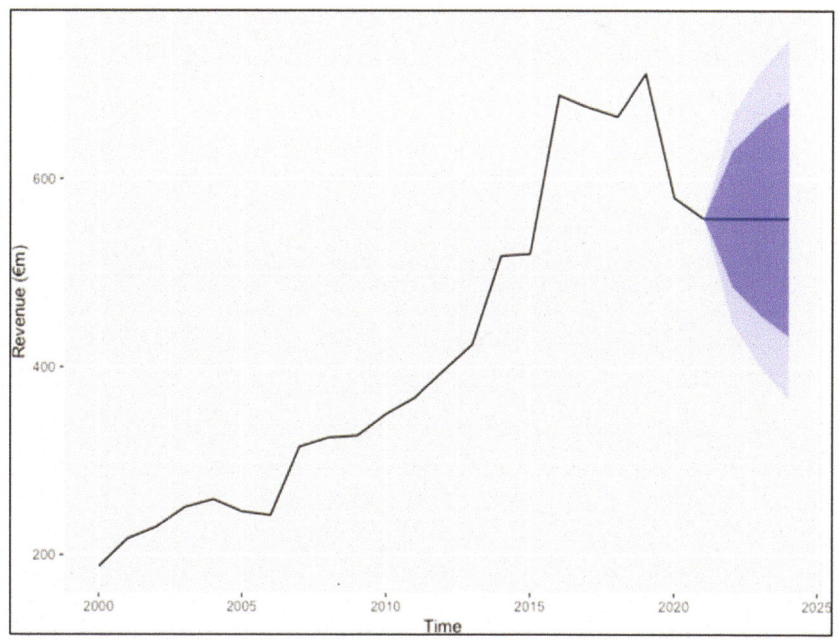

FIGURE 8.9
Manchester United Naive Predictions Graphically.

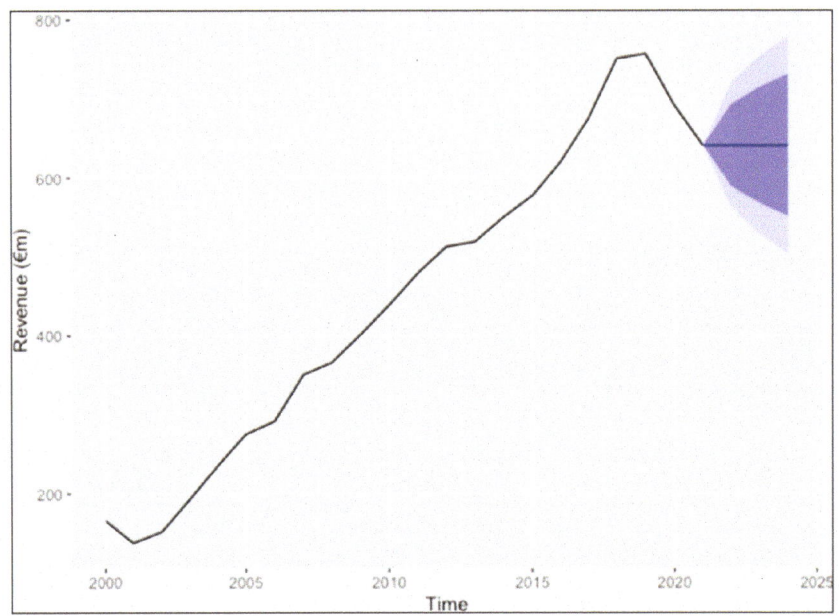

FIGURE 8.10
Real Madrid Naive Predictions Graphically.

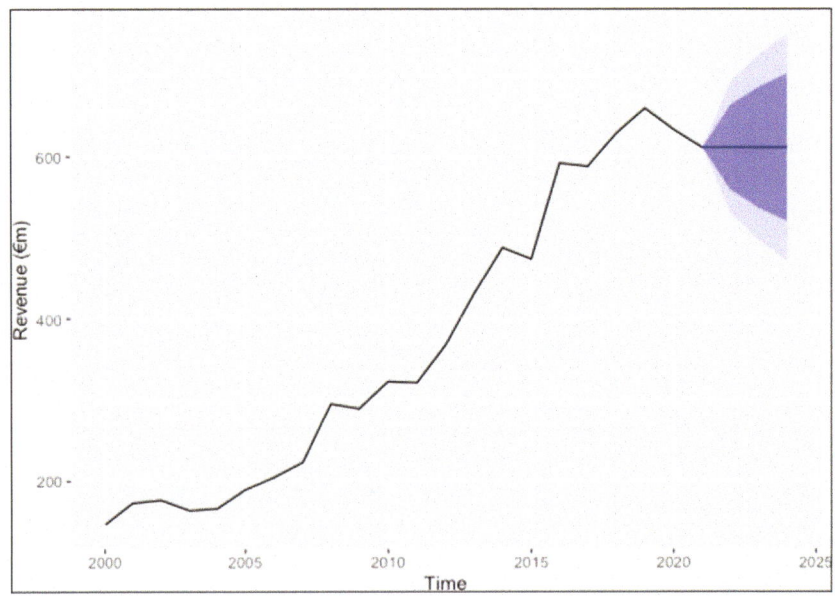

FIGURE 8.11
Bayern Munich Naive Predictions Graphically.

8.11 graphically represent the results obtained in Table 8.2 to visualize the predictions for the next 3 years with their relative confidence interval using the naïve method. According to the results obtained from the naïve method presented in Table 8.2, we can identify that the total revenue forecast for Real Madrid for the next 3 years will be €641m, with the confidence interval increasing every year, and a 95% chance that the total revenue will be within the interval for every year. According to the results obtained from the naïve forecasting method presented in Table 8.2, we can identify that the total revenue forecast for Bayern Munich for the next 3 years will be €611.4m, with the confidence interval increasing every year, and a 95% chance that the total revenue will be within the interval for every year. Figures 8.9, 8.10, and 8.11 represent the naïve predictions of Manchester United, Real Madrid, and Bayern Munich.

8.4.5 Simple Exponential Smoothing (SES) Method

According to the simple moving average, which forecasts the total revenue for the upcoming 3 years using historical data and a smoothing coefficient, we obtain Table 8.3.

According to the results obtained from the simple exponential smoothing (SES) forecasting method presented in Table 8.3, we can identify that the total revenues for Manchester United forecast for the next 3 years will be €558m, which is the same result as the naïve method. However, the confidence interval in SES differs slightly from naïve, where we can identify smaller intervals, for a 95% confidence prediction for total revenues. According to the results obtained from the SES forecasting method presented in Table 8.3, we can identify that the total revenues forecast for Real Madrid for the next 3 years will be €641m which is the same results as the naïve method. In addition to

TABLE 8.3

SES Method Forecasting Results

	Manchester United		Real Madrid		Bayern Munich	
Date	Point Forecast (€m)	95% Confidence Interval	Point Forecast (€m)	95% Confidence Interval	Point Forecast (€m)	95% Confidence Interval
2022	558	[444, 672]	641	[559, 723]	611.4	[523, 699]
2023	558	[397, 719]	641	[526, 756]	611.4	[487, 736]
2024	558	[361,755]	641	[500,782]	611.4	[523, 699]

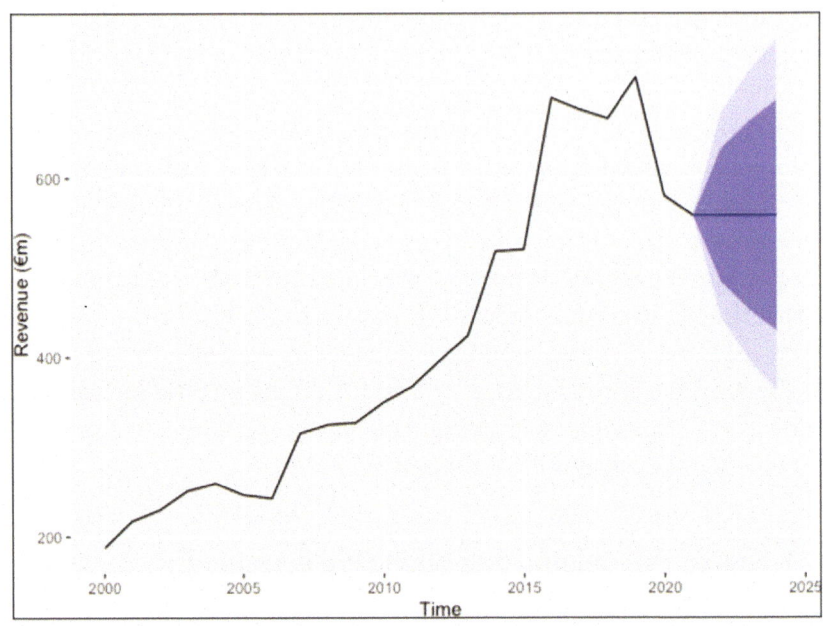

FIGURE 8.12
Manchester United SES Predictions.

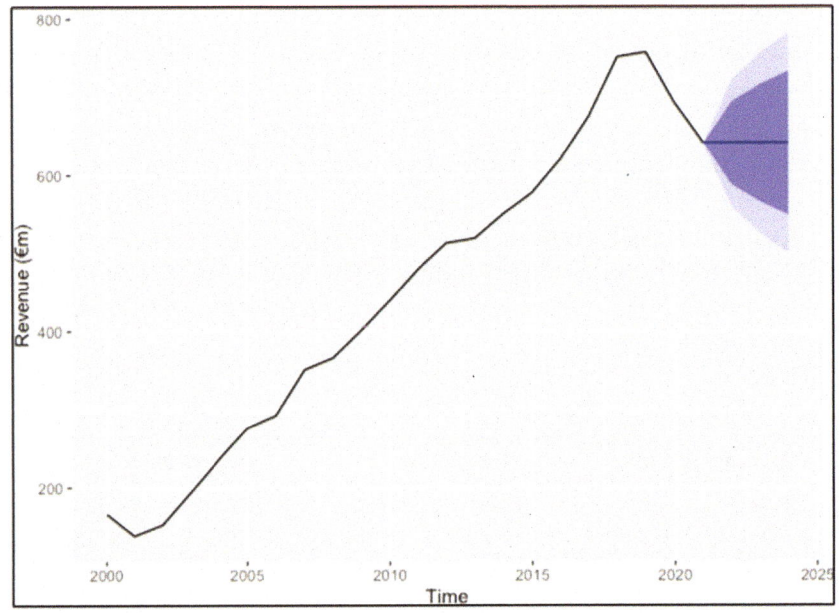

FIGURE 8.13
Real Madrid SES Predictions.

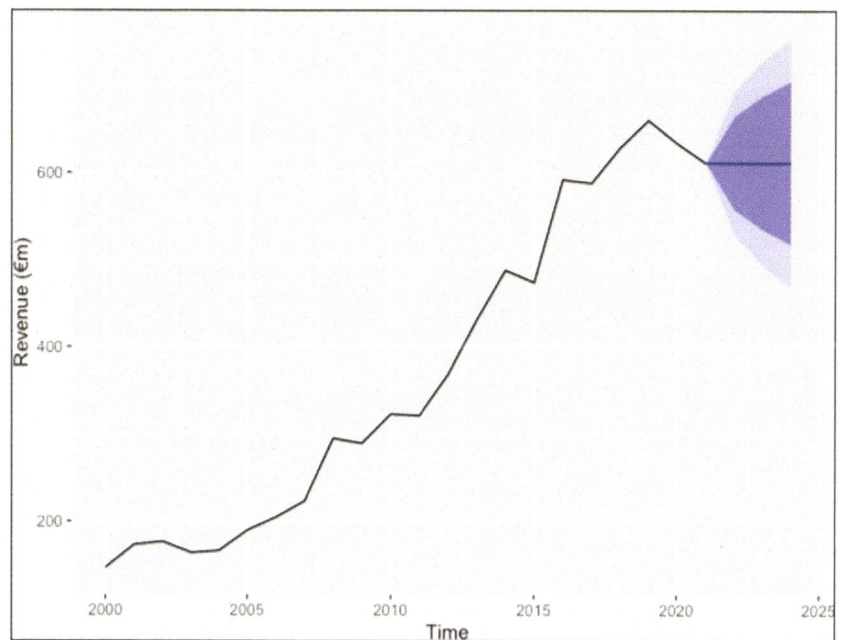

FIGURE 8.14
Bayern Munich SES Predictions.

that, the 95% confidence interval is almost the same for both models, with slight differences. According to the results obtained from the SES forecasting method, we can identify that the total revenue forecast for Bayern Munich for the next 3 years will be €611.4m, which is the same result as the naïve method. In addition to that, the 95% confidence interval is almost the same for both models, with slight differences. The graphical representations of the results obtained by the SES method are presented in Figures 8.12, 8.13, and 8.14.

8.4.6 Holt Winter's Method

Holt Winter's forecasting method is also a smoothing method to predict total revenue for upcoming years. Table 8.4 presents the forecasting results for total revenue for Manchester United using Holt Winter's method.

According to the results above, Holt Winter's forecasting method predicts that Manchester United's total revenue will keep on decreasing following the trend that started in 2020 due to Covid-19. In addition to that, total revenue is not expected to surpass €600m in any of the upcoming 3 years, where the 95% confidence intervals are maximized at €600m in 2024. According to the

TABLE 8.4

Holt Winter's Method Forecasting Results

	Manchester United		Real Madrid		Bayern Munich	
Date	Point Forecast (€m)	95% Confidence Interval	Point Forecast (€m)	95% Confidence Interval	Point Forecast (€m)	95% Confidence Interval
2022	481.5	[366, 597]	663.77	[589, 738]	642.6	[570, 715]
2023	405	[226, 583]	686	[581, 791]	665.3	[571, 760]
2024	328.6	[58,600]	708.4	[580,837]	688	[575,801]

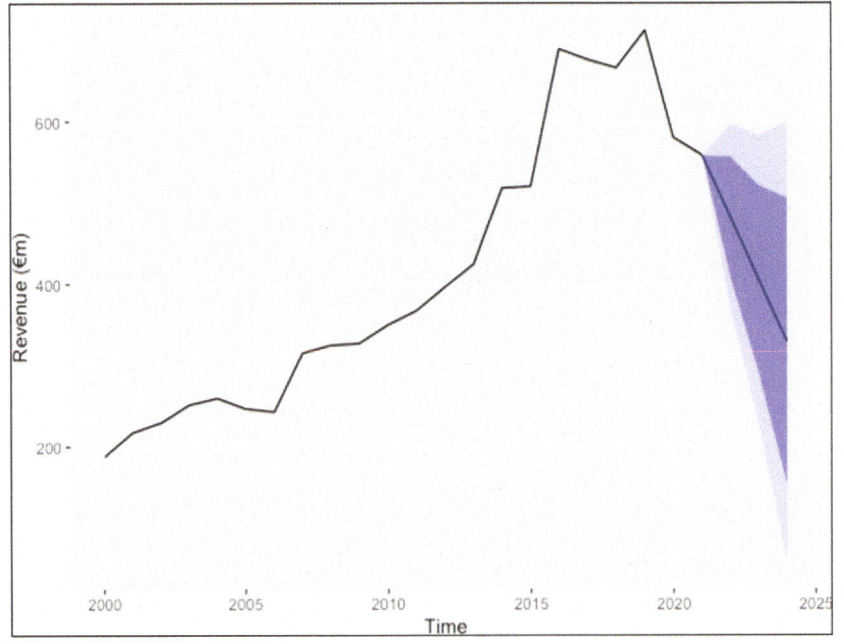

FIGURE 8.15
Manchester United Holt Winter's Predictions.

results above, Holt Winter's forecasting method predicts that Real Madrid's total revenue will start to increase in 2022, following 2 years' decrease in 2020 and 2021 due to Covid-19. Total revenue is expected to increase by around €20m every year from 2021 until 2024. Confidence intervals also suggest that there is a 95% chance revenue will not drop below €580m in any year and might reach more than €800m by 2024. Figures 8.15, 8.16, and 8.17 graphically represent the results obtained in Table 8.4 to easily visualize the predictions and their respective confidence intervals.

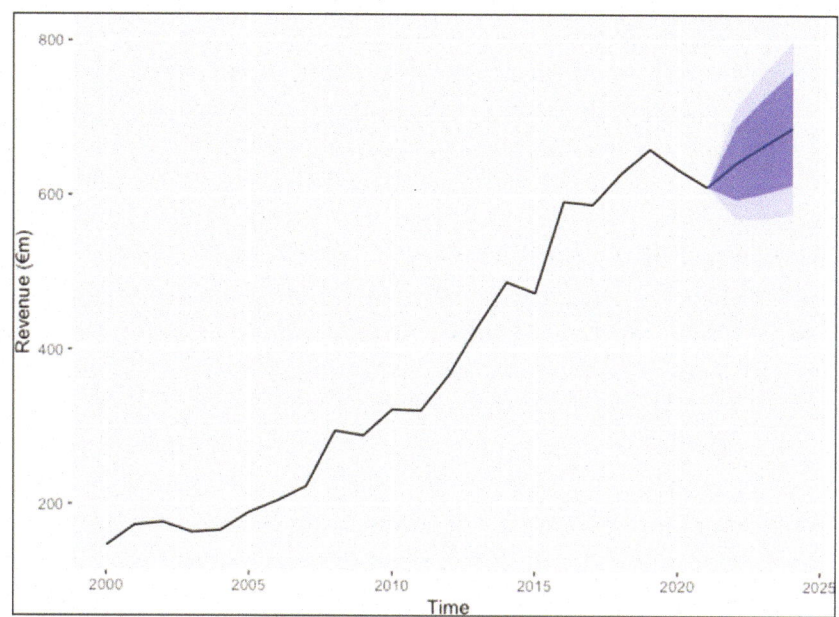

FIGURE 8.16
Real Madrid Holt Winter's Predictions.

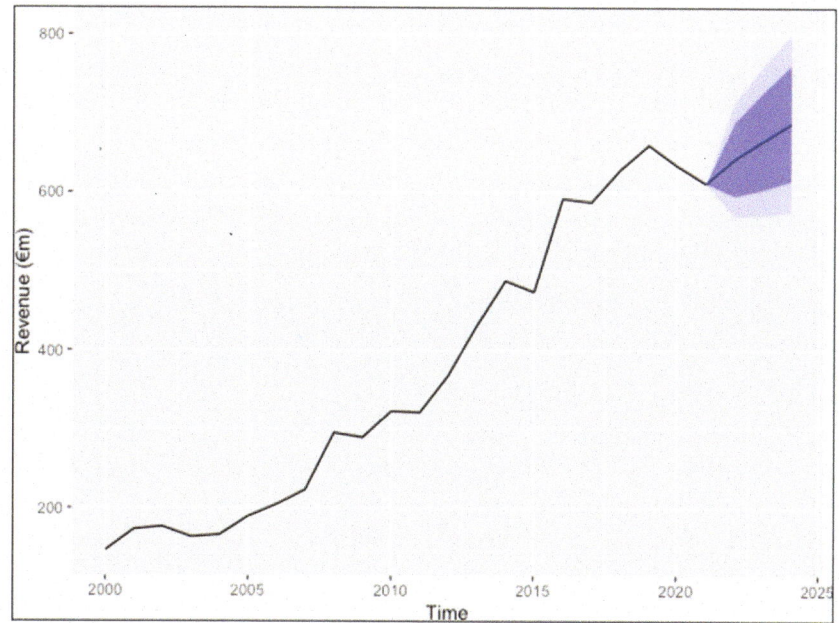

FIGURE 8.17
Bayern Munich Holt Winter's Predictions.

8.4.7 Auto-ARIMA Method

The Auto-ARIMA forecasting method forecasts the total revenue for the upcoming 3 years using an autoregressive integrated moving average method which accounts for trend, noise, and seasonality of the data. However, no features of the time series were identified before forecasting as everything was set automatically by the model. Table 8.5 presents the forecasting results using the Auto-ARIMA method.

Auto-ARIMA's prediction for Manchester United total revenues was a constant €558m for the next 3 years with the confidence interval increasing every year, which has very similar results to the naïve and SES methods. Figures 8.18, 8.19, and 8.20 represent the results obtained by the Auto-ARIMA method in Table 8.5 graphically. According to the results obtained by the 4 different forecasting models above, we can identify that the forecasting results using Auto-ARIMA were similar to the result obtained by the naïve and SES methods, where the model predicts that the total revenue will be constant at €558m for the next years, whereas Holt Winter's method predicts that Manchester United's total revenue for the next 3 years will continue to decrease. We can also recognize that the lower bound of the 95% confidence interval is decreasing after every year, but the upper bound is increasing as well, creating a bigger interval for a higher 95% chance prediction.

According to the results obtained by the 4 different forecasting models above, we can identify that the forecasting results using Holt Winter's method were the most logical, as we expect to see an increase in Real Madrid's revenue after the pandemic. Auto-ARIMA predictions were slightly similar, but predicted revenues for the next 3 years were less, but with similar confidence intervals. Results obtained by the naïve and SES methods were the same, where the models predicted that the total revenue will be constant at

TABLE 8.5

Auto-ARIMA's Method Forecasting Results

	Manchester United		Real Madrid		Bayern Munich	
Date	Point Forecast (€m)	95% Confidence Interval	Point Forecast (€m)	95% Confidence Interval	Point Forecast (€m)	95% Confidence Interval
2022	558	[447, 669]	628.3	[573, 684]	633.5	[564, 704]
2023	558	[401, 715]	643.6	[525, 762]	655.7	[557, 754]
2024	558	[366,750]	643.6	[459,829]	677.8	[557,799]

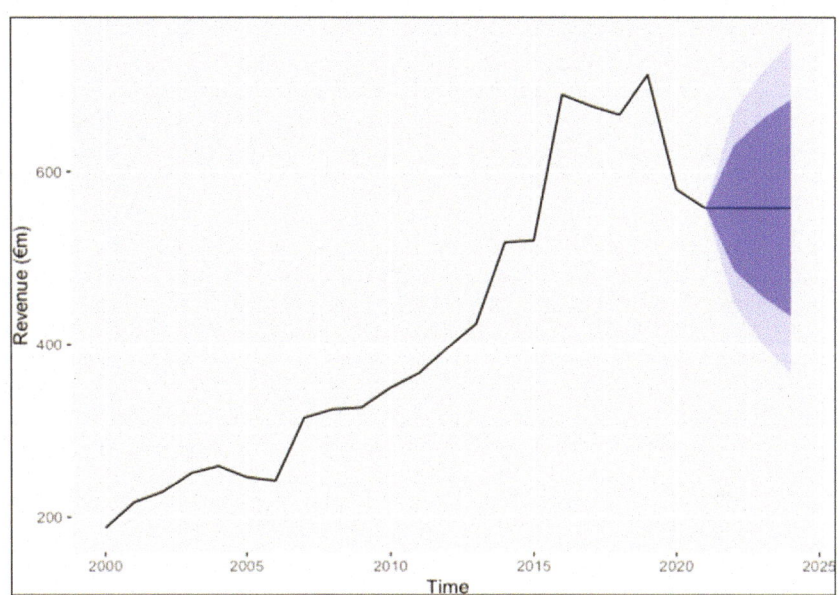

FIGURE 8.18
Manchester United Auto-ARIMA Predictions.

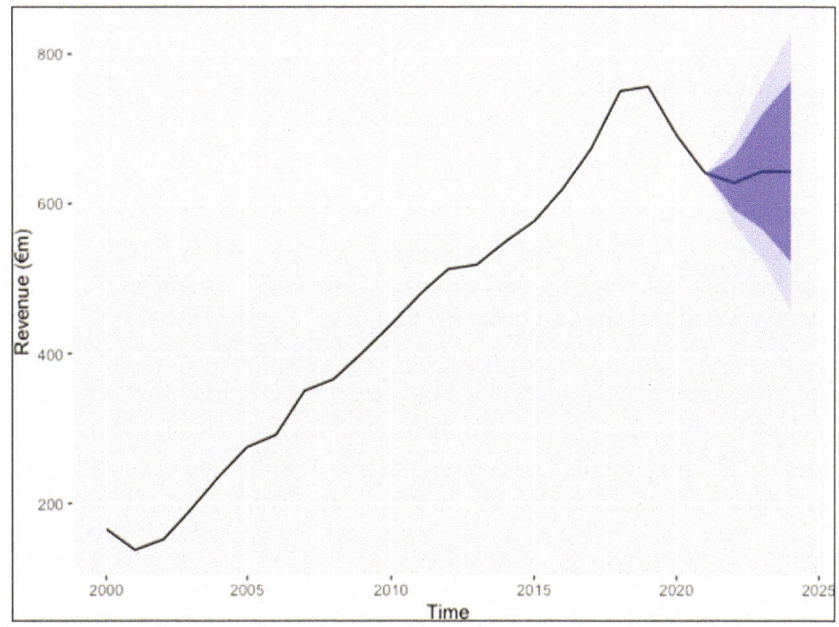

FIGURE 8.19
Real Madrid Auto-ARIMA Predictions.

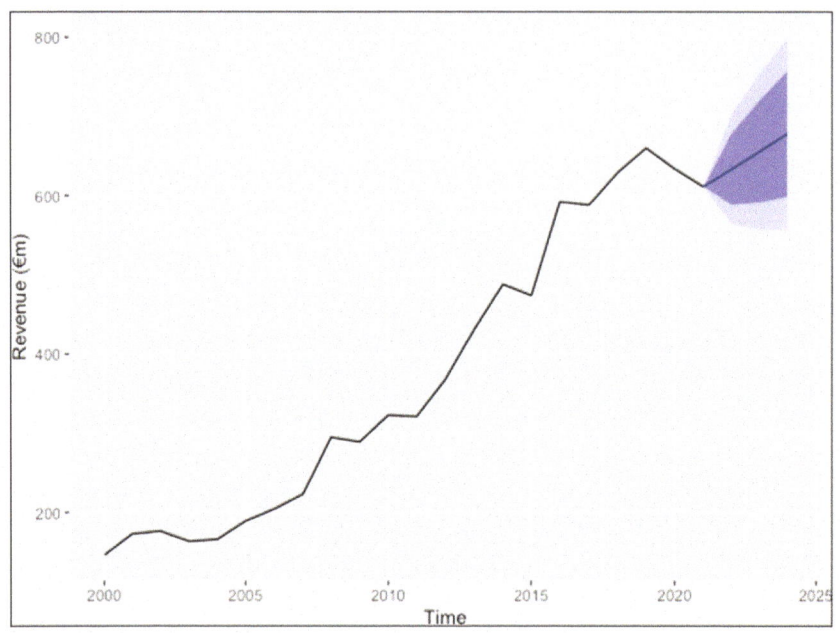

FIGURE 8.20
Bayern Munich Auto-ARIMA Predictions.

€641m for the next three years. We can also recognize that the lower bound of the 95% confidence interval is decreasing after every year, but the upper bound is increasing as well, creating a bigger interval for a higher 95% chance prediction.

According to the results obtained by the 4 different forecasting models above, we can identify that the forecasting results using Holt Winter's method and Auto-ARIMA were the most logical, as we expect to see an increase in Bayern Munich's revenue after the pandemic.

Predictions of both models were similar, with slight variations in point forecast and confidence intervals, but the general trend is the same where the models expect that Bayern Munich's total revenue will increase starting next year. Results obtained by the naïve and SES methods were the same, where the model predicts that the total revenue will be constant at €611.4m for the next years. We can also recognize that the lower bound of the 95% confidence interval is decreasing after every year, but the upper bound is increasing as well, creating a bigger interval for a higher 95% chance prediction.

8.5 DISCUSSIONS AND CONCLUSION

In this chapter, we have provided a comprehensive review of sports analytics, areas of application, data available, and data analysis techniques applied. The analysis of this research allows researchers, sports organizations, or anyone who is interested in the field of sports analytics to understand its vast applications and level of complexity. The analytical approach sheds light on the interrelation between on-field and financial performance, an area not researched enough, and it has several opportunities for sports clubs. Explanatory data analysis using visualization, correlation, and clustering has led to the conclusion that sports clubs' performance strongly impacts on their financial revenues. In addition to that, exploring financial data for football clubs allows their management to understand their best and worst streams of income and leverage data analytics to increase their financial perform-ance such as commercial revenue generated from commercial activities. Forecasting total revenue for clubs allows them to estimate the expected revenues for the upcoming years and determine if they will improve finan-cially. This will allow sports clubs to tweak some aspects within the club such as new signings, invest in more social media marketing, and develop and implement new training and game strategies. All these changes, if done successfully, will allow a club to assess and improve its performance, win more titles, and satisfy their fan base, thus bringing in more revenues in the upcoming years compared to the forecasts.

8.5.1 Limitations of the Study

Despite all the advancements that the sports analytics industry has gone through in the past decade or two, some major challenges and limitations arise, such as the following:

Finding the right analytics people: The hardest aspect of sports analytics is deriving the most meaningful insights for the club. Multiple models are developed and implemented by analysts to assist their sports clubs in achieving better results.

However, few people can do high-quality and useful analysis using sports data and derive valuable and unique information for the sports team. Communication between analysts and non-technical people is crucial. Analysts must share their models and results with coaches, scouts, players, and more, and to do that they should have a deep understanding and full knowledge of the processes, model built, and its implementation within the team. Coaches who receive information from their analysts but are not communicated with properly might disregard their work and not use it.

Communication between analysts and non-technical people: Mr. Melville shed light on an important challenge in sports analytics according to his experience. Analysts must share their models and results with coaches, scouts, players, and more, and to do that they should have a deep understanding and full knowledge of the processes, model built, and its implementation within the team. Coaches who receive information from their analysts but are not communicated with properly might disregard their work and not use it.

Data Loss: With hundreds of millions of data points being generated yearly from multiple sports events and competitions, one issue that organizations face is data loss (Wallace, 2021). Data can be lost due to mishandling or mismanagement of the data, poor collection of data, hacking, or cyber threats. Sports organizations should understand the importance of the data at hand and implement strict data protection measures to keep the data safe.

Privacy and Ethical Concerns: Data collected by sports organizations on athletes – whether it is performance statistics, health-related information, or personal information – all contain valuable information. This data is also shared with third parties for commercial activities and more, which means the data is more at risk of being leaked or shared more. The sports ecosystem should address this challenge and understand the severity of its implications. Data protection with regulatory and ethical requirements should be applied and athletes should give their explicit consent before data is shared (Deloitte Analytics, 2022).

8.5.2 Future Scope

Sports analytics has a bright future ahead. This field is only starting to emerge and is expected to grow even more in the next decade. New technologies are expected to make their way into the sports analytics field such as motion capture and more advanced wearable sensors. This will allow for improved performance evaluation for athletes and generate more data points which contain more useful insights and information. Virtual Reality headsets can also make their way to the sports industry as fans could virtually watch games while staying at home. Every sport will evolve as more data will be generated and more data analysis techniques to be applied. Mr. Melville supports that, saying more data will become available for sports organizations and then to the public where valuable research will be published. Teams who buy into the good analytical ideas early on with the accurate data and relevant analysis will achieve success.

REFERENCES

American Gaming Association. (2022). Legal sports betting. www.americangaming.org/polic ies/hot-issue-sports-betting/

Apostolou, K., & Tjortjis, C. (2019). Sports Analytics algorithms for performance prediction. In *2019 10th International Conference on Information, Intelligence, Systems and Applications (IISA)* (pp. 1–4). IEEE.

Bai, Z., & Bai, X. (2021). Sports big data: Management, analysis, applications, and challenges. *Complexity, 2021,* 1–11. https://doi.org/10.1155/2021/6676297

Caulfield, J., & Jha, A. K. (2022). Stadiums and digitalization: An exploratory study of digitalization in sports stadiums. *Journal of Decision Systems, 31*(suppl 1), 331–340.

Deloitte Insights. (2021). The hyperquantified athlete: Technology, measurement, and the business of sports. www2.deloitte.com/us/en/insights/industry/technology/technol ogy-media-and-telecom-predictions/2021/athlete-data-analytics.html

Deng, Z., Lin, X., Huang, Z., Meng, J., Zhong, Y., Ma, G., Zhou, Y., Shen, Y., Ding, H., & Huang, Y. (2021). Imaging techniques: Recent progress on advanced imaging techniques for lithium-ion batteries. *Advanced Energy Materials, 11*(2). https://doi.org/10.1002/ aenm.202170007

Dixon, M. J., & Coles, S. G. (1996). Modelling association football scores and inefficiencies in the football betting market. *Journal of the Royal Statistical Society: Series C (Applied Statistics), 45*(2), 265–280. https://doi.org/10.2307/2986068

Ikotun, A. M., Ezugwu, A. E., Abualigah, L., Abuhaija, B., & Heming, J. (2023). K-means clustering algorithms: A comprehensive review, variants analysis, and advances in the era of big data. *Information Sciences, 622,* 178–210. https://doi.org/10.1016/ j.ins.2022.11.139

Kashyap, H. (2021). A primer on sports analytics: A new dimension of sports. *Analytics India Magazine.*

Kemble, J. (2022, May 19). Real Madrid secure €360 million deal with Sixth Street and Legends for Bernabéu redevelopment. Football España. www.football-espana.net/2022/05/19/ real-madrid-santiago-bernabeu-boost

Khan, R. U., Salamzadeh, Y., Iqbal, Q., & Yang, S. (2022). The impact of customer relationship management and company reputation on customer loyalty: The mediating role of customer satisfaction. *Journal of Relationship Marketing, 21*(1), 1–26. https://doi.org/ 10.1080/15332667.2020.1840904

Liu, A., Mahapatra, R. P., & Mayuri, A. V. (2023). Hybrid design for sports data visualization using AI and big data analytics. *Complex & Intelligent Systems, 9*(3), 2969–2980. https:// doi.org/10.1007/s40747-021-00557-w

Mondello, M., & Kamke, C. (2014). The introduction and application of sports analytics in professional sport organizations. *Journal of Applied Sport Management, 6*(2), 11. https:// trace.tennessee.edu/jasm/vol6/iss2/11

Pantzalis, V. C., & Tjortjis, C. (2020). Sports analytics for football league table and player performance prediction. In *2020 11th International Conference on Information, Intelligence, Systems and Applications (IISA)* (pp. 1–8). IEEE.

Patel, D., Shah, D., & Shah, M. (2020). The intertwine of brain and body: A quantitative analysis on how big data influences the system of sports. *Annals of Data Science, 7*(1), 1–16. https://doi.org/10.1007/s40745-019-00239-y

Patil, A. (2018). *Exploratory data analysis using R.* Packt Publishing.

Razzaq, A., & Yang, X. (2023). Digital finance and green growth in China: Appraising inclusive digital finance using web crawler technology and big data. *Technological Forecasting and Social Change, 188,* 122262. https://doi.org/10.1016/j.techfore.2022.122262

Reep, C., & Benjamin, B. (1968). Skill and chance in association football. *Journal of the Royal Statistical Society: Series A (General), 131*(4), 581–585. https://doi.org/10.2307/2343878

Ridder, G., Cramer, J. S., & Hopstaken, P. (1994). Down to ten: Estimating the effect of a red card in soccer. *Journal of the American Statistical Association, 89*(427), 1124–1127. https://doi.org/10.2307/2290947

Romanov, D., Molokanov, V., Kazantsev, N., & Jha, A. K. (2023). Removing order effects from human-classified datasets: A machine learning method to improve decision making systems. *Decision Support Systems, 165,* 113891.

Sarlis, V., & Tjortjis, C. (2020). Sports analytics: Evaluation of basketball players and team performance. *Information Systems, 93,* 101562. https://doi.org/10.1016/j.is.2020.101562

Sestino, A., Prete, M. I., Piper, L., & Guido, G. (2020). Internet of things and big data as enablers for business digitalization strategies. *Technovation, 98,* 102173. https://doi.org/10.1016/j.technovation.2020.102173

Srivastava, P. R., Eachempati, P., Kumar, A., Jha, A. K., & Dhamotharan, L. (2023). Best strategy to win a match: an analytical approach using hybrid machine learning-clustering-association rule framework. *Annals of Operations Research, 325*(1), 319–361.

Tiwari, S., Sharma, P., & Jha, A. K. (2024). Digitalization & Covid-19: An institutional-contingency theoretic analysis of supply chain digitalization. *International Journal of Production Economics, 267,* 109063. https://doi.org/10.1016/j.ijpe.2023.109063

Wallace, B. (2021). Sports industry execs share challenges and approaches to creating analytics. Network Computing. www.networkcomputing.com/data-center-networking/sports-industry-execs-share-challenges-and-approaches-to-creating-analytics

Worville, T. (2021). *How football's finest are using analytics to find an edge.* https://studycrumb.com/alphabetizer

Zadeh, A. H. (2021). Quantifying fan engagement in sports using text analytics. *Journal of Data, Information and Management, 3*(3), 197–208. https://doi.org/10.1007/s42488-021-00052-4

9

Summary

Jillian McNiff Villemaire

The convergence of data science and sports has been explored through diverse examples throughout this book, showcasing the significant innovations shaping the industry today. The contributions highlight how analytics, AI, and emerging technologies have redefined performance, strategy, and fan engagement across various sports disciplines. The reader has been able to delve into a variety of examples and current applications of analytics and data science to the sports industry. The vast and diverse research conducted by contributing authors showcases the depth and range of ways that data is currently being applied to the sports industry. Additionally, the reader has had the opportunity to explore where the sports industry and data science are moving together with innovations and adaptations of existing models into this industry.

The chapters presented in this book underscore the profound impact that data analytics, artificial intelligence, and emerging technologies are having across various facets of the sports industry. Each year, new and previously unconsidered developments emerge. As evidenced from this and previous innovations in data volumes, the world of analytics is constantly evolving. The editors of this volume spent considerable effort to showcase a range of models and sports industry applications. This effort was made to allow this text to demonstrate the variety of applications data science has on the sports industry. Additionally, the hope is to prompt the reader to consider new and emerging ways to use data science to inform decision making.

From predictive models enhancing recruitment to virtual reality reshaping training, these innovations demonstrate a paradigm shift. Furthermore, the book emphasizes the role of interdisciplinary collaboration, which is critical for driving advancements in areas like injury prevention, player

DOI: 10.1201/9781032665191-9

development, and operational efficiency. From the intricate analytics revolution in the NFL to the integration of biomechanics and machine learning in golf, these innovations are not only enhancing performance but also democratizing access to advanced analytical tools for a broader audience. The convergence of these technologies with traditional sports frameworks has led to new interdisciplinary collaborations and expanded opportunities for both professional and amateur analysts. The integration of technologies such as IoT, machine learning, and blockchain promises continued evolution in both professional and amateur sports. These tools are transforming the way teams and organizations analyze performance, manage finances, and strategize. Beyond technical applications, this book underscores a broader cultural shift where data science is democratizing access to insights, empowering smaller organizations, and fostering inclusivity.

Technologies presented in this book are revolutionizing not only the way games are played and analyzed but also how they are experienced by fans, both in person and virtually. The application of game theory in sports management and the predictive analytics used to forecast financial outcomes for football clubs further highlight the strategic advancements being made in the industry.

As we look to the future, the intersection of sports and technology will continue to evolve, offering new insights and opportunities for athletes, coaches, analysts, and fans alike. The ongoing integration of AI, IoT, and big data will not only reshape the sports landscape but also redefine how success is measured, both on and off the field. This book serves as a testament to the transformative power of these technologies and a guide to understanding their current and potential impact on the world of sports. Looking ahead, the continued synthesis of sports and data science will offer groundbreaking opportunities for innovation. By fostering collaboration between analysts, technologists, and practitioners, the sports industry can continue to unlock new potentials, pushing the boundaries of what's achievable on and off the field. This volume stands as both a celebration of current advancements and a call to action for readers to envision the next wave of transformative ideas in the sports analytics revolution.

Index

2D Gaussian function, 43
3-D motion capture, of body movements,
    28–29
5G networks, 1

A

Advanced data analysis techniques, 73
Adventure tourism, 77
    AI-assisted recommendation systems for,
        78
Affective Reality Theory, 19
Age-related diseases, use of AI in detection
    of, 90
Amateur analytics movement, 32
American Development Model, 10
Anti-doping system, 78
Application programming interface (API),
    35
Artificial intelligence (AI), 1, 5, 17, 50, 52,
    123, 169
    adoption in sports, 78
    application in
        analyzing large quantities of data from
            multiple sources, 95–96
        cricket umpiring, 78
        cutting security costs, 97
        data analytics techniques to forecast
            patterns and decision-making, 71
        detection of age-related diseases, 90
        enhancing cybersecurity, 97
        enhancing security of stadiums, 94–95
        freeing security staff for other activities,
            97
        improving athletic performance, 98
        management of stadium, 88–91
        metal detectors, 96
        monitoring spectators' behavior and
            detecting threats, 96
        recognizing security shortcomings and
            suggesting improvements, 96
        smart stadiums, 3
        streamlined food and ticket purchasing,
            99

China's AI assisted lottery system, 75
China's economic growth based on, 75
mobile fitness apps (MFA), 69
for prediction of sport outcome, 130–133
predictive and cognitive skills of, 55
rise in demand for, 105
in stadium market regional analysis,
    103–104
Artificial Intelligence in Stadium Global
    Market Report 2023 (Business
    Research Company), 100
Artificial Intelligence of Things (AIoT)
    adoption and propagation in sports sector,
        59
    applications of, 55
    background and significance of, 52
    block diagram of evolution of, 55
    convergence of IoT and AI, 54–55
    emergence of, 53–54
    impact on sports ecosystem
        addressing of ethical concerns, 78
        changing of national avenues, 76–78
        societal norms and regulatory
            frameworks, 74–76
    implementations in sports, 71–74
        expert recommendations, 73–74
        injury and rehabilitation, 72
        insightful data, 73
        pandemic scenarios, 71–72
        range of possibilities, 71
        real-time analysis, 73
        scalable fan engagement, 72–73
        training, 72
    integration into public sector enterprises,
        71
    other IS theories in, 68–71
        Attachment Theory, 68–69
        cognition-based models, 69–70
        Goal-Setting Theory, 69
        Neuro-fuzzy Prediction Models, 69
        self-determination theory, 70
        theory of reasoned action, 70–71
People, Process, and Technology (PPT), 56

PPT framework-based visualization of, 56
purpose and scope of, 52–53
schematic representation of, 54
in sports industry, 55
sports teaching and training capabilities,
    72
technology acceptance theories, 59–68
    Diffusion of Innovations (DOI) theory,
        62–64
    Technology Acceptance Model (TAM),
        60–62
    Theory of Planned Behavior (TPB),
        64–66
    Value-based Adoption Model (VAM),
        67–68
and virtual reality, 71
Artificial Neural Networks (ANN), 72, 73,
    132–133
Athletic performance, use of AI in
    enhancing, 98
Atomic Golf, 7
Augmented reality technologies, 3
Auto-ARIMA forecasting method, 5,
    162–164
Automated journalism, use of AI in, 100

B
Bagga, Gurshish, 37
Baldwin, Ben, 35–36, 40
Banner, Joe, 33
Bargaining theory, 122
Baseball, game of, 33, 116
Bayern Munich, 155
    Auto-ARIMA's prediction for, 164
    naive predictions graphically, 155
    SES predictions, 159
Bayesian Network, 133
Beach sports, 78
    role in development of tourism, 77
Beane, Billy, 139
Bet365, 143
Betway, 143
Big data, 143, 145
    analytics, 4, 54, 77–78
    emergence of, 138
    impact on the development of the sports
        industry, 141
    power of, 29
Big Data Bowl, 2, 5, 31, 34, 40–46

Biomechanical time series, 27
Biomechanic analytic tools, benefits of, 20
Biomechanic data technologies, 2
Biomechanics, 15, 78, 170
    data, 127
    technology, 9, 20, 25
Blaire, Zac, 23–24
Blockchain, 72, 170
Boosting, 133
Box score, 138
Boylesports, 143
Brighenti, Caio, 44
Broadie, Mark, 21–22, 26
Buzz (Salzman et al., 2003), 50

C
Camera technologies, 8
Career path certifications, 9
Carnegie Mellon University, 35, 45
Center of mass (COM) displacement, 27
Center of pressure (COP), 27
Chadwick, Henry, 138
Chatbots, 54, 89, 90
    AI-powered, 91, 99
Chief technology officers (CTO), 52
Cisco Systems, 102–103
Clark, Kevin, 31, 33
Classification algorithms, 133
Closed circuit television (CCTV) cameras,
    92, 94, 96
Cognitive Affective Personality System
    theory, 19
Cognitive capabilities, of human, 75
Cognitive Reasoning Sports Teaching Model
    (CRSTM), 70
Communication, between golfers and
    instructors, 20
Completion Probability (CP), 37, 44
Compound annual growth rate (CAGR), 90
Computer vision algorithms, 123
Conditional probability distributions, 43
Context data, 127
Convolutional neural network (CNN), 38,
    41
Correlation matrix, 148–151
Cournot, Antoine Augustin, 110
COVID-19 pandemic, 71
    challenges for sports event managers due
        to, 101

impact on AI adoption in stadiums, 3, 100–102
lockdown, 100
measures taken by AI to solve the problems caused by, 101
monitoring by facial recognition, 102
outbreak of, 100, 105
Cricket umpiring, use of AI in, 78
Critical thinking, 53
Crowd disasters, 94
Crowd management systems, 104–105
AI-based, 91
Crowd metrics, AI-powered surveillance tools for detecting, 101
Cybersecurity, use of AI in enhancing, 97

D

Data analysis, 54, 62, 73, 130, 133, 139–140, 144–145, 165–166
Data cleaning
process of, 146
and standardization, 128
Data collection, methods of, 128
Data-driven analytics, 29, 50, 169
AI-based, 68, 71
applications in golf, 25–28
to forecast patterns and facilitate informed decision-making, 71
personal development through, 9
use of, 2
Data extraction, from websites, 128
Data imbalance, dealing with, 128
Data labeling, process of, 146
Data loss, 166
Data mining, 73, 142, 145
Data science, 1, 124, 129, 169–170
Data security and privacy, 78
Data storage, 71
Data streaming, real-time, 105
Decision-making, 1, 4, 18–19, 38, 92, 111, 121, 169
data-driven, 105
in the game of football, 32
game theory-based, 73
in-game tactical decision-making, 123
of managing a stadium, 87
public finance decisions, 122
statistical models used for, 37
strategies for, 38

use of AI-based data analytics techniques for, 71
Decision trees, 73, 131, 133
Deep learning algorithms, 132
Deep neural networks, 133
Diffusion of Innovations (DOI), 3, 53, 60, 62–64
Digital content management, 105
Digital information, 54
Digital technologies, 5, 57, 67, 72
Digital transformation, of sports industry, 1
Disease management, 90
Disruptive technologies, 52
Djokovic, Novak, 119–120
Doping in sports, use of AI in detection of, 78
Douglas, Joe, 32
Drapkin, Zack, 44
Drive Shack, 7
Dr. Kwon's Golf Biomechanics Instructor Training Program, 10
Dwaine Knight Center for Golf Management at the University of Nevada, Las Vegas (UNLV), 9

E

E-commerce, 60, 68
Edge Computing for the Internet of Things (EC-IoT), 53
Elbow Point Technique, 151
optimal number of clusters using, 152
Elite athletes, use of technology and technology acceptance for, 17–21
Elite sports, 76
impact on society, 77
societal effects arising from, 76–77
Ellis Park Stadium disaster (2001), 94
Emerging technologies, 50, 79, 169
Emotional information processing, 19
Ensemble Methods, 133
E-sports, 74
European football clubs, 5, 140
European sports ecosystem, 59
Evaluation systems in competitive sports, use of AI in, 75
Evolutionary Computation, 73
Evolv Technology, 89
Expert systems, 73
Exponential smoothing forecasting method, 5

F

Facial recognition, 3, 89, 91
    AI-assisted, 99
    pandemic monitoring by, 102
Fan engagement analytics, 125
Fan's experience, leveraging AI to elevate,
    98–100
Feature engineering, 128, 129
Fédération Internationale de Football
    Association (FIFA), 139
Fever detection, use of AI in, 101–102
Finau, Tony, 23–24
Fitness trackers, usage of, 70
FlightScope, 2, 8
Football, game of, 31, 117
    10-digit game identification numbers, 35
    American football game, 118
    calculation of individual win probability
        (WP), 35
    decision-making in, 32
    gamesmanship of, 34
    logistic regression approach for estimation
        of play's expected points (EP), 35
    Pederson's approach to blending
        traditional and analytical approaches
        to, 32
    play-by-play information, 35
Four-person games, 110
Full Swing simulator, 7, 9

G

Game payoffs, determination of, 111–114,
    116, 118–121
Game strategy analysis, 125
Game theory, 4–5, 73
    application in sports management, 170
    elements of, 111
    four-person games, 110
    mixed strategy solutions, 113–115
    multiple-player game technique, 122
    Nash equilibrium, 112–113
    origin of, 110–111
    Prisoner's Dilemma, 112, 122
    probability assignment in, 121
    sports examples of, 115–120
    three-person games, 110
    two-person games, 110
    utilizing analytics and, 120–122
Gamification, process of, 9

Generalized additive models (GAM), 21–22,
    35
Global sports, ethics of technology use in, 78
Golf analytics, 2, 21–25
Golf biomechanics laboratories, 11
Golf club, 11, 15
Golf, game of
    applications of data analytics and machine
        learning in, 25–28
    Atomic Golf, 7
    benefits of interdisciplinary collaboration,
        15
    biomechanics and fitness exercises related
        to, 10
    biomechanics certifications, 10
    biomechanics technology, 9, 13, 25
    communication between golfers and
        instructors, 20
    consumer base, 8
    data analytics of, 21–25
        benchmark functions from putting, 23
        benchmark functions from various
            lies, 21
    data collection and analytics in, 9
    Elite Golfers Performance Evaluation, 25
    Executive Management certification, 10
    golfers using the ground force, 15
    Golf Operations certification, 9–10
    instruction technologies, 8
    on-course participation for golfers, 7
    pelvis rotation data, 14
    relationship of variance and strokes
        gained, 27
    role of technology in, 6–8
        performance outcomes, 11–16
        specialization of teaching and coaching,
            8–11
    rotational velocity of the golfer's pelvis, 14
    simulators, 7
    "strokes gained" metric, 11
    tracking of golf swings, 27
    translational motion, 13
    use of technology and technology
        acceptance for elite athletes, 17–21
    velocity and acceleration, 13
Golf instructors, certification for, 10
Gordeev, Dmitry, 40
GPS Tracking System, 142
Greens in regulations (GIR), 22

Ground reactionary force (GRF), 27
Group statistics, 101
Gymnastics, AI-aided system in, 75

H
Halaby, Alec, 32
Hierarchical clustering, 131
Higher education, 9
Holt Winter's forecasting method, 5, 159–161
Hoppen, Sam, 38–39
Horowitz, Maksim, 35
Human behavior, complexity of, 19
Human–computer interaction, 69
Human interaction dynamics, 52
Hype Cycle for Emerging Technologies, 50–51

I
IBM Corporation, 103
Impact factor (IF), 133
Individual win probability (WP), 35
Industrial Internet of Things (IIoT), 53
Industrial Robotics of Things (IRoT), 53
Information processing, 19
Information systems (IS) theories, 52
In-game play statistics, 123
In-game tactical decision-making, 123
Injuries, sports-related, 72
Injury data, 125, 126
Injury risk management, 125
Institutional Review Board (IRB)
    Elite Golfers Performance Evaluation, 25
Integrity and fraud detection, use of
        predictive analytics for, 126
Internet of Medical Things (IoMT), 53
Internet of Things (IoT) technologies, 1, 3, 5,
        50, 54, 94
    advent in sports, 78
    data monetization techniques in, 54
Internet of Vehicles (IoV), 53
Intrinsic motivation, 70

J
James, Bill, 138
JavaScript Object Notation (JSON), 35

K
Kaplan-Meier estimator, 43
Kinematic sequence (rotational velocity)
        graph, 14

K-means clustering, 5, 41, 144, 151–154
    clusters obtained using, 153
K-Nearest Neighbors, 131, 133
Knowledge-based economy, 75
Knowledge innovation, 72

L
Lewis, Michael, 50
Lifelong learning, 9
Linear discriminant analysis, 133
Linear regression, 26, 37, 69, 131, 133
Logistic regression, 35, 37, 133
Lopez, Mike, 40
Lottery system, AI assisted, 75
Love Parade disaster (2010), 94

M
Machine learning (ML), 1, 5, 28, 37, 73, 88,
        99, 123, 132, 141–142, 170
    advancements of, 4
    applications in golf, 25–28, 29
    learning algorithms, 4, 26
        deep learning, 132
        for prediction of sport outcome,
            130–133
        reinforcement, 132
        semi-supervised, 132
        supervised, 131
        unsupervised, 131
Magnetic resonance imaging (MRI), 90
Major League Baseball (MLB), 31, 139
    "moneyball" movement in, 34
    Oakland Athletics, 123
Manchester City, 139, 146
Manchester United, 155
    Auto-ARIMA's prediction for, 162, 163
    naive predictions graphically, 156
    SES predictions, 158
Match results data, 127
Metal detectors, AI-powered, 96
Microsoft Analytical Tools, 139
Mobile application platforms, governance
        of, 74
Mobile fitness apps (MFA), 69
Moneyball (book), 123, 139
Moneyball (movie, 2011), 50, 139
"Moneyball" movement, 31, 34
Monte Carlo simulations, of the NFL regular
        season, 36

Morgenstern, Oskar, 110–111
Movement mechanics, 125
Multiple-player game technique, 122

N
Naïve Bayes, 133
Naive forecasting method, 5, 155, 157
Nash equilibrium, 4, 111–115
Nash, John F., 111
National Basketball Association (NBA), 31, 139
  Atlanta Hawks, 35
  development of the {nflscrapR} project, 35–36
National Collegiate Athletic Association (NCAA) Division, 26
National Football League (NFL), 2, 31
  amateur analytics movement in, 33, 37, 40–45
  application programming interface (API), 35
  Big Data Bowl, 5, 31, 40–45
  copycat league, 32
  data analytics, 31
    in game planning, 33–34
    lowered barrier of entry for, 35–40
    public-facing analytics work, 39
    R package for, 35
  decision-making strategies, 38
  Detroit Lions, 44
  Philadelphia Eagles, 32
  Plus-Minus metric, 39
  user-created models for simulation of NFL seasons, 36
    Completion Probability Model, 37
    Draft Surplus Value model, 37
    Expected Points Model, 37
    Win Probability Model, 37
Neural networks
  artificial neural networks (ANN), 72, 73, 132–133
  convolutional neural network (CNN), 38, 41
  deep neural networks, 133
  used in team sports for risk assessment and performance prediction, 73
New York Times, The, 142
Non-cooperative games, 4, 111–112

O
Oakland Athletics (Major League Baseball team), 123, 139
Off-field data analytics, 126
Officiating analysis, for training and recruitment, 125
Off-the-tee (OTT), 22, 24
On-field data analytics, 125–126
Operational efficiency, 5, 103–105, 170
Ordinary least square (OLS) linear regression, 26
Outcome prediction, use of ML models for, 125
Outdoor adventure tourism sports, 77

P
Paddy Power, 143
Paris Saint Germain (PSG), 146
Pattern recognition, AI-based, 72
Patton, Steve, 39
Pederson, Doug, 32
Pelvis displacement, 27
People counting, 101
People, Process, and Technology (PPT), 56
Performance evaluation and contract negotiations, 126
Performance prediction, 63, 73, 123, 142
Personal learning styles, 19
PhilSports Stadium stampede (2006), 94
Play-by-play information, 35
Player performance
  analysis of, 125
  in fantasy sport games, 123, 126, 128
Players' sport injuries, management of, 123
Player-tracking data, 40
Ploenzke, Matt, 44
Predictive analytics, 3–4, 89, 92, 135, 170
Principal component analysis (PCA), 27, 39, 131
Priority Matrix for Emerging Technologies, 50
Prisoner's Dilemma, 112, 122
Problem-solving, 53
Professional and Amateur Sports Protection Act 1992 (PASPA), 142
Professional Golfer's Association (PGA) of America
  career paths, 9
  Coach program, 10

Life Learning Model, 9
Shotlink system, 21
Teaching and Coaching certification, 9
types of stroke gained used by, 22
Pro Football Focus (PFF), 31, 34, 39
Public sector enterprise, integration of
AI-IoT-tech in, 71
Python (computer programming language),
31, 34

Q
Quality of life, 71

R
R (computer programming language), 31,
34–35
RandomForests, 28
algorithms, 37, 133, 135
Conditional Density Estimate Model, 43
Rationality, model of, 111
Real estate management, 87
Real Madrid, 139, 146–147, 155
Auto-ARIMA's prediction for, 163
naive predictions graphically, 156
SES predictions, 158
total revenues forecast for, 157
Real-time analysis of athlete performance,
use of IoT data and AI techniques
in, 73
Real-time videos, 101, 104
Reasoned action, theory of, 70–71
Regression modeling, 133
Rehabilitation, after sports injury, 72
Reinforcement learning algorithms, 132
Research questions (RQ), 140
Return on investment (RoI), 102, 141
Ringer, The (Kevin Clark), 31, 33
Risk assessment, 62, 73, 77
Roseman, Howie, 32
Rotational acceleration, 13–14
Rubenstein, Ariel, 111
Rule Set, 133
Russia-Ukraine war, impact on global
economy, 90

S
Sabermetrics, 33, 139
Scoring, use of AI for, 75
Scouting data, 127

Searchveillance, 102
Security screening, AI-based, 89
Self-regulation skills, 17
Semi-supervised learning algorithms, 132
Sense-Model-Plan-Act (SMPA) loop, 53
Sequential Modeling, 41
ShotLink+, 2, 21
Shunjiang Ma, 69
Silhouette Method, 151
optimal number of clusters using, 152
Simple exponential smoothing (SES)
method, 157–159
Singer, Phillip, 40
Sixth Street and Legends, 147
Smart cities, environmentally sustainable,
71
Smart machines, 55
Smart Sport Training (SST), 73
Smart stadiums, 88, 91–92
application of artificial intelligence in, 3,
92–98
for enhanced entertainment, 93
for enhanced safety and security, 94–97
for greater commercial opportunities
and improved customer service, 93
improving athletic performance, 98
for reducing environmental impacts
and energy costs, 97–98
sustainable development, 97–98
concept of, 91
infrastructure of, 89
Smart tools
implementation of, 88
integration in stadiums, 88
Smart watches, 70
Social behaviors, 19
Social media interaction, 143
Social recreational sports, 71
Societal transformations, 78
SoFi Stadium, 89
Sport management, 9, 29
Sport outcome, prediction of
accuracy of, 123–124
computational methods for, 130–133
data collection and preprocessing
techniques for, 126–129
data for
types of, 126–127
use of, 123

feature selection and engineering
techniques, 129–130
future directions and challenges in,
134–135
goals of, 128
machine learning algorithms for, 130–133
match outcome modeling, 123
NBA game winners, 129
predictive analytics for, 124
application of, 124–126
review papers on, 133
role in sports decision-making, 124
through computational prediction,
133–134
Sport-related physical activity, during
tourism, 70
Sports analytics, 1, 4, 32, 139
Auto-ARIMA forecasting method,
162–164
correlation matrix, 148–151
data sources for, 145–146
descriptive measures, 146–148
growth of, 142
Holt Winter's forecasting method,
159–161
K-means clustering model, 151–154
literature review of, 141–144
method for analysis of, 144–146
naïve method, 157
simple exponential smoothing (SES)
method, 157–159
study for understanding of
future scope of, 166–167
limitations of, 165–166
purpose of, 140
Sports betting, 126
Sports biomechanics, for technique
evaluation and movement
optimization, 73–74
Sports clubs, 5, 139–140, 143, 165
Sports culture, development of, 124
Sports ecosystem
AI-IoT-tech in
emergence of, 53–54
impact of, 74–78
in Europe, 59
theories in, 56–59
Sports education, 69
Sports & Fitness Industry Association
(SFIA), 89

Sports fraternities, 53
Sports gambling and betting, 143
legalization of, 142
Sports industry, 3, 103, 123
applications of analytics and data science
to, 169
digital transformation of, 1
growth of the global AI in, 105
impact of big data on development of, 141
integration of AI with IoT, 52, 100
Sports Info Solutions (SIS), 31, 34, 44
Sports innovation, 15
Sports lottery, economic potential of, 75
Sports management, application of game
theory in, 170
Sports organizations, functioning of, 52
Sports science, 73, 133
Sports teaching and training, use of AI-IoT-
tech for, 72
Sports technology, 78
Sports tourism, 77
Sports training, educational aspects of, 70
Sports wagering, legalization of, 142
Stadium. *see also* Smart stadiums
AI-based video surveillance system at, 101
COVID-19's impact on the use of AI in,
100–102
Ellis Park Stadium disaster (2001), 94
energy efficiency renovations in, 98
integration of smart tools in, 88
Love Parade disaster (2010), 94
management of
decision-making of, 87
real estate, 87
use of AI in, 88–91
PhilSports Stadium stampede (2006), 94
real-time information on space use in, 88
security system, AI-based, 94–95
traffic flow optimization, 99
Stadium Electricity-Artificial Intelligence
(SE-AI), 98
Stadium market
major market players in, 102–103
opportunities for AI in, 104
Stern, Alex, 43
Stern, Benjamin, 38
Stimulus-organism-response (S-O-R)
framework, 68
"Strokes Gained" analysis, 2
Subbaiah, Meyappan, 44

Supervised learning algorithms, 131–132
Support Vector Machines (SVM), 131, 133,
    135

T
Talent identification, for scouting and
    recruitment, 126
Teaching and coaching, role of technology
    in, 8–11
Team momentum, 130
Technologies in sports, adoption of, 3
Technology Acceptance Model (TAM), 3,
    17, 53
Technology innovation, 52
    AI-driven, 104
Tennis game, 119
Text analytics, 72
Theories, in the sports ecosystem, 56–59
    mixed embeddedness theory, 57–59
    Olympism for Humanity Theory and
        Praxis, 59
    Pressure-State-Response (PSR) model, 59
    'Sport Ecosystem Logic' theory, 57
    stakeholder theory, 59
Theory of Planned Behavior (TPB), 3, 53
The Suzy and Jim Broadhurst Golf
        Teaching and Research Center, at
        The Pennsylvania State University
        (PennState), 9, 11
    golf biomechanics course, 9
Time maximizing variance, 27
Time series analysis, 133
Titleist Performance Institute (TPI), 10
Tomlin, Mike, 34
TopGolf, 7
Torso displacement, 27
Tourism Economics, 89
Tracking data, 28, 34, 40–41, 126
Tracking devices, 1
Trackman simulator, 2, 7, 8

Tucker, Albert, 112
Two-person games, 110

U
UEFA Champions League, 154
United States Golf Association, 10
United States Olympic Committee, 10
UNLV College of Hospitality, 10
Unsupervised learning algorithms, 131
The Use of Machine Learning in Sport
        Outcome Prediction: A Review, 133

V
Value-Based Adoption Model (VAM), 3
Ventura, Sam, 35
Video analytics, 3
    AI-based, 94
Video footage, real-time monitoring of, 94
Video games, design of, 111
Video monitoring solutions (VMS), 94
Virtual reality (VR), 3, 71, 89, 91, 166, 169
    AI-powered, 99, 104
Von Neumann, John, 110–111

W
Wearable technologies, 1
Web of Things (WoT), 53
Web scraping tools, 128
Weight training, 72–73
Win probability estimates, inclusion of
        variance and uncertainty in, 38

X
XGBoost, 28, 37, 43

Y
YouTube Theater, 89

Z
Zelus Analytics, 44